AMERICA'S FIRST FROGMAN

Portrait by Alice V. Knight

AMERICA'S FIRST FROGMAN

The Draper Kauffman Story

Elizabeth K. Bush

NAVAL INSTITUTE PRESS

Annapolis, Maryland

This book has been brought to publication by the generous assistance of
Marguerite and Gerry Lenfest.

First Naval Institute Press paperback edition 2012.

Naval Institute Press

291 Wood Road

Annapolis, MD 21402

ISBN 978-1-59114-069-6

Library of Congress Cataloging-in-Publication Data

Bush, Elizabeth K., 1922–
America's first frogman : the Draper Kauffman story / Elizabeth K. Bush.
p. cm.
ISBN 1-59114-098-6 (alk. paper)
1. Kauffman, Draper. 2. Admirals—United States—Biography. 3. United States. Navy. Underwater Demolition Teams—History. 4. World War, 1939–1945—Regimental histories—United States. 5. World War, 1939–1945—Naval operations, American. 6. United States. Navy—Officers—Biography. I. Title.
V63.K38B87 2004
940.54'5973'092—dc22

2004014368

Printed in the United States of America on acid-free paper ♾

First Printing.

Contents

This book is dedicated with love to my husband, Pres, whom Draper so greatly admired, and without whose encouragement this story would never have been written.

—E. K. B.

Foreword

THIS BOOK IS ABOUT a true American hero. It is about "duty, honor, and country." It is about service and sacrifice.

When Adm. Draper Kauffman's sister, my own sister-in-law, asked me to write this brief introduction, I set aside my policy of not writing forewords or blurbs for books. I did this because of my great respect for Adm. Draper Kauffman, about whom this book is written.

In the summer of 1944 my torpedo bomber squadron, VT-51, based aboard the carrier USS *San Jacinto* covered some of the landings on Guam and Saipan. I remember vividly the sight of those Marines going ashore in the face of severe enemy fire. I remember thinking rather selfishly, "Thank God I am a pilot, not one of those Marines going in there to face hell. In an hour I'll be back aboard ship in clean clothes, in great quarters, and with great food, and these guys will be trying to advance one hundred yards in the face of enemy fire."

What this nineteen-year-old navy pilot didn't know at that time was what had transpired before the Marines landed. I knew nothing about the frogmen, nothing about those courageous underwater men who bravely paved the way for the Marines.

I didn't realize that Draper Kauffman, whom I barely knew then, was not only a pioneer in the field but also a fearless leader who put his own life on the line right next to the men whom he had trained and whom he led into harm's way.

This book tells of the heroism of the underwater demolition teams. It also tells about Draper's service in France in 1940, his being taken prisoner by the Germans, and of being part of a truly brave group of men in the British navy in 1940–41 who rendered safe the German time bombs and mines.

In 1941 he transferred to the U.S. Navy, where he developed a bomb disposal team, joining again with selfless, courageous volunteers in this still-vital work.

In telling us about her brother's life of service and dedication, Beth Bush also defines sacrifice and heroism.

The question is rhetorically asked, "Where do we find such men?" My answer is that when a crisis arises, the United States will always find such men. We found them in Desert Storm, in Vietnam, and in Korea. Surely we found them in World War II, and now we find them in Afghanistan and Iraq. Draper Kauffman is one such man who brought honor and credit to the uniform he wore.

Day in and day out, he laid his life on the line for his country. He was a true leader. He always put his men first. He went in early and often. He led by his own courage. Draper Kauffman, proud officer in the U.S. Navy, defines for me what service to country is all about.

I was very proud to have been a lowly lieutenant (jg) in the navy during WWII. There I learned firsthand about service to country. And I learned a lot about sacrifice and patriotism.

Much later, as president of the United States, I was proud to have been the commander in chief of our armed forces. In both these incarnations, my appreciation for those who served was honed, my appreciation for real heroes sharpened to a fine edge. My respect for the U.S. military knows no bounds.

Adm. Draper Kauffman's commitment to service and his exemplary record have reinforced my views on duty, honor, and country.

Who says there are no American heroes? Draper Kauffman was a true hero. This book tells us why.

George H. W. Bush

Preface

In July 1942 *Time* magazine ran an article about an American who had joined the British navy. It told how, in November 1941, in the lobby of London's Savoy Hotel, some reporters got to chatting with a fellow American who, they noticed, was wearing a uniform of the Royal Navy. The reporters wanted to know why. The American said he had been in the Royal Navy exactly one year and was going stateside for a month's leave the next day.

"I'm supposed to be a naval officer," the young man said, "but they won't let me go to sea!" He wore spectacles, and after a pause he added, "Bum eyes. They threw me out of the U.S. Navy." His voice was bitter. "They've got me on shore duty, nursing those goddam land mines. Nothing like what those pilots do," he mourned.

The reporters looked at one another, silent. They knew that land mine duty in Britain took at least as much courage as being a fighter pilot.

His name was Draper Kauffman, he said, and his father was Rear Adm. James L. Kauffman, then commander of U.S. Navy defenses in the Gulf of Mexico.

"Fat lot of good that connection did me," said Lieutenant Kauffman. "Eyes went bad on me just after I finished at Annapolis."

The article concluded: "While Lieut. Kauffman, R.N., was on leave in the U.S., the Japanese attacked Pearl Harbor. The U.S. Navy then found Draper Kauffman's eyes and experience good enough for war. Last week Secretary Knox awarded Lieut. Kauffman, [USNR], the Navy Cross for exceptional heroism. His deed: unloading and examining a live, 500-lb., Japanese bomb, which failed to explode when it hit an Army field in Hawaii, last Dec. 7."

Draper Laurence Kauffman was my brother, and that Navy Cross was just one of a series of distinctions that would make his unique career. This is the story of Draper Kauffman, who graduated from the Naval Academy in 1933 but failed to gain a commission on account of defective eyesight, and who, despite this inauspicious beginning, went on to become a hero in World War II, an admiral, and—ironically—superintendent of the U. S. Naval Academy. It is the record of a naval career that was not only successful but also, in the annals of the U.S. Navy, surely one of the most unusual.

After being forced out of the navy in 1933, Draper was employed by a New York–based steamship company, the U.S. Lines, which sent him to Germany at the very time Hitler was hammering into shape that country's collective mind-set. Draper's deep-seated reaction to events unfolding in Nazi Germany would shape the course of his life for years to come. It would compel him to travel to wartime France, where he served in the American Volunteer Ambulance Corps and was taken prisoner by the Germans; he became a British naval officer and eventually, when the United States had its rude awakening at Pearl Harbor, found himself back in the fold of the U.S. Navy. Draper's subsequent career setting up the navy's first bomb disposal and underwater demolition schools, and later serving as a UDT (underwater demolition team) commander in the Pacific, is a story of great leadership and undying determination.

This is also the story of Draper Kauffman's relationship with his family—most notably, with his father, Adm. James Laurence Kauffman, who had an impressive career in his own right as well as a profound influence on Draper's development.

Both my brother and my father had a genius for leadership. Dad focused his talents on his great loves—the sea and ships, especially destroyers—and inspired a generation of officers who commanded surface ships. Draper was superb at revolutionizing groups and creating new organizations from scratch. He loved the navy deeply and thought that it brought out the best in people. It is no accident that the Naval Academy's Leadership Prize is named for Draper Kauffman.

Both men, at one point or another, appeared sidetracked in their naval careers and still went on to make flag rank. Both had a passion for command. They relished the role of having final responsibility and were unhappy if the buck did not stop with them.

Both were lucky enough to have supportive wives who enjoyed the challenges of navy life, who were uncommonly adept at handling them, and who brought their influence to bear on several generations of navy wives, an accomplishment not to be taken lightly.

Both believed deeply in serving their nation; both turned down lucrative civilian jobs to remain in the navy. Both believed that the opportunity to "make a difference" was a far greater reward than fame or wealth. Draper's son, Draper Jr., once jokingly chided his father for not parlaying his conspicuous wartime role into fame and fortune. His father replied that it was rare for anybody to be given the chance to serve his country in an important way—that the opportunity alone was worth far more than wealth and left a legacy far more enduring than fame. That was a belief he shared with his own father, one that above all defined their lives.

WHILE I WAS writing this book, a great nucleus of information was Draper's oral history, produced under John Mason's program at the U.S. Naval Institute. Dr. Mason had a deeply intelligent, sensitive approach to oral history and developed great rapport with Draper. He ended the oral history saying, "These interviews are fitting and perceptive accounts of a dynamic, innovative officer, a humanitarian par excellence—a thoroughly lovable man!" I also availed myself of numerous speeches, letters, and articles by and about Draper.

A source for writing the first chapter about Draper's time in France was Col. J. A. Frécaut, whom I had the good fortune to meet in Alsace-Lorraine while he was doing his own research on the war. He escorted my husband, Pres, and me, and Draper's daughter Kelsey Kauffman to the villages where Draper had driven his ambulance. Colonel Frécaut also took us to the location of the German prisoner-of-war camp in Lunéville, where my brother was held. When he finished his own research into the war in that region, he kindly sent me a copy of his published account, "La Vie en Lunéville, 1939–1945."

For the second chapter, about bomb and mine disposal in Britain, I had invaluable help from men involved in that dangerous work—men who possessed the inimitable British gift for understatement and who were inordinately modest, though many had been awarded Britain's prestigious George Cross for their heroic accomplishments: Lt. Comdrs. John Ouvry and Horace Taylor, Capt. Roger Lewis, Adm. Geoffrey Thistleton-Smith, army captain A. B. Waters, and Maj. J. D. Hudson. Maj. Arthur Hogben, author of *Designed to Kill,* kindly gave me a tour of the explosives museum outside London that houses samples of the German bombs and mines Hitler rained down on Britain. I was given a tour as well of HMS

Vernon and was surprised to find that the people there are still deeply involved in bomb disposal work. I also had helpful visits with Moe Archer, who worked with my brother on a George mine in England and later at Pearl Harbor, and with Philip David, also briefly in England, who later followed in Draper's footsteps as head of the U.S. Navy Bomb Disposal School. Philip wrote a history of the school, which he kindly loaned me.

For later chapters, I'm indebted to James Barnes and the board of directors of the UDT–SEAL Museum in Fort Pierce, Florida, for giving me access to source materials. The executive director H. T. Aldhizer painstakingly removed photographs from the museum walls after hours and had them photocopied for my use. My heartfelt thanks also go to board member Bob Marshall, who during the Pacific war served as executive officer of UDT 5, which Draper commanded, and who fought alongside my brother. Bob has filled me in on innumerable details and recounted some funny stories.

Draper's wife, my sister-in-law and best friend, Peggy Tuckerman Kauffman, gave me needed encouragement when I first set out to write this book. Sadly, she died soon after my brother. How I miss her, and how I wish she had been here as the story of her husband took shape. Draper's eldest daughter, Cary (the baby in this book), a beloved Unitarian minister, gave me welcome advice from time to time; sadly, she too has died. Draper's son, Draper Laurence Kauffman Jr., and daughter Kelsey Kauffman—both PhDs and published authors—were tremendously generous with their help. I also relied on notes that Draper Jr.'s wife, Susan, jotted down when my brother was still alive, telling his unforgettable stories.

Pres's and my children were a source of inspiration. Over the years, our daughter, Kelsey Bush-Nadeau, found background books that were invaluable to me as I was writing, and our son Jamie Bush was a tireless advocate, putting me in touch with Hugh Hewitt, a writer and TV and radio show host, and through Hewitt, the authors Merrill Bartlett and Michael Levin. Our son, and Draper's godson, Prescott Bush III recorded thoughtful comments about his uncle.

While dwelling on family, I want to express special gratitude to Pres's brother, George Bush. Former presidents are flooded with requests to promote books, and though George has a policy of refusing such requests, he graciously agreed to pen the foreword to this book. George had a great rapport with my brother; he has been the speaker at a number of events in his honor, including the christening of the USS *Kauffman*, a guided missile frigate named after Draper and my father.

I am also profoundly grateful to men like Robert Eigell, Jim Warnock, Dan Dillon, Tony Watson, and Bruce Beame, who, when they heard what I was writing, recorded their memories of Draper, some of which have found their way into these pages.

And then there is the contribution of Peter Blanchard. Peter was always on call to tame my word processor and keep me from throwing it out the window. Without his computer expertise and his patience with a woman who was schooled in longhand, I would have been composing the manuscript with a pen.

Three people are most responsible for this book in its civilized state. The first is Al Viebranz. After writing the first few drafts, I became discouraged and was ready to walk away from the whole enterprise. Then Al, a neighbor and friend as well as a published writer, read it and was so intrigued by the story that he offered to show me how to put things together. Thanks to his know-how, ability, and enthusiasm, I was back in business.

But I was still not satisfied, and Al understood how I felt. A friend and author, William Ewald, asked *his* friend and author, Capt. Edward L. Beach (author of *Run Silent, Run Deep*), to give me advice. Captain Beach had served in the navy with my father, about whom he told some marvelous stories. He put me in touch with Constance Buchanan, a superb freelance editor and a delight to work with; she helped me put the manuscript into almost final form to go to the Naval Institute Press where executive editor Paul Wilderson has a marvelous talent for leading frustrated authors through to publication.

Last and most important, there is my eternally patient husband, Pres, who supported me without question when it seemed as if I was eternally writing. Pres was always there to help me choose the right word or phrase, a wonderful talent of his. His enthusiasm for Draper's story never dimmed (no brothers-in-law could have been closer), and that, more than anything, kept me going until the end.

In the preface to her book about her mother, *Clementine Churchill: The Biography of a Marriage,* Mary Soames writes, "One curious effect of writing about my parents is that as time and the book go on, I myself from being an observer in the wings become involved as a witness in the story, and a background 'incidental' participant in events which have shaped and shaken all our lives" (vii). That is precisely how I felt as I delved into my brother's career. In the beginning, I kept my presence to a minimum. Then I realized that Draper's story couldn't be separated from my story or that of the rest of our family—or indeed, from the events that shaped so many millions of lives during World War II. Like Mrs. Soames, I became an incidental participant in the tumult of that era.

Of course, there's a big difference between being an incidental participant and an active one. Time and again, my brother Draper placed himself in the middle of the fray—in France, in Britain, and in sundry spots in the vast Pacific. All of this put his character to the ultimate test, and each time he rose to the challenge. Draper was born with charisma and drive; over time, he became a dynamic and outstanding leader. Draper's courage was contagious; those who followed him became as courageous as he. Through active participation in the war, Draper Kauffman did his part to shape the future, and it is that, above all, that inspired me to write this account of his remarkable service during and after World War II.

AMERICA'S FIRST FROGMAN

1

An Ambulance Driver in Alsace-Lorraine

Early in the morning of 10 May 1940—not long after midnight—Draper Kauffman reported to his job in the French region of Alsace-Lorraine. It was his first day, officially, as an ambulance driver for the French army. The decision to go to France was made without considering the feelings of his immediate family. "STOP HIM IMMEDIATELY!" his mother had cabled his father at sea as soon as she caught wind of Draper's resolve. He was getting embroiled in a war that the United States wanted nothing to do with. But no amount of stern lecturing from Capt. James Laurence "Reggie" Kauffman, USN, could persuade his son to veer from the rocky road down which he was heading. As his mother once said about Draper, "He always says 'Yes dear,' then does exactly what he pleases."

Kauffman's first day as an ambulance driver happened to be the very day that western Europe came apart at the seams. On 10 May German armies invaded Holland, Luxembourg, and Belgium, smashing through what was thought to be the impassable Ardennes Forest toward France.

Hitler's actions in May 1940 were the starkest indication yet of his designs on Europe. In 1938 the führer had annexed Austria and invaded Czechoslovakia, managing to justify his actions to France and Britain, which, only twenty years after the Great War and the loss of almost an entire generation of young men, were anxious to maintain peace at any cost. Not until September 1939, when Hitler marched into Poland, with which France and Britain had a treaty, did those countries feel compelled to declare war on Germany. The declaration, however, had no effect on Poland's fate; without armed Allied support that nation quickly succumbed.

An uneasy quiet settled over Europe, an eight-month lull that became known in England and the United States as the phony war; in France, the *drôle de guerre*. Under cover of silence, Hitler was consolidating his gains—plundering resources from the territories he'd invaded or overrun, transporting entire factories with hundreds of workers to Germany, establishing concentration camps, and strengthening his war-making capabilities and his defenses. It is hard to believe today how little of that behind-the-scenes activity got through to the rest of the world, or rather how entrenched that world was in wishful thinking. That see-no-evil stance had less to do with Hitler's gagged press than with a world grown weary of war and depression.

One of the führer's efforts during the phony war was construction of a series of defenses known as the Siegfried Line. The Siegfried Line lay along the French-German border, almost parallel to France's own defensive Maginot Line. In some places, including Alsace-Lorraine where Draper Kauffman would soon be, the two lines were a mere ten miles apart. The Siegfried Line fooled the French into thinking that Hitler planned to fight a war of fixed defenses. Far from it. Unbeknownst to French military leaders, the führer's intention was to launch a swift, aggressive invasion of France, and to send the bulk of his forces around or over, not through, the Maginot Line.

The Maginot Line was a series of fortifications in the east of France where that country bordered on Switzerland, Germany, and Luxembourg. This elaborate defensive frontier consisted of six-story underground forts, pillboxes, barracks, hospitals, power stations, miniature railroads, and casements with their guns pointed east toward the potential enemy. The French government had built it at enormous cost after World War I and convinced the French people that it was impregnable. So secure did the French military feel with this snaking steel and concrete colossus that they had cut conscription and neglected to update weaponry—they did not have a single new tank. During the phony war, French army divisions stationed on the Maginot Line made no attempt to shell Germany's portion of the Saar River, which was industrialized and within easy range of their heavy artillery. In fact, the French did little more than probe the Siegfried Line around Saarbrücken, in northeastern France. Captured German soldiers apparently claimed not to know that war had been declared between their country and France—which only confirmed the French army's sense of security.

The problem with the Maginot Line was that it stopped short of the supposedly impenetrable Ardennes Forest to the northwest. That, as events proved, was a fatal miscalculation. On 14 May 1940 German army divisions that had muscled their way through a gap in the Ardennes crossed the River Meuse at Sedan, France, easily outflanking the Maginot Line, while additional army divisions pressed against that line to keep French army units pinned down in the east of France. The divisions that had broken through at Sedan made a swift drive west toward the English Channel. By early June the Germans had routed British, French, and Belgian troops and gained control of northern France. At that point, Hitler abandoned an attempt to cut defending troops off from the sea, husbanding his precious panzers for a drive southward through France, and the routed Allied divisions were evacuated at Dunkirk. With his objective in northern France secured, Hitler's Armies A and B launched their broad attack against points south while Army C continued pressing against the Maginot Line at points east, including where Draper Kauffman was stationed in Alsace-Lorraine, south of Saarbrücken.

On 10 May 1940, as Hitler initiated his opening thrust against western Europe, Kauffman reported for ambulance duty. He was stationed near the town of Sarre Union, about ten miles short of the Maginot Line.

He had arrived there by an unconventional path. Kauffman had graduated from the Naval Academy in 1933 but was refused a commission when he failed to pass the eye exam. He went to work for the U.S. Lines Steamship Company in New York, where he had a good job that he enjoyed—until they sent him as an assistant operations manager to survey their Berlin office in early 1939. There Hitler's huge army and emotional following of thousands struck him as frighteningly ominous. Germany, he had not the slightest doubt, was planning to go to war. When indeed that happened, Kauffman joined the American Volunteer Ambulance Corps because at the time, with isolationist sentiment strong in the United States, it seemed the only way he could play a part in helping to slow Hitler's advance. He arrived in Paris in March and went through ambulance driver training.

On 10 May he volunteered to go to an advance post six miles beyond the Maginot Line, just four miles short of Hitler's Siegfried Line, a no-man's-land between the two lines that was patrolled by a volunteer group from the French army called the Corps Franc. The Corps Franc was an extraordinary collection of elite fighters—"as brave a group as I've ever come across," Kauffman would later write in a rare, twenty-page letter home to the family. At the time his mother and sister were living in California; his father was commanding a squadron of destroyers in the Caribbean. "You were either accepted by the Corps Franc or you weren't accepted," Kauffman went on, "and the two were miles apart." In the horrible weeks that were to follow, as French troops staved off German attacks across the Maginot Line, Kauffman would be inspired by the valor and tenacity exhibited by the men of the Corps Franc. "There wasn't anything they wouldn't do for you," he wrote. "If one member of the patrol was trapped and there were five others, they would attack fifty Germans to try to free the one man who was trapped."

For Draper Kauffman, that first day at his post was truly a baptism by fire. A couple of Corps Franc men came racing up on bicycles exclaiming that they had many men wounded near Frauenberg and requesting an ambulance to go for them. Kauffman volunteered for the duty and picked as the chief stretcher-bearer a man by the name of Gauvoi, who looked the calmest of the would-be volunteers. "I never would have done this if I'd known what it would be like," Kauffman confessed in his letter. "So many shells exploded in the road ahead . . . that my only instinct was to drive as fast as possible and I damn near wrecked the car doing it. When we picked up the wounded, the attendant calmly asked me to drive slowly so as not to jolt them. I . . . kept below twenty kilometers an hour—

though every second on that road it seemed to me increased their chances of really getting killed. After we got them transferred to another ambulance to go back to the hospital, I sat in my driver's seat and started shaking like a leaf." From that moment on, Kauffman understood how an infantryman could freeze, and how a soldier could run away.

While he was collecting himself, several more Corps Franc men came tearing down the road on bicycles and asked him to go again. He wanted to refuse. "I certainly would have if I'd been a Frenchman," he offered candidly, "or an American with Americans, but I couldn't very well disgrace us with them. I'll never again be as scared or feel as sick, but I think I covered it up so they thought I was cheerfully volunteering. The second trip was as bad as the first, with terribly wounded ones to be lifted and carried. Incidentally, both Gauvoi and I got Croix de Guerres for those trips. But more important at the time was my invitation to dinner that night with the Corps Franc."

On the first night at dinner there were 120 volunteers of the Corps Franc—of those only 14 would be alive and uninjured when Hitler's army breached the Maginot Line near Saarbrücken on 16 June. Draper Kauffman took his place among them, struggling to *tutoyer*. His schoolboy French was barely adequate to the task of the formal *vous,* and now he was being called upon to address this close-knit group with the familiar *tu*. He sat between a nineteen-year-old lieutenant named Toine and the fellow who had asked him to drive to the scene of carnage, Marcel. Toine was small, a gentleman of the finest, most sensitive type, and, in spite of his young age, very old school in his courteous manner and courtly bearing. Marcel was a large strapping farmer of twenty-eight, rough in bearing and manners. But their obvious differences mattered not at all. The Marcels and the Toines were brothers in the Corps Franc.

The elaborate dinner ritual struck Kauffman as a scene he might see in a movie. Each man killed since the previous night was solemnly toasted. Next someone read out the names of the wounded and they were toasted. Then the assembly drank to the American in their midst and he was allowed to make the final toast. "Confusion to Hitler and long live France!" The reigning spirit of selflessness was so grand it was contagious, and from that time on it enabled Kauffman to perform his job without caving in to fear.

He received a separate invitation to dinner each night, though he could accept only three more times because he almost never had enough time to sit down to eat. The friendships that these get-togethers nurtured were in one way good, but they made the war and its horrors far more personal and terrible for Kauffman because every time he went to collect the wounded there was at least one in each load who was a friend. "You sincerely call a man a friend in a very short time when things are hot," he wrote in his letter home. "This climaxed one day when I picked Toine off the field with his face half gone, one arm shot to pieces, and his left foot gone. When we got him into the light of the Poste de Secours I almost gave way, and he didn't help any by winking at me with his good eye and squeezing my hand with his good one."

In early June Kauffman was sent to a rear post called Berig, in the French countryside, for some rest and recreation. There he wrote his mother to reassure her:

> Today I am feeling like a million dollars! I have had twenty-eight hours' sleep, a shower, and a delicious hot meal, the first in nearly three weeks. I am in a post in the rear getting a rest and fully enjoying it. That shower was the most marvelous thing you could imagine!
>
> Another driver and myself are billeted with a wonderful French peasant family, with lots of milk, bread, butter—oh, all the things we've wanted. This is really R&R. The war is going on all around us but doesn't touch us. There is a large open hospital here where we make only about one trip a day, and that is usually to hospitals farther back, so they are not dangerous at all. The French treat us all like kings. From their soldiers second class to their generals they are all marvelous to us.
>
> You and Dad may have thought the French didn't really need us, but that is most definitely changed. They have needed us badly these last few weeks, and I feel we have saved the lives of many who would have died if we hadn't been here.
>
> One incident I think of. I went out as a stretcher-bearer the other day (the regiment was short of stretcher-bearers) and we picked up a young junior lieutenant, age twenty-two. His leg had been shot away but a quick tourniquet around the stump kept him from bleeding to death. We didn't say a word till we got to the car

> that had the American flag on it. He then asked in slow, perfect English, "Are you an American?" I said yes and he replied simply, "Thank you so much that you are here," and then passed out cold. . . .
>
> I wish I knew what America is thinking now. I have had no news . . . since leaving our base. I suppose all stories from this side are labeled propaganda but there are two simple facts for which I can vouch.
>
> One: the Germans frequently and obviously fire on the Red Cross when there is no chance of mistaking it. . . . We have all begged the directors in Paris to let us take the Red Cross off our cars as well as the American flag. They have agreed to our camouflaging the top and removing the Red Cross there, but they want it kept on the sides—I think from a public relations standpoint.
>
> Two: The French treat German prisoners who are wounded with the greatest care in the world. If I bring in four wounded—two French and two German—they are treated in the order of the seriousness of the wounds and no favoritism shown. I have had German wounded who spoke English and who have told me that they couldn't understand it. . . . Well, every nation has its ruffians and gangsters, but Germany seems to be a nation of gangsters, when in military uniform anyway.

In Berig, Kauffman grew close to a group of junior doctors, much like American interns, with whom he dined. On 10 June while they were eating together, the president of France came on the radio to announce that Italy had joined Germany in the war. There was a feeling of great bitterness toward Italy, and when the radio began playing "La Marseillaise" everybody jumped to their feet. "It must be the most exhilarating national anthem in the world," Kauffman declared to his family.

By 14 June German forces advancing from the north of France had reached Paris. French troops on the Maginot Line fought valiantly and refused to surrender, but the main German thrust outflanked them and took them from the rear. On 16 June Hitler's Army C quickly breached the demoralized Maginot defenses at Saarbrücken and Colmar, while the French army reeled into a headlong southern retreat, slowed by the panicked exodus of civilians seeking safety in southern France. The roads were clogged, and German pilots in Heinkels roared over at tree level, strafing the helpless tide. More fervently than ever, Draper Kauffman prayed that America would intervene. It seemed as if his prayers had been answered when, during a power blackout, notices appeared at the Berig town hall announcing that the United States had entered the war. Apparently similar notices were posted in other towns. The French reacted with wild enthusiasm—and then, thirty-six hours later, came the grim news that it had all been a mistake and the United States had not declared war after all. "It was brilliant propaganda on the part of the Germans, if they did it," Kauffman explained in a letter home, "because the enormous relief was followed by an even more enormous letdown." And yet "the French never showed resentment to us. . . . I'd have thought they would."

A few days after Kauffman left Berig news came that his doctor friends had all been killed. It seemed that they were in their medical tent marked with a huge Red Cross when German bombers released their deadly cargo.

Despair overcame the French in the latter half of June as the German invasion advanced and pushed south. Kauffman joined the wave of French army units retreating before this juggernaut. The French used American ambulances for the last-minute evacuation of towns and hospitals because, as the French general explained, troops seeing an American ambulance going back up north to the front to get the wounded was good for morale.

Kauffman drove the last vehicle out of Baccarat, southeast of Nancy, and the last one out of nearby Lunéville before the bridge there was demolished by French forces hoping to slow the German advance. Then he was sent back north to Sarre Union to evacuate civilians who had been given two days to leave. It was tragic—the very old and the very young in carts, the rest walking and carrying what little they could and dropping much of it along the way. This was not the first time the older people had been forcibly evacuated from their homes because of the Germans. It was not surprising that they felt bitterness toward the Germans and also toward their own government for being so ill prepared.

At one point Kauffman and three other ambulance drivers, to avoid being swamped by the flow of refugees, retreated to the top of Mont Repos, where the weather was perfect and the scenery breathtakingly beautiful. The passing cavalcade made for a pitiful contrast. As he explained, "It wasn't just that the men were in tatters—cloths wound about shoeless feet . . . , blood-stained shirts, improvised bandages on head, arms, legs with blood showing through. The animals . . . trudged along as though each step were to be the last one, and in many cases it was, as there were eleven who had to be shot in our view. The most tragic, however, were the shoulders. That had happened overnight. It was not the sag of exhaustion, it was the complete slump of utter despair coupled with the blank expression of a chaotic bewilderment."

The Germans had overrun the area and there was no hospital nearby. A French general sent for a volunteer to take wounded fighters through enemy lines to a hospital that had been seized by the Germans. So Kauffman loaded up his ambulance and took along another driver, a lieutenant by the name of Steel who had lived in Europe most of his life and spoke perfect French, German, and English. Upon their arrival at the forward French post, they were told that the German post was only a few kilometers up a winding road. They continued along at a crawl, so slowly that the white flags on the front and top of the ambulance barely flapped in the breeze, while Kauffman continuously dinged the bell and held the door ajar so as not to appear threatening to the enemy.

"I remember the cows browsing in that beautiful scenery," he wrote, "and finally we came around a bend and saw something move. Jeepers! With no bravery whatsoever, I jammed on the brakes, jumped out of the car, threw my hands in the air, and like a grade C movie yelled 'Kamarad!' About a dozen Germans had machine guns pointing at us, and there were about eight guns behind the ambulance, pointing at this potential Trojan horse, while we opened the doors. They found that yes, there really were badly wounded men. They actually let us take them to the hospital. But then, when we tried to make a second trip, we heard motorcycles charging up behind us and we knew we'd lost the game."

On 22 June, just six weeks after he had reported for ambulance duty, and one day following the armistice signed by the French and the Germans at Compiègne, Draper Kauffman and his codrivers were hauled off to prison camp at Lunéville.

Several thousand Frenchmen and some fifteen Americans were in that German prison camp. When the captured men arrived they were given a questionnaire that included the query, "Have you ever been in Germany?" Kauffman checked no. The prison commandant, who spoke fairly decent English, sent for him one day. As Draper stood before him he looked down on the desk where there was a thick file. He could read his name upside down on the top page.

The commandant said, "Now, have you ever been in Germany?"

"No sir!"

"I suppose," said the German officer, "you are not the Draper Kauffman who went to Germany in 1930 while he was a midshipman at the U.S. Naval Academy and who in 1939 went back to Germany—specifically to Berlin—as an employee of the U.S. Lines Steamship Company?"

Somehow the German military had come up with striking details about Kauffman's most recent jaunt to the German homeland, including the fact that on Good Friday 1939 he was at the Four Seasons Hotel in Berlin, where the concierge had been able to get him a ticket to *Parsifal,* and had said, "How wonderful to see *Parsifal* on Good Friday!" When the concierge had asked how he liked the performance, the young American had replied, "I hate to say so, but I thought it was dreadful." On Easter Sunday, the commandant rattled on, Kauffman had gone out to Sans Souci by bus and been observed talking to a couple on a bench, who had said they were from Iowa. "You know," the commandant quoted Kauffman as saying, "if I were a bomber pilot with orders to bomb a place like this I don't think I could do it." Furthermore, the commandant continued, Kauffman had represented the U.S. Lines at a North Atlantic conference on the shipment of gold, which was flowing out of Europe and was enormously profitable for the steamship lines.

THIS INCREDIBLE German intelligence made a mockery of Kauffman's answers on the questionnaire. Everything the commandant had said was correct. When Kauffman finally agreed that he had been to Germany, the man burst out laughing. "He's doing this just to show me Germany's omniscience," thought the American. It was frightening. How many buildings had Hitler devoted to housing minutely detailed records like these?

If the Germans were diligent at spying, they were masters at propaganda. In prison camp they showed a film of the German air force sinking five British battleships. Not until later did Kauffman learn that the entire battle had been faked.

A number of German guards had studied English and wanted to practice their language skills. During those sessions young Kauffman, who became known as a troublemaker, gave them a piece of his mind. "There's no way you're going to keep the United States out of this war," he told them, "and as soon as the United States comes in, it's all over as far as you're concerned. It was proven in 1917–18 and it will be the same thing all over again." The guards discounted what he said. They were firmly convinced that the world had reached a stage where it needed to be run by a homogeneous, efficient group of people, namely, the Germans. As proof of their superiority they now could point to the demolition in several hundred days of Poland and France, not to mention the subjugation of Austria, Czechoslovakia, Belgium, and Holland. Draper Kauffman's outspoken declarations did not appear to worry them. But occasionally the suggestion of American involvement in the conflict seemed to send a very small cloud into their very blue sky.

The Americans were separated from the French, who had become dispirited, and, except for an occasional kick, the Germans generally left the Americans alone. The Yanks spent most of their time planning to escape, until one day a Frenchman managed that feat. The Germans put the names of all the French prisoners in a box, drew out ten names, lined them up, and shot them while the Americans were forced to watch, aghast. They then said, "If an American escapes, we'll draw ten of your names out of the hat and shoot you." That put an end to any American escape plans. Kauffman and his compatriots made a solemn pact never even to try.

In the United States, Draper's mother had received a typed postcard purportedly from her son announcing that he was safe, in good health, and being well treated by the German army. It bore no postmark or signature. This was at least more encouraging than the only news she had had before, which consisted of a brief newspaper clipping that listed his name among a number of men who had been awarded the Croix de Guerre. Because most of the people mentioned, she discovered, had been killed, Mrs. Kauffman had been racked with miserable uncertainty. Now it seemed that at least he was alive, even if he had been captured. At about this time, Capt. Roscoe Henry Hillenkoetter, U.S. naval attaché in Paris, sent Reggie Kauffman a message at sea saying he had heard his son was safe in a prison camp.

The greatest annoyance in prison camp was boredom. But it gave Kauffman considerable time to think about his life up until that point and the family he had left behind. They were small as families went, a close-knit foursome—Draper and his sister, Betty Lou, eleven years his junior, and their mother and father.

Elizabeth Draper Kauffman (known as Elsa) was a charming, beautiful, witty woman who loved to travel, entertain, and tell stories. Her son, Draper, supplied plenty of material for her stories. When he was five his dad was a lieutenant junior grade with the Naval Experiment Station in Annapolis, researching the structure of various fuel oils for navy ships. The family lived on the Naval Academy grounds. His mother often chuckled about the time her five-year-old, who spent every waking minute outdoors playing from dawn to dusk, was summoned into the house for disobeying her. He ran in and said, "Hurry up and spank me so I can go back out and play!" Draper was independent at an early age.

Draper and his mother were very close. Because his sister was born so much later and his father was frequently away at sea, for many years it was just the two of them at home together, wherever they happened to pitch their tent as an itinerant navy family. No matter how often they moved, Elsa Kauffman never let go of her firm intention to raise her son in the best possible way, which included making sure he received a good education. The very week he was born in 1911 she began saving twenty cents a week toward his college. In later years, strong-minded and ever resourceful, she took great pains to make sure that he applied himself at Kent School, and she searched for means to combat the nearsightedness that threatened to bar him from entry into the Naval Academy.

In 1917–18, when Reggie Kauffman was away at war, Elsa was stricken with a life-threatening case of flu during the epidemic that killed more people than did the war itself. She was living with Draper at the Peggy Stuart Inn just outside the main gate of the Naval Academy. She quarantined herself and arranged for a maid at the inn to give Draper his meals and take him to and from school. The maid would leave a tray for Mrs. Kauffman outside her closed door, though for quite some time she was too ill to get out of bed and fetch it. One day Draper asked the maid why the Navy Chapel bells rang all day long. "Them's all the funerals," she replied. It was unsettling for Draper to have his mother so very ill. Elizabeth Kauffman did eventually recover. In order not to worry her husband she did not say a word about her illness to him until after he came home from the war.

Elsa Kauffman's personality made her a good match for her naval officer husband, who shared her zest for life and her sense of humor. He was a man of decision who always laughed about the man who was passed over for captain "because he never could decide whether to say yes or no when either would have done." Reggie Kauffman's own favorite approach to decision making he summed up with a chuckle: "So we compromised and did it my way." But his humor was not the mark of a shallow man. On the contrary, he was philosophical and deeply religious. And he truly loved the navy. Like many midwestern boys—he hailed from Miamisburg, Ohio—he had been drawn to the sea and was happiest aboard ship, happiest of all in command. There was no doubt about that.

He had transmitted that love to his son. While Draper was still quite young his father took him on several short cruises, which were a thrill for him. He looked up to his dad and wanted to be just like him. When he was about nine, his mother took him to meet his father's ship at Coronado, California, where the family had moved from the East Coast. Reggie Kauffman had become a snappy dresser in London during World War I after discovering Gieves and Company, maker of Royal Navy uniforms and top-of-the-line civilian clothes. When Elsa and Draper Kauffman headed down to the dock they found themselves standing next to a burly navy chief. When Reggie Kauffman came off the ship with a dapper walking stick from Gieves, Draper's mother commented mischievously to the chief, "*That* looks like a nice man coming down the gangway." "Listen lady," replied the chief with obvious pride, "don't let them fancy clothes deceive you none. That's Stormy Kauffman, the toughest destroyer skipper in the navy!" Draper never forgot that.

Although Reggie Kauffman had served on battleships and cruisers, his true love was the destroyer, small enough to "turn on a dime." You knew what made a destroyer tick—each mechanical part—and you got to know every member of her crew personally. It was Draper Kauffman's dream to be a destroyer skipper just like his dad.

He had big shoes to fill, for his father had a naval career that was growing more distinguished with each year. During World War I his first assignment had been as head of the armed guard on a troopship, the SS *Tenadores,* carrying American soldiers to fight in France, the first U.S. troopship to land on those shores. He was then ordered to a destroyer headed for Queenstown, Ireland, where U.S. ships served under the command of the Royal Navy. By the time the Great War was over—when his wife and son watched him step off his ship with that walking stick—Kauffman was a lieutenant commander and captain of his own destroyer. He had been awarded the U.S. Navy's highest medal, the Navy Cross, for distinguished service while engaged in the hazardous duty of patrolling and escorting convoys through waters infested with enemy submarines.

In November 1920 Reggie Kauffman was ordered to Washington, D.C., to head up the Bureau of Engineering's new radio division. During his three years there he was in charge of procuring radio equipment for the navy. He had been offered several civilian jobs, including one with an oil company at many times his navy salary, but he could not imagine giving up a career for which he harbored such a passion. In Washington the Kauffmans had three precious years of family life. Draper attended Saint Alban's School. In 1922, when he was eleven years old, his sister, Elizabeth Louise (Betty Lou), was born. By sheer happenstance, Wallis Spencer, the future wife of the Prince of Wales, served as one of Betty Lou's godmothers. The baby had been diagnosed with a life-threatening ear infection and her distraught mother had asked the minister to come and christen her. A close friend, Marianna Sands, was called in as godmother, and the baby's father was summoned home and directed to bring someone to act as godfather. At this inauspicious moment Wallis, whose first husband, Winfield Spencer, had just left her in a drunken rage, stopped at the house to pour out her woes to Elsa Kauffman. Elsa told her visitor, "I haven't got time to listen now, Wallis—but would you like to be Betty Lou's other godmother?"

Draper was to take a very dim view of his sister's godmother, the future Duchess of Windsor. Wallis Spencer had begun an affair with a handsome young secretary at the Argentine embassy and later that year, no doubt owing to the resulting scandal, was dropped from the guest list for a party given by the Italian ambassador. It was considered the event of the year in Washington. Wallis was livid. Having decided it was Elsa Kauffman's fault because the Italian ambassador was a good friend of the family, she stormed into the house, swept past Draper, and lit into his mother with a stream of abuse the likes of which his tender eleven-year-old ears had never heard. "No one has ever spoken to me like that in my life and that's the last time I'm ever going to speak to you!" Mrs. Kauffman snapped, and promptly showed Wallis out of the house.

Several years later Elsa Kauffman was visiting Wallis Spencer's cousin in England, Corinne Murray. "You know, Elsa," her hostess said, not aware of the earlier contretemps, "Wallis is seeing quite a lot of the Prince of Wales, so I've asked them over for drinks while you're here." To which Draper's mother replied, "Since I don't speak to her in my country, I don't know why I should speak to her over here," and found an excuse to absent herself for the evening. She confessed later with a laugh to her son, "I wish I hadn't been quite so principled!"

The Kauffman family had only three years together as a family in Washington, for in 1925 Draper went off to Kent School in Connecticut. When he was a sophomore the family left him behind and moved to Rio de Janeiro, where Reggie Kauffman was sent as a member of the U.S. naval mission helping Brazil, at its request, to improve the caliber of its destroyer force. Draper was fifteen at that time but his little sister was only four, and the family's sojourn in Latin America resulted in a story that Reggie Kauffman always told with amusement about his children's age difference. In his work with the Brazilian navy he came to admire many of the officers he met. But there was one problem: he was having a very difficult time persuading the Brazilian officers in a destroyer group to stay out at sea, even overnight. He argued with them, saying that in a professional navy officers often had to stay at sea for extended periods. He eventually was able to get a few of them to stay aboard his destroyer for almost a week. One morning over coffee in his cabin, one of the Brazilians noticed a picture of Draper and Betty Lou. "Ah, Commandante," he remarked admiringly, "those are two of your children?"

"Yes," replied Kauffman, "my only two."

"But there are many years between them?" the man said, surprised.

"Eleven years."

The Brazilian's face fell. "They keep you that long at sea in your country?"

Despite their age difference and the years of separation, Betty Lou adored her brother. He was as charming and funny with his young sister as he was with the rest of the world, and like so many others, she came under his spell. It helped, of course, that when she was small Draper took time to read to her, frequently *Winnie the Pooh* and *Alice in Wonderland*. He told her that he planned to be a writer, and that he had heard *Alice in Wonderland* was a good thing for aspiring writers to read.

During his years at Kent School, Draper discovered girls. When he was fifteen he sailed down to Rio de Janeiro for summer vacation and during the journey he and a Brazilian boy his age, Luiz, became fast friends. Luiz told him how much he was looking forward to his sixteenth birthday. "Why?" asked Draper. "Because I'm going to be given a girl for my birthday!" replied his friend. When Draper requested the same from his father, he was firmly told that a more North American way was to capture a girl's heart with flowers. He noticed that American ladies seemed crazy about orchids, which were a dime a dozen in Rio. En route back to the States in the fall he fell for a movie star on the ship. Drawing on his newfound knowledge of the power of exotic flowers, he ordered her two dozen orchids when he arrived back in New York and had the bill sent to Kent. Being penniless, of course he sent the tab off to his dad, who was more than a little annoyed.

It was at Kent School that Draper Kauffman realized he wanted to go into the navy—and that he had better start preparing. He was having trouble with his eyes, so his mother left Brazil with Draper's sister in tow to try to help him out. She took him to see John Burke, a well-known ophthalmologist in Washington, who told her that her son's eyes were weak and that he would never pass the Naval Academy physical. Reggie Kauffman, taking Dr. Burke's word as gospel—and also because he worried that his son's choice of the navy had been made out of loyalty to him—enrolled Draper at Princeton. He had not, however, reckoned on Draper's perseverance, or on his wife's discovery of Dr. Bates, a new and unorthodox eye doctor who introduced her son to a daily regimen of lengthy eye exercises, including "palming," in which he had to hold his hands over his eyes for a full hour. Though the regimen was, in Draper's words, "excruciatingly boring," and he could seldom afford the time for it, his eyes did seem to improve.

Another problem soon appeared. An Ohio congressman had promised Draper Kauffman an appointment to the Naval Academy, but this benefactor died suddenly. His successor, moreover, already had his own list of appointments drawn up. Draper thereupon did what he knew was inexcusable. He wheedled a hundred dollars out of his grandmother, left school without telling anyone where he was going, and made his way to Washington, D.C., where he camped out at the YMCA. By the time he resurfaced at school, it could be safely said that his parents and Father Sill, headmaster at Kent, were ready to shoot him. Draper Kauffman had a one-track mind; when he decided something was important he pursued it to the end—a trait he retained throughout his life, and for which his father repeatedly criticized him.

While he was in Washington, Draper managed to see twenty-two congressmen who had not filled their appointments. His most difficult task was bluffing his way past their secretaries; having gained the inner sanctum, he would tell each congressman how badly he wanted to attend the Naval Academy. He knew how to appeal to people's sympathies and touch a heart if there was one to be touched. He played his woebegone story for all it was worth and in the end he found three representatives willing to help. But he later received a letter from the Navy Department informing him that he could have only one appointment to the academy, and that he was to choose his sponsor. In the end, he had the luxury of selecting another Ohio congressman, Roy G. Fitzgerald.

No amount of charm, however, could fix Draper Kauffman's eyes. He passed his academic entrance exams for the academy but failed the eye test. A sty in his left eye gave him an excuse to come back and take it again. The second time he had poison ivy in both eyes, and so was given yet another chance. The test was further delayed on account of his sister, Betty Lou. On the Fourth of July, Draper, his mother, and his sister joined friends for an idyllic picnic on the flat rocks at Beavertail in Jamestown, Rhode Island. As they were departing, Betty Lou spotted a firecracker that had not been lit and begged her brother to do the honors. Obliging his little sister, Kauffman struck a match and the firecracker exploded in his eye. He was a good sport about it—he never said a cross word to his sister, and again the Naval Academy postponed his eye test. At the end of July the academy finally examined his eyes and decided he could be admitted.

Kent School had given Draper Kauffman such a good background academically that he did not have to study strenuously during his plebe year, which was a pleasant surprise after navigating such an obstacle course just to get into the academy. The work became more challenging in his second or Youngster year, but his dad kept a watchful eye on him from Brazil and somehow he squeezed through. The summer of that year Kauffman took his "Youngster cruise," and he sent his sister presents from the countries he visited. He knew how to keep a hold on her heart. From Germany he mailed a large porcelain doll with eyes that opened and closed, a gift Betty Lou cherished not least because no other girl she knew was lucky enough to possess one, but even more because they did not have a brother like the one she doted on. Betty Lou's mother outfitted her in smocked Liberty Lawn dresses complete with bloomers, and when Draper's beautiful doll arrived in the mail, she had it dressed to match. Betty Lou's joy was complete.

In the summer of his second-class (junior) year Kauffman had his first taste of responsibility as a battalion commander; to his surprise he liked it. It was only one of many experiences at the Naval Academy that he reveled in. He rowed on the crew in his second-class year as captain of the lightweights (his mother pumped him full of bananas and chocolate milkshakes to get up his weight for varsity, but he always rowed off all the extra calories). He had a hand in organizing the Quarterdeck Society, devoted to public speaking and debate, and in reorganizing the Trident Society, a literary group. In addition, he was on the reception committee, the pep squad, and the yearbook staff. During his first-class or senior year he had the lead in the drama society, the Masqueraders.

Despite Draper Kauffman's varied accomplishments, his father was difficult to please and frequently came down hard on him, which he would continue to do in later years. It was a tribute to his good nature that he managed not to let his dad's recurring admonitions wear him down, and over the years they maintained a close relationship. Among issues that the senior Kauffman brought up repeatedly were his son's mediocre grades (he kept a chart in Brazil tracking Draper's monthly academic performance) and, after the Naval Academy, his failure to engage in regular exercise (Reggie Kauffman was an avid walker, swimmer, and golfer). Moreover, in his father's mind Draper did not pay enough attention to how he looked in his civilian clothes. Commander Kauffman was particular about his appearance and felt that his son should live up to the same standard.

But all else paled next to Draper's greatest filial shortcoming: his disinclination to write. As much as he admired and appreciated his mother and father, he became so engrossed in his own projects that, except in times of great urgency, their letters would pile up, unanswered. Unlike his father, who was a faithful, voluminous, and articulate letter-writer, Draper often simply could not make himself set pen to paper. Nearly every Thursday when Reggie Kauffman went to meet the mail boat in Rio de Janeiro, he would note in his journal, "Again no letter from Draper." Years later in prison camp, when Draper Kauffman finally had all the time in the world to communicate and, at last, the inclination, there was no stationery for prisoners. He determined that when he got out he would write the family about his experiences in France—which he did, primarily in one long letter.

DESPITE KAUFFMAN'S SUCCESSES at the Naval Academy, his eyes continued to hold him back. During the Depression the U.S. Congress had passed a law that would permit only half the graduates of the classes of 1932 and 1933 to be commissioned. Midshipmen were being carefully screened with physicals, and when the eye standard for graduating was raised from 18/20 to 20/20, Draper Kauffman could not squeeze by. June Week—graduation time—was a sad passage for him and the half of his class who ended up without commissions.

Draper's mother and sister arrived in Annapolis several weeks before graduation. Betty Lou was only ten, and she spent much of her time roller-skating on the academy grounds and keeping a sharp eye out for her brother. One day she saw him, marching by in formation. "Dray, Dray! Look, it's me!" she shouted. The midshipmen were not allowed to turn their heads while marching, but Draper nonetheless bestowed a friendly grin on his little sister and immediately got put on report.

Because of Betty Lou's youthful indiscretion, her brother missed a big dinner out on the town that his family had planned. He never said anything to her, but her mother did.

Reggie Kauffman was exceedingly upset about Draper's missing out on a commission. Moreover, it was June 1933 and his only son, full of promise, had no prospects in the midst of the severest depression that had ever hit the United States. Although Draper Kauffman approached job hunting with naive confidence, he quickly gained an appreciation for the breadlines that midshipmen were inclined to think other people stood in, not themselves.

He managed to survive, however. Shortly after graduation a troupe arrived in Annapolis to make a B-grade movie called *Midshipman Jack*. A technical director was needed, and Kauffman was suggested on the strength of his experience as the lead in the Masqueraders. He accepted the job immediately for what in those days was a princely sum, fifty dollars a day. His bank account was further padded when senior officers at the Naval Academy said that the hero, Bruce Cabot, could not wear the midnight blue uniform with which he had been outfitted—it would have to be regulation navy blue. Draper Kauffman, who happened to be about the same size as Cabot, offered his cruise box full of uniforms, which he no longer needed since he did not have a commission. The movie director, grateful that the production would not be delayed by this hitch, presented Kauffman with an eight-hundred-dollar check in return. On top of that, he got to know the eighteen-year-old star, Betty Furness, of movie and later early television fame, because she and her mother had taken up temporary quarters at the Peggy Stuart Inn where his mother and sister were staying. Mrs. Furness approved of the Kauffmans, which meant that Draper was the only young man in Annapolis allowed to date the toast of the town. A movie star! His sister was highly impressed, not least when he informed her that he had given the actress the miniature copy of his academy ring.

As it turned out, Kauffman did not have to wait long for a real job, not by depression standards. The same talent that got him into the offices of twenty-two congressmen in Washington as a lowly prep school student eventually landed him a job, now as a Naval Academy graduate. After a single summer of searching, he was offered a position at the U.S.

Lines in New York. He rose quickly through the ranks and became assistant operations manager, and in 1939 he spent two months in the company's British office, two months in the French office, and then two unforgettable months in the German office.

By the time Kauffman returned to New York he was convinced that a war was coming unless the United States pronounced that it would join hostilities if they broke out. He also strongly believed that if there were a war and the United States stayed out, Germany would completely overwhelm both France and Britain. With his head full of these thoughts, Kauffman joined a so-called free lecture circuit, traveling to various bureaus in the New York–New Jersey area and speaking before whatever audience happened to assemble (lectures were free of charge). Four nights a week he delivered a stump speech urging the United States to issue a statement that it would join Britain and France if Germany declared war, but he could have stayed in bed for all the enthusiasm he was able to arouse. The prevailing antiwar sentiment in the United States was reflected in the size of its military. In 1938 when Hitler invaded and easily crushed Czechoslovakia, that country had a better-equipped army than the United States, which was only a third-rate military power at that time. Kauffman's argument that the United States should join the war was proffered with a plea that the country strengthen its armed forces.

On 1 September 1939, when Germany marched into Poland, his appeals grew urgent. The United States should enter the war immediately, he stated baldly. His audiences went from apathetic to antagonistic, particularly women. "Frog lover! Limey lover! Why don't you go over and join them yourself and leave us out of it? Don't send my son to war!" These were the responses he heard most frequently. He did not make any converts—not one. If he was devastated at the turn of events and his own inability to influence them, his friends were mildly amused by his maverick stance and they gave him a good deal of ribbing.

In more ways than one, this was a time of soul-searching for Kauffman. The wife of his boss and mentor at the U.S. Lines, Basil Harris, was a devout Catholic and often invited the young man to their weekend homes on Long Island and in Rye, New York, along with a priest, Father James Keller, who was a deeply intelligent man with a magnetic personality. Following many late nights of talk, Kauffman became convinced that he should leave the Episcopal church and become a Catholic. In a rare letter to his mother in California, he informed her that he had been baptized and that afterward Mrs. Harris had given him a celebratory luncheon at the Waldorf in New York. This was upsetting to Elsa, who had insisted that Draper's father become an Episcopalian before they were married. She was as devout an Episcopalian as Mrs. Harris was a Catholic. Several years later, Kauffman put his mother's mind to rest by returning to the church of his boyhood.

The one who bore the brunt of Kauffman's religious conversion was his sister, Betty Lou. At the time she was at the Dominican Convent of San Raphael, a boarding school in California and the only school that, as an itinerant daughter of the navy, she had ever hoped to attend for three consecutive years. She had ended her junior year on a happy note, having won the English prize, been elected president of the Shakespeare Club and the Poetry Club, selected as editor of the yearbook, and nominated for president of her class. Under the influence of her brother's conversion, she half jokingly mentioned to her mother that she had thought of becoming a nun. That was too much for Elsa Kauffman. Near the beginning of Betty Lou's senior year her mother whisked her out of the convent so fast she barely had time to blink and packed her off to a boarding school in San Francisco, Miss Hamlin's, allaying the pain of transfer with promises of visits to the theater, the ballet, and the ski slopes of Yosemite. Mrs. Kauffman, like her son, had amazing powers of persuasion.

Draper Kauffman finally decided that he was not doing any good with his speeches on the free lecture circuit. But he was determined to do something about what he saw happening in the world. He had heard about the American Volunteer Ambulance Corps, which had placed itself under the direct orders of the French army, and he went to see its head, a Colonel Thompson. Thompson turned out to be a great help, because Kauffman had no way of meeting the financial requirements. All volunteers were required to put up $3,000 for an ambulance—a phenomenal sum at that time—and have an additional $500 at their disposal to take care of expenses and food while in the French army. Kauffman had enough for the subsistence but could cough up only $500 toward the ambulance. Colonel Thomson through various channels was able to scrape together the remaining $2,500 and, later, another $3,000 when Kauffman had an ambulance shot out from under him.

Kauffman now had two tasks ahead of him. One was to inform the U.S. Lines. The other, a more daunting prospect, was to tell his family. His bosses at the U.S. Lines were none too pleased, but he managed to persuade them to grant their wayward employee a six-month leave of absence. As for his mother and dad, they were exceedingly perturbed. After shooting off a cable to her husband demanding that he stop Draper, his mother called Betty Lou at the University of California at Berkeley, where she was a freshman, with instructions to write her brother and tell him how foolish it would be for him to ship out to France. Betty Lou honored her request, more or less. But her brother's decision only increased his stature in her eyes. She never admitted it to her mother, but she could not resist saying how proud she was of him for wanting to go.

In spite of family resistance, Kauffman did not regret his decision to join the French effort—that is, not until he landed in German hands. Wasting away in prison camp, he did have second thoughts. His frustration was compounded when it dawned on him why his mother and father were so strongly opposed to his abandoning his job as a shipping company manager in New York to drive an ambulance in France. It was his fault, he began to see, for not expressing to them long ago his passion about this war. With his dad at sea and his mother and sister in California, and he, as always, delinquent in letter writing, Kauffman had neglected to fill them in on his trip to Berlin for the U.S. Lines and his reaction to Hitler's raving speeches, not to mention the German public's frenzied embrace of their leader. Upon his departure for France he had written his father to inform him of his plans, adding, "I think there are times when a thing is worth fighting for, even if it is not in your best self-interest at the moment." But that failed to communicate the depth of his commitment to helping defeat Hitler. It was the poignant experience of seeing Germany firsthand that distinguished Draper Kauffman from so many of his fellow Americans who turned a blind eye and a deaf ear to the ominous rumblings in Europe.

In the German prison camp, the Americans had been penned right alongside the double-gated entrance to the camp. One day, as the ambulance drivers were playing one of their endless games of poker with twigs in the dirt, a mysterious visitor appeared. As Kauffman told it later, "We heard a woman's voice—a very high, shrill American voice berating the guard at the entrance. There was this lady who seemed well along in years (probably fifty). It was a hot day, but she was dressed like what I thought missionaries wore—a long black dress that covered her from her neck to her ankles. She was giving the guard hell because she was an American citizen and had a perfect right to visit this prison camp. Of course he didn't understand a word of her English. Finally she took her umbrella and whacked it down on the guard's helmet (it couldn't have hurt, but it certainly surprised him), marched past him and through the inner gate."

Assuming she would be promptly thrown out, the prisoners hurried to scribble down their names and addresses and rushed them over to her, hoping to get word to their families. The commandant surfaced immediately and ordered her to leave. No, she said, raising her voice as she cited the Geneva Convention rules and argued that they should have traded the Americans by now, that their actions were illegal. The man just looked at her and wrung his hands. Nothing in his book instructed him how to handle a case like this, and finally he walked away, after saying that she could have a word with the men.

They could not believe this was happening—an American woman spending an hour in their company, asking them questions about themselves. Talking to Lieutenant Steel, who had lived in Germany, she shifted into what he later said was perfect German. He said, "I'm curious—why didn't you speak German to the guards or the commandant?" Her reply: "You never want to speak German to them; it gives them a sense of superiority, and God knows they've got enough of that!" Kauffman heard later that the woman may have been a member of the Morgan Group, an American Quaker organization based in Paris. She invited them to come out and see her ambulance, which was new and sported elaborate equipment, but the men remembered their pact never to attempt escape and politely declined.

"So," concluded Kauffman, "thanks to her getting back to our embassy (we heard later that she put on this performance at some eleven German prison camps and secured the Americans' release at all of them), the day came when we were put in a cattle car with two guards and delivered to the U.S. embassy in Paris."

Captain Hillenkoetter, who was not only U.S. naval attaché but also, because the American ambassador to France had been called home, chargé d'affaires, officially received the prisoners when they arrived in the cattle car at the embassy. The men had to sign statements saying that they would never join any armed force against the German Reich, and the Germans withheld their passports. The embassy issued new passports good for travel only through France, Spain, and Portugal en route to the United States. Also stamped on the documents (apparently as part of the deal struck with the Germans to free the Americans), was the disclaimer "Not valid in the United Kingdom," something that would later cause Kauffman some trouble.

The Morgan Unit was a godsend. It found the former prisoners rooms in the Hotel Bristol and rounded up a doctor. During the weeks in prison, where the Germans gave them almost no food, they had all become emaciated. Draper Kauffman had dropped 40 pounds, from 165 to 125. The doctor put them on a regimen of five meals a day, but they had to be small. One of the group said, "To hell with this!" went out and got himself a hearty meal, and was sick as a dog for a couple of days.

Kauffman had an odd experience in Paris while he was getting ready to go south to Lisbon. He was walking along the street and a man with a British accent came up to him. "I know your background at the U.S. Naval Academy and I understand you're going to Lisbon," he murmured. Then he mentioned an airfield that the Germans were preparing near Paris. They were laying cement around all the trees but had not cut the trees down. "I want you to pass this on to Sir Noel Charles, who is our minister in Lisbon," the man went on. Thinking this could be a trap, Kauffman acted noncommittal, but he did memorize the information.

The six gaunt ambulance drivers left Paris with two girls from the Morgan group and an American nun and proceeded through occupied France to the Spanish border, unescorted. They were U.S. citizens, and they did not expect trouble because the United States was not at war with Germany. The wild confusion that reigned in France during the early weeks of the occupation delayed them; it took eight days for them to cross the two borders and reach Lisbon. There they saw a U.S. Navy cruiser at anchor in the harbor. Kauffman discovered that Adm. David LeBreton, a friend of his father's, was on board. In his wrinkled French army uniform he paid a call. LeBreton, who had been expecting Kauffman, welcomed him with open arms. Apparently Reggie Kauffman, though informed by Captain Hillenkoetter that his son had been in a prison camp, had not yet received Hillenkoetter's follow-up message about Draper's release, and he had been overloading all the navy circuits to Europe with urgent requests as to the fate of his son. LeBreton treated Kauffman to a good American meal and they discussed his plans, which, despite the disqualifying statement on his passport, included a trip to England. Nothing could deter him now. Not surprisingly, he had grown even more violently anti-German. "It took me years after the war to get my senses back and be comfortable with German nationals," Kauffman later said, "which I'm embarrassed about, but it was true." In his mind, traveling to England would be the quickest way to fulfill his goal of opposing Germany's lust for world power.

He went to see Sir Noel Charles with the story about the airfield and the cement-encircled trees. Charles promised, "We'll send it to England." Kauffman took the occasion to add, "I would like very much to join the British navy when I get there. Do you think that's possible?" Sir Noel agreed to put that in the message as well. He received return word that the British government had heard about the airfield but also that it was useful to get confirmation. As for Draper Kauffman's application to the Royal Navy, it would be given every consideration.

"How are you going to get to England?" Sir Noel asked him.

"Sir," he replied, "that was my next question to you!"

Charles sent for an expert in such matters, who said, "We can put him on one of the small freighters that has cabin accommodations for twelve. Of course, he'll have to sign on to make it legal." This was duly arranged, and thus did Draper Kauffman, graduate of the U.S. Naval Academy, become a lowly second pantryman on the SS *Spiro*.

The SS *Spiro* was a coastal 2,500-tonner. German Focke-Wulfs were thick over Lisbon Bay, but that did not scare Kauffman, who assumed they would hit other ships—not his.

The captain had received orders that Draper Kauffman was to be put in one of the passenger cabins, which led to a peculiar situation because second pantryman was as low as possible in the ship's hierarchy. The captain had no problem with this unorthodox arrangement; he understood that Kauffman was primarily a passenger. But he went on to say, "I need a second pantryman badly and you're signed on."

"What the hell," thought Kauffman, "I don't mind. It gives me something to do." It sure did. He later pointed out, "There's a great social gulf between a second pantryman and a first pantryman. The first pantryman does the dishes and peels the string beans. The second pantryman does the pots and pans and peels the potatoes, and there's a hell of a difference there. Boy, do the British ever eat potatoes!"

The *Spiro* took forty-three days to go nonstop from Lisbon to Methil, Scotland. First, in convoy but unescorted, she crossed the South Atlantic to a point near the mouth of the Amazon, then followed the American coastline up to Boston, where she joined an escorted convoy and came back across the Atlantic without incident. Kauffman had a fine time:

> Every afternoon I set up three chairs on the no. 3 hatch, put two buckets in front of each—each bucket was half full of spuds—and in five minutes I had people on either side of me peeling potatoes so that they could talk to this peculiar Yank.
>
> One time one of the regular lookouts got very sick. When I was asked to be a lookout I was a little dubious because of my near-sighted eyes, but there was a young French soldier aboard who, though he spoke no English, had good eyes, so we stood watch together. He'd spot a *lumière la-bas* and I'd yell down, "There's a light over there!"

2

A Yank Joins the Battle of Britain

In September 1940 the SS *Spiro* and its second pantryman arrived at Methil, Scotland. Draper Kauffman came, as he had to France, at an eventful time. September was the month that Hitler decided to intensify his bombing of Britain, going after more than just industrial and military targets. Earlier, his objective had been to bomb the Royal Air Force out of existence before sending seaborne infantry troops to invade Britain. Civilian areas, including London, were not to be targeted. But the Royal Air Force was proving more formidable than expected, not least because it was outproducing the Germans in fighter planes. In August a German pilot racing back to the motherland unintentionally jettisoned a bomb over England's capital city. Churchill seized upon this event to order a reprisal raid on Berlin, and the Battle of Britain quickly heated up. On 7 September, finally given the green light by Hitler to go after civilian targets, the Luftwaffe launched an around-the-clock bombing raid on London that would last for seven days, result in the deaths of thousands of civilians—the Royal Family barely escaped a bomb that landed on

Buckingham Palace—and leave scars across a cityscape where once there had been ancient churches, handsome buildings, and beloved historic monuments.

When he arrived in Scotland wearing the uniform of the French army, Kauffman found himself saluted by every noncommissioned officer and soldier he passed. Technically he was still in the French army, having never been discharged, and he was still carrying the passport that the Germans had stamped "Not valid for travel to England." That "gosh-darned" document, as he referred to it, came back to haunt him when he tried to land at Methil. Scottish officials packed him off to London with instructions to the chief of police there and to the American consul. He went into the consular office first and said, "I have a mistake on my passport. Would you correct it for me? The passport says 'Not valid for travel to England.' Well, I'm already in England so obviously that's wrong."

The young lady at the desk was very obliging. "Why certainly," she said, and stamped out the offending phrase. Without questioning him, she added a new one saying Kauffman's passport was valid for travel in the United Kingdom for six months—a gesture that so amused him that he kept the passport for years afterward. Thus freshly equipped, he proceeded to the chief of police and slid like butter through the bureaucratic chute. His next stop was the British Admiralty, where he announced that he would like to join the Royal Navy, proffering a copy of the message from whoever had sent it to Sir Noel. Told to explain his background in writing for the secretary of the Admiralty and to get some verification, Draper approached Capt. Alan Kirk, the American naval attaché and a friend of his father. Captain Kirk took him to lunch and afterward penned a short, noncommittal cover note saying, "As far as I know, everything in his dossier is correct," adding, "I've known him all his life and know his family very well." This was turned over to a Captain Barry, naval assistant to the first sea lord, who interviewed Kauffman at length and sent him for a slap-dash medical exam that instantly proved his eyes were not any good and that he was still underweight (despite forty-three days of peeled potatoes).

Nevertheless, several weeks later he was able to write home giving his address as HMS King Alfred and announcing that he was now a full-fledged member of the Royal Navy Volunteer Reserve (RNVR). "Can you imagine," he wrote, "an alien getting into our navy between nine o'clock in the morning and five o'clock in the evening! But of course they are at war and shorthanded—and I never would have gotten in if I hadn't graduated from our Naval Academy."

Draper Kauffman was commissioned a sublieutenant RNVR Special Branch, a nonseagoing billet, and sent immediately to HMS King Alfred, which was not a ship but rather an RNVR officer training school at Hove, a suburb of Brighton on the southern coast of England. (In Britain, even shore stations were designated HMS for His [or Her] Majesty's Ship. The Royal Navy was amused by German propaganda that claimed they had sunk HMS King Alfred.) The majority of Kauffman's compatriots at the school were cadets, who had had from three to nine months at sea as enlisted men, then came to Hove and graduated as officers RNVR. A minority were already officers when they arrived because of special training, in Kauffman's case, the U.S. Naval Academy. Having forgotten a good deal in the seven years since graduation, he was further set back by the (to him) strange terminology that was British nautical English. Because of his poor vision he could not go to sea as a watch officer, and he wrote home that he would have a fit if he got stuck in some office job, a dread that would follow him throughout his career.

So Kauffman buckled down and commenced to study harder than he had ever done at home. As the only American then serving in the Royal Navy, he kept reminding himself that he represented the United States and had to do a good job because of the human tendency to judge a country by an individual. Despite the work, he found time to enjoy his peers and was elected senior class officer during the second week. "This sounds nice but entails a lot of extra work so it merely meant that I looked like a sucker," wrote Kauffman. Each week at dinner one man would serve as vice president of the mess. When Kauffman's turn came, he did his part to establish some transatlantic camaraderie. As he explained:

> Thursday night was the formal night—the "dining-in evening," as they called it—when the port was passed in exactly the right manner. God help you if you let number two port pass number one—and all that sort of stuff. At the end of the meal the President would stand up and say, "Mr. Vice—the King!"
>
> And the Vice President was to stand up and say, "Gentlemen,

> the King!" I went to the executive officer, who was sort of a father confessor to us all, and said, "Commander, I'm supposed to do this tonight. Would it be very bad taste of me to say in the toast, "Gentlemen—the President and the King"?
>
> "Why," he said, "I don't know, Draper, but that's a very interesting idea, and I will certainly raise no objection if you decide to do it." I'd have been much happier if he'd said yes or no.
>
> But I got to my feet and said, "Gentlemen—the President and the King!" And bless their hearts, there wasn't a murmur—every single person echoed, "The President and the King!" At that moment I was very nervous. But mind you, they are not looking to embarrass or infuriate an American at this time.

The students were billeted in hotels and at a former girls boarding school, which—to the amusement of all—provided a buzzer and a sign above each bed saying "Ring for Mistress." There were some five hundred trainees, officers and officer candidates alike, in residence, among them a Davis Cup player, a well-known yachtsman, the author G.F.G. Pollard, and a producer for the Westminster Theater in London, Lord Selsden, each of whom, Kauffman commented wryly, received the "princely" sum of fifty-four dollars a month. That had to be stretched. He wrote home with a request for some Chesterfield cigarettes and Maxwell House coffee, finding the British equivalent awful.

Kauffman missed more than the small things in life. "What I wouldn't give for just one weekend home where blackouts and air-raid shelters are unknown and where I would be with people I know and love," he wrote wistfully. He was not alone in yearning for loved ones. Many British citizens themselves were separated from their families. Armies of English children had been evacuated to the countryside and to the United States while parents stayed behind in urban battle zones to defend their nation from air attacks. It took considerable fortitude to put up with separation and the deprivations of an air war—the prolonged keening of sirens, sleep deprivation resulting from nightly attacks, food shortages, lack of heat, blackouts, collapsed buildings, fires, homelessness, and of course, death. In London some people slept in air raid shelters, but many others packed themselves like sardines into the Tubes, the subway stations.

Through all this the British people remained stalwart and courageous, utterly defiant of Hitler and inspired by Churchill's leadership. Their prime minister's eloquence brought out the best in the British character, and the best in Draper Kauffman as well:

> We shall not flag or fail, we shall fight in France, we shall fight on the seas and the oceans. We shall fight with growing confidence and growing strength in the air. We shall defend our island, whatever the cost may be. We shall fight on the beaches, we shall fight in the fields and streets, we shall fight in the hills. We shall never surrender. And even if, which I do not for a moment believe, this island . . . were subjugated and starving, then our Empire beyond the seas, armed and guarded by the British Fleet, would carry on the struggle until in God's good time, the New World, with all its power and might, steps forth to the rescue and liberation of the old.

At that stage of the war, roughly a quarter of the bombs Germany dropped on British targets were duds that dug ten to thirty-five feet into the ground. People did not pay much attention to them, just lived and worked around them. When, however, the Germans began attacking with delayed-action bombs, which had timing devices that could be set to trigger an explosion minutes or hours after a bomb hit the ground, it had to be assumed that any bomb might detonate at any moment. A large area was cleared around each bomb so that it could be defused and later detonated in an unpopulated area. Within a week of the delayed-action bomb's deadly debut, London was gridlocked. Even an emergency vehicle took about eight hours to get from one side of the city to the other because so much real estate was roped off for unexploded bombs.

This turn of events put Draper Kauffman in a quandary. Not wanting to worry his mother, he wrote his father at sea. The elder Kauffman was then commander of the Caribbean patrol, charged with covering Axis ships operating in the Gulf of Mexico and keeping a close watch on Vichy French forces in Martinique. Draper explained to his dad that just before he had arrived at Hove a call had gone out for volunteers in bomb disposal work, and that another call was sure to go out while he was there. He weighed the pros and cons of stepping up. First, he would be fulfilling his self-imposed goal of contributing to the war effort, and in a positive way because, as he wrote, "much as I loathe . . . the Germans for what they are doing, if I could be of more use saving property and lives than destroying them I might feel better about it in the end." Second, bomb disposal work might save him from the miserable tedium of an office job. But over and against those pros was "mainly one thing—fear—and that decided me against."

Then came the day of reckoning. About two weeks after Kauffman got to Hove, a bomb dropped perilously close to the mess hall. Since officials at HMS King Alfred didn't know whether it was a dud or not, they sent for a newly formed army bomb disposal squad headquartered nearby. The students, meanwhile, picked their way around the bomb as they headed for their classes. When they came back for dinner there was nothing left of the bomb but a large crater—and, sadly, nothing left of the bomb disposal squad. The next morning, a Friday, the students were called to attention and officers asked for six volunteers. "The timing couldn't have been worse," Kauffman wrote. "I didn't move and only three came forward. But for the next two hours I fought the damn thing out, pro and con, finally going up to volunteer at lunchtime. To my surprise, fourteen other fellows did the same, so there were eighteen of us. To be honest, I would never have gone up if I'd known they had enough."

The volunteers were all duly interviewed by Capt. L.E.H. Llewellyn, director of the Royal Navy's brand new Unexploded Bomb Department. "Good grief, Kauffman, what did you volunteer for?" Draper kept asking himself as one after another of the courageous souls filed in for a grilling. His loss of confidence was compounded when he stopped by the scene of destruction and stared down into the heart of the crater. When it came time for his own interview, Captain Llewellyn's first question was: "Are you frightfully keen for this type of duty, young man?"

"No, sir," Kauffman replied with a sigh of relief, thinking he had been let off the hook. But as it turned out, that was the deciding answer. Anyone who said yes was immediately crossed off the list, being deemed excessively zealous for a type of duty that required the steadiest of nerves.

According to Arthur Hogben in his book *Designed to Kill,* the only thing Llewellyn would tell his prospects about qualifications was that bomb disposal required common sense, courage, tenacity of purpose, and the ability to keep tight-lipped about what they had been taught.

Wags altered this list of qualifications. To do bomb disposal work, they said, a man had to be strong, unmarried, fast on his feet, and fully prepared for the afterlife.

Llewellyn was an inflexible Welshman whose active dislike of Englishmen had earned him the nickname Captain Bligh. But he got along well with the Australians, the Canadians, and the sole American. In the end Kauffman was chosen to be one of the six volunteers. That was Friday evening. The men were notified that they would leave the very next day, at noon. So that night Kauffman's class threw a party for him, since he was the only representative of their bunch of fifty. "They did me proud, so much so that I barely made it to a party the Canadians asked me to, and they finally put me to bed at 6 AM," he later recalled.

The next day a Commander Head, who was executive officer of HMS King Alfred, rounded up the six volunteers for a hasty orientation. He thanked each heartily for offering his services and told them that they could quit the game and finish up their courses at King Alfred at any point and that he, personally, would see they got whatever jobs they wanted within reason after they finished. Kauffman was specifically promised a job at sea in a fighting ship. "This Commander Head is probably the best known and best liked man in the British navy," he enthused, finally glimpsing his dream on the horizon.

The six volunteers were to report to a Royal Air Force station on Sunday to commence their course. On the train Kauffman got to know his five companions, who all shared his misgivings about the job. For better or worse, that was comforting. "I was glad that they also were nervous and that they were inclined to laugh too much and talk in too high pitched a voice," he wrote to his father. "I want to tell you about them, but maybe I'll send that in a letter to you all, so Mother will feel somewhat included. I think she'll get a kick out of hearing about them."

That was an optimistic thought. Kauffman later wrote a letter to his mother alluding to a "special project" that he could not elaborate on, otherwise his letter would be censored. He described his fellow volunteers with great enthusiasm, inadvertently including such comments as "Phil joined us because he believes every officer should volunteer for every nasty job" and "George Cook joined because he wanted to see if his nerve is any good." Of course his mother's antennae shot right up, and when Reggie came home briefly she badgered him mercilessly until he gave her a bare glimmer of what their son was up to. After her husband went back to sea she took aside Capt. Scott Moncrief and Comdr. Geoffrey Poe, two British officers who were assigned to her husband's staff, and asked them what bomb disposal meant. The two men were so impressed by what they had heard of this type of work that they went into more detail than necessary, not realizing how much this would scare their anxious listener. They explained that if a bomb implanted itself thirty feet in the ground, a squad of sappers, or enlisted ratings (usually Royal Engineers), would dig thirty feet down and shore up the sides of the hole to prevent it from collapsing and detonating the weapon. Then the bomb disposal officer would go down and tackle the fuse. One small mistake and he could be blasted to smithereens. Draper's mother, needless to say, was worried sick. When Kauffman wrote to his father, however, he emphasized that 99 percent of bomb disposal work consisted of the unglamorous job of digging holes.

That may have been true, but there was good reason for his mother's informants to be impressed by Draper's line of work. As Maj. A. B. Hartley explains in *Unexploded Bomb: A History of Bomb Disposal,* "this was a Heroic Age of bomb disposal, a period of individual prowess, when urgency and a lack of knowledge and equipment led to the taking of fantastic risks. . . . It was, however, a Heroic Age whose protagonists remained obscure, since their actions were kept from the public for reasons of security. It was obviously undesirable to publish reports that might help the enemy to estimate [your] ability to deal with weapons."

Kauffman and the other five volunteers were together for the next two and a half weeks, first at an RAF school, next a naval school, and then at the Admiralty in London, where they drew their assignments. Finally after a bang-up evening on the town they split up. They had a beautiful dinner at L'Ecu de France with all the trimmings, then gave the London nightspots the once-over after picking up some girls at the Overseas Club. They danced till three, took the girls home, and talked through the night and on into morning, at which point their various trains departed. By now there was such a nonstop demand for disposal officers that there would be no chance for such camaraderie in the future, and Kauffman never mentioned that great group of intrepid bomb-disposal pioneers again.

A battle of wits was being waged between the German designers of the delayed-action bomb fuse and the British bomb disposal people. The British had designated "bomb cemeteries" in places like parks where a bomb could be dumped and detonated without harm to people or buildings. As Kauffman recounted, "We'd hoist a bomb out of the ground, put it in a truck whose nose was painted bright red, race through town to a bomb cemetery and dump it. There was always a police car that went ahead of us with loudspeakers telling everybody to get out of the way. But as soon as people heard them . . . they'd all come dashing around to see the truck go by. Definitely our glamorous period! You couldn't walk into a pub and pay for a drink. The place was yours!"

Then, through British newspapers they got hold of in Dublin, the Germans discovered that the disposal people had learned to dig down to a bomb and defuse it. In response, the Germans added an antiwithdrawal device, so that yanking the fuse would set the bomb off. Now the bomb disposal officer wore a field phone (walkie-talkie) through which he would communicate with an enlisted man a safe distance away who would jot down each comment the officer made as he went through the painstaking task of defusing the explosive: "I'm now about to unscrew nut number three a quarter of a turn to the right, then another quarter of a turn." If anything happened, at least the next person would not make the same mistake. In this way bomb disposal teams learned to get around the Germans' antiwithdrawal device, though the solution, tragically, was far from infallible.

The next step in the game was forced when the Germans began installing antidisturbance devices that caused bombs to detonate if they were moved. Now the disposal teams could not cart their deadly cargo to the bomb cemeteries. At the National Physical Laboratory and HMS Vernon—the Royal Navy's Torpedo Mining School at Portsmouth where weapons were taken to be evaluated and experimented with—it was discovered that the insertion of a liquid into the fuse would congeal and freeze the antidisturbance device. This was tricky because the liquid had to be heated and inserted gingerly through two tiny holes drilled, very delicately, at the top of the fuse. If the fuse was ticking, of course, this operation also had to be conducted swiftly. The bomb disposal officers began to notice that the Germans always printed numbers outside their fuses. If the number ended with 5 it was a standard action fuse, if it ended in 7 it was a delayed-action fuse; if it started with 4 it had an antiwithdrawal device, and if it began with 1 it was an antidisturbance fuse. The orderly Germans wanted to be able to handle their own fuses if one of their planes crashed. It took some time before the British disposal officers were finally able to make sense of all of this, and many remained skeptical to the end.

Kauffman was given the job of bomb safety officer in north Wales, with one petty officer and several men. As the fall of 1940 passed, Hitler, hoping to bring Britain to its knees before the planned but delayed invasion, intensified his night raids on cities across the United Kingdom. Late in the year the Luftwaffe inflicted a three-night blitz on Liverpool, and Draper Kauffman was called in from Wales to help with bomb disposal in that beleaguered English port.

As it turned out there were few bombs to be dealt with in Liverpool, so he was referred to a newly established navy mine disposal command under Capt. C.N.E. Currey. (This all-navy group, based in London and known as the Land Incident Section, consisted of twenty-five officers, of whom a third were eventually lost.) Captain Currey got through to Draper's boss in London, Captain Llewellyn, and requested permission to use him. To Draper's surprise—he knew nothing about mines—he was welcomed with open arms and sent immediately to assist on a job. What he would be helping with was not mines in the harbor, but rather a lethal weapon the Germans had recently introduced: parachute-borne land mines. Adapted from magnetic sea mines that had been used against Allied ships, land mines were eight feet long and weighed more than two tons. Released at a great height, the mines would slowly float to the earth under their silken chutes and upon contact detonate with a force that in some cases opened up a mile-long scar. When some of the mines failed to explode, of course, they had to be defused, a harrowing task. While the disposal officer fiddled with the fuse he would listen very intently. If he heard a buzzing sound, it was time to bolt—for any second, up to a maximum of seventeen seconds, the mine could explode. The British were frantic because the blitz on Liverpool was the first time parachute mines had been used in numbers, and there were nowhere near enough disposal officers to handle them. At that point in the war nobody was an expert in mine disposal. The bomb disposal people had to learn quickly.

Kauffman never forgot the first parachute mine he helped with.

It had come down in a crowded section of Liverpool and got tangled around a chimney. The nose was resting comfortably in an overstuffed chair in the reception room of a sumptuous house of ill repute. This place was not exactly vital to the war effort, but it was surrounded by scores of factories and dockworkers' homes. Some prematurely hung Christmas streamers were wrapped around the mine, giving it a ludicrously surreal appearance.

Kauffman was soaked with perspiration when "Mother" Riley, the mine disposal group's oldest officer and the most experienced, having handled two or three of these monstrous weapons, calmly started working on the mechanical fuse and showed him what to do. (The officer defusing the weapon would work alone unless, as in this case, he was training someone.) This particular job was relatively simple. Lieutenant Riley made quick careful turns on the keep ring that held the fuse in position while every instant Draper expected the terrible buzzing sound that signaled the end of everything. Nothing happened. Riley eased the fuse out, and when it was in their hands and away from the mine, a triumphant feeling overcame them. But confidence, Draper Kauffman reminded himself, was a dangerous indulgence in this business.

They had lost a couple of officers earlier that morning and so Kauffman inherited a set of tools along with an outstanding petty officer by the name of Martin. Soon thereafter he and Martin were dispatched to Cholmondeley near Chester to defuse a mine buried next to the greenhouse and residence of a Mr. Carter and his family. Ruefully, Kauffman gazed at the neat greenhouse and the Carter home. The easiest and safest way to deal with this mine was to work a hole down alongside it and blow it up. There was nothing nearby that was vital to the war effort—nothing that an explosion would harm.

"I'm sorry, but your property will be destroyed," he informed the owner.

Mr. Carter didn't ask to save his property. In fact, he didn't say a word. Perhaps that's why Draper changed his mind and determined to dig the thing out. He had Martin and another enlisted man with him, Seaman Bentley—a novice—and also some Royal Engineers for the heavy digging. The mine was buried deep, and when they finally gouged out a hole big enough to work in, cold water had seeped up to their armpits.

Kauffman retrieved the mechanical fuse, which also contained a magnetic fuse for underwater detonation. About a week after the job's completion, he received some snapshots of the owner's home and nursery with just this note: "Enclosed find pictures of my house and nursery thanks to you. Sincerely, Carter."

Lieutenant Kauffman and Petty Officer Martin handled eight mine jobs during that blitz, all with easily accessible fuses. Martin would be at the other end of the walkie-talkie, taking notes that his commanding officer relayed to him while he was defusing. The new director, Captain Currey, Kauffman was convinced, sent him only on easy jobs for several reasons: he was new; he was borrowed from a bomb disposal squad; and since he was the only American officer in the Royal Navy at that time, Currey did not want to deal with the bureaucratic red tape should anything happen to him.

Kauffman established an immediate rapport with Captain Currey, as did all the intrepid band of about twenty-five officers who worked with the mines. A man who inspired complete confidence in his officers, Currey was dynamic and unhesitatingly purposeful. One of this small group, Lt. Horace Taylor, RNVR GM GC (GM stood for George Medal, GC for George Cross, both awarded for exceptional bravery in a noncombatant situation) commented, "We could get through to him on the phone at any hour of the day or night for advice, taking precedence over anyone else of whatever rank; he paid no attention to bureaucracy. Just the man for our unprecedented type of work about which so little was then known." Draper Kauffman was readily accepted by his new peers, as Taylor pointed out:

> It was mandatory of course that we should always work solo when attempting to render a mine safe, unless the circumstances of access to it made that impossible. In the meantime between jobs, we did many experiments to try to improve our knowledge and techniques, and it was in that context that I met Draper, an American who, to everybody's curious surprise, managed to join the British Royal Naval Volunteer Reserve and our bit of it in particular, for its very existence was supposed to be secret. He, being a very charming and self-effacing type of chap, was quickly assimilated into our party. It was known for a short time as Admiralty RMS (Rendering Mines

Safe). That was soon changed for reasons of security to LIS (Land Incident Section).

Kauffman gradually learned more about mines and, at the request of the U.S. naval attaché, Captain Kirk, wrote a paper explaining how they worked. The original German sea mine, he wrote, was set off by the magnetic field of a ship passing over. One day in late September 1940, a sea mine landed by mistake on a small town on the banks of the Thames, causing far more devastation than a regular 2,000-pound bomb—first, because the mine was 95 percent explosive instead of 50 percent, and second because it did not lose any of its force by penetrating the ground like an ordinary bomb. This incident was played up by the British press with detailed pictures of the tragic results, which reached the German embassy in Dublin the next day. Within a month, the Germans had added a new fuse to their mines, a bomb-type fuse designed to activate up to seventeen seconds after impact unless by that time the mine was in fifteen feet or more of water. There were three small holes at the top of the fuse, and water pressure exceeding that of a fifteen-foot depth would stop it from operating, allowing the weapon to act as a mine. Thus if the weapon landed on soil it acted as a bomb, but if it plunged into the water it became a mine.

The bomb fuses were poorly and cheaply designed, in startling contrast to the ingenious, expensive mine fuses housed in the same casing. The bomb fuse had two flat round discs, one above the other. The shock of hitting either land or water caused a detent to fall, releasing the top disc. Spring pressure then made this disc complete a circle in eight and a half seconds, at the end of which a second detent dropped and the bottom disc circled around in eight and a half seconds. If, when seventeen seconds was up, water pressure had not short-circuited this fuse, a third detent dropped and the mine went off. But the bomb fuse had a defect that caused it to malfunction more than a third of the time. When the weapon hit the ground, one of the discs might be jolted and sent slightly off center, so that when it revolved it might graze the other disc and come to a stop. If the disposal officer disturbed the mine at all, he could free the discs from each other and reactivate the fuse. Once he heard the dread buzzing noise, he had anywhere from one to seventeen seconds to escape. Thus land mine disposal was much more of an open gamble than bomb disposal. If a delayed-action bomb went off, the end was simply at hand. If a mine fuse started buzzing, however, there was a fifty-fifty chance of getting away.

Draper Kauffman's report on all this must have satisfied Captain Kirk's curiosity, as he wrote Draper a note in November 1940: "Thanks ever so much for your letter. I think you are on a very sporty job—in fact I am rather reluctant to tell your father and mother exactly what you are doing. However, when I get home I will whisper it in Reggie's ear."

In early December, back in Wales, Kauffman wrote his father again telling him about his new involvement with land mines and begging him to keep it from his mother:

> The English newspapers went on a tangent about land mines because of one under St. Paul's and they magnified the risk out of all proportion. Mother may have gotten hold of one of those papers and would imagine all sorts of things, whereas I am really only taking a normal war risk not nearly as dangerous as an office job in London or a destroyer job like yours in the last war. . . .
>
> I wonder what this New Year will hold for you and me. Will we be fighting side by side—allied—or in the same Navy? If we came in, I would not want to change a job over here for a job in our own Navy in an office in the States. I know I am doing something worthwhile here, and there are so many people with bad eyes to file reports in the Navy Department at home. . . . Wouldn't it be fun though for the two of us to get together in London? There are several good places there that need a little pepping up. Well, whatever it holds I hope that 1941 will give us a Victory and end this mess.

At Christmastime the Germans unleashed another blitz over Liverpool, and Kauffman returned to the scene of his baptism in land mines. On Christmas Eve he and his team entered a run-down area and evacuated some thousand people from their homes. Mine disposal was time consuming, painstaking work. Not until midnight on Christmas Day had the mine been deactivated and the residents returned. But that job was easy compared to the next one, in a neighborhood where a mine had smashed into a cellar and scattered explosive all over the place. Aside from the fact that working with explosive caused dermatitis, Kauffman's team had to sweat it out among all that tinder trying to find the fuses, which they finally eliminated. Then firefighters were called in to burn the house down and thereby prevent additional devastation.

Kauffman's wake-up call took place in his bailiwick of Holyhead, Wales, in January. A mine had landed precipitously close to a vital railway track. He went to work. Like any good disposal officer—or experienced bank robber—he sized up his getaway first. The nearest shelter was a railway embankment some fifteen seconds away if he crossed the rough ground at a dead run. The air was bitterly cold and his hands were numb—a disadvantage when it came to the delicate work of fuse deactivation. On the top center of the fuse casing was a small round device the size of a threepence piece—the "thruppenny bit," disposal men called it. This had a pair of holes into which was inserted a nonmagnetic wrench with nubbins on it. Then a dartlike device was carefully applied to hold back the spring-drive striker while the fuse assembly was withdrawn. Kauffman later recalled:

> I had just put the wrench into one of the turn holes when my hand slipped and hit the mine. It was just a faint slap against those hundreds of pounds of steel and explosives—but enough. I heard that low harsh mechanical buzzing start. Never have more things gone through my head faster. I knew Petty Officer Martin would be standing where I directed him to stay—on the railway embankment. "Down, Martin, down!" I yelled at him, and I was on my feet. All the directions I had ever been given raced through my mind. Drop—relax—roll when you were running and a bomb let go. I was forty yards away when it went. A lot of interested townsfolk had been watching from the standard four hundred yards. They told me afterward that I was right alongside a little tree when the explosion came. The tree and I left the ground simultaneously and landed together twenty-two feet away. All I remember was seeing the stuff flying up into the air and covering my head with my hands. I passed out. . . . Captain Currey's official comment read as follows: "It is apparent that Lieutenant Kauffman accomplished the equivalent of a nine-second 100-yard dash. This world record may have been induced by a sense of urgency."
>
> I thought that was beautifully British!

Captain Currey had a rule that no officer or enlisted man should go back to disposal work after a mine had blown up on him. So Draper Kauffman, with an egg-size bump on his forehead—when he got back to the United States months later, it was still there—and suffering from injured kidneys, was dispatched to peaceful Oban, Scotland, to recuperate for a couple of months.

His father continued to write him regularly, in spite of getting little response. He could always think of topics related to Britain. Reggie Kauffman's new job in conjunction with lend-lease was to survey the various British Caribbean islands. (Lend-lease was an agreement to "lend" the British navy fifty U.S. destroyers in return for Britain's "leasing" the United States bases on certain Caribbean islands. This was one of the ways President Roosevelt managed to help the British without declaring war.) The U.S. Navy captain wrote almost whimsically of visiting Antigua where he had gone to see Lord Nelson's house "looking for inspiration."

In another letter he mentioned Bianca Clement, one of Draper's "girls," whose younger sister, Kitty, was a favorite friend of Betty Lou's. This being a "coming out" year, Kitty's aunt wanted to give a big dinner-dance for Kitty, who persuaded her instead to spend the money to buy part of a Spitfire, Britain's most renowned front-line fighting plane.

On 21 January 1941 the elder Kauffman wrote his son from his squadron flagship, the USS *Sampson,* which was en route to the Caribbean for operations with the Atlantic Fleet. He had just recently received a letter from Draper that had been two months in transit and included nothing about the accident. Thus none of the home contingent knew about it. Captain Kauffman expressed his fascination for Draper's description of handling delayed-action bombs and said he was very pleased to hear about his promotion to lieutenant and his congratulatory message from the first sea lord. However, he added,

> I do hope you will cut out this time-bomb business and get back to the Navy. I can understand that the Navy has charge of mines, etc., but they also have considerable to do with boats and ships which, when all is said and done, is the major mission of the Navy. Also when we get into the war I hope you will immediately go around to Alan Kirk and arrange for a transfer to the U.S. Navy. I

have discussed the matter with him and there will be no difficulty in your transferring and you will not be put in the supply corps or made a civil engineer to dig ditches; also you will be transferred at the same rank you hold in the R.N.V.R. I have discussed this with Admiral Nimitz, who is chief of the Bureau of Personnel.

Please do me a great favor. Have your picture taken in your French ambulance corps uniform and also in your British uniform. It will give your mother a great deal of pleasure. Things at home are O.K. except your mother worries more and more about you. Please write her the intimate details of your life—where and how you live—what you do off duty.

His father's admonition about getting back to the true business of the navy—boats and ships—hardly seemed fair, since as he well knew Draper had been blocked from sea duty on account of bad eyes. But doubtless his dad was referring to administrative rather than seagoing duty, the pencil pushing that his son hated the thought of, and doubtless too Captain Kauffman's sense of urgency in this matter stemmed in part from his wife's intense anxiety.

Soon thereafter the elder Kauffman arrived in Washington on leave and filled Draper in on the climate at home: "This place is a hotbed of rumors of war and gossip. People are violent on all questions. Of course all discussions center around the lend-lease bill."

There are many people in this country who remember that after the last war, England went out for trade in a big way, and absolutely opposed paying any of her debts to us. . . . Those things still annoy people as they did me at the time. . . . England has been ruthless in her day. . . . Again I am for giving all aid to Britain, including going to war. Of course everything at present is being done to give England aid—as far as this country can go without war actually being declared. . . . I have the job I am best fitted for and I have every reason to expect that my "boats" will be ready for any duty they may be called on to do.

Please take care of yourself—most accidents happen when you get accustomed to things and careless. You are of more value to the R.N.V.R.—not to mention yourself—alive and physically fit than when otherwise.

Draper Kauffman was on rest and recreation in Oban, Scotland, for several months. The presence of an attractive young woman there greatly sped along his convalescence, but his mind was clearly more focused on matters of war than on love, for when he finally left Scotland she started each letter with the complaint, "Bombs, darling—Why haven't you written?"

While still in Scotland he was given the job of special services officer to keep him busy, and he organized football (soccer) tournaments among the crewmen of former trawlers that were now acting as patrol craft along the coast. Since they came into port mostly on Sunday, he waged a battle with the Scottish kirk, which had strong laws against soccer and other activities on Sunday. The first time Kauffman proposed a change to the law he was defeated seven to nothing; the last time he lost only four to five, which was great progress. Despite the disagreement, he had fun getting to know the seniors of the kirk and he admired them a great deal.

In February 1941, ignoring his orders not to meddle with bombs in Scotland, Kauffman could not resist the challenge of handling an unexploded one in a merchant ship, the *Baron Renfeld*. She was at sea, off the island of Mull, the crew having deserted her on account of her deadly cargo. According to Kauffman this was not a particularly risky job. Though the bomb looked menacing, embedded in a bunker and covered by several feet of soft, shifting coal with just a bit of tail fin visible, it proved to have just an ordinary dud fuse. The ship was listing about thirty degrees and rolling in uncomfortably heavy seas. "There is something rather eerie about being alone on a deserted ship," he later wrote home, "especially under those peculiar circumstances. When I finally got the darned thing defused I got my Petty Officer aboard and we hoisted it over the side. I looked and felt like a chimney sweep who hadn't had a bath in a year." Several years later, while in the U.S. Navy, he was pleasantly surprised to receive a belated award for salvage from the Royal Navy. He had not realized that British naval officers got salvage awards, since Americans did not.

In March the Germans, having given up on a seaborne invasion of Britain, unleashed a mind-numbing blitz on Glasgow as part of a stepped-up campaign to subdue the British once and for all with air power. Kauffman was only a few hours' drive from Glasgow and, again unable to resist temptation, he asked permission of Captain Llewellyn, via Captain Currey, to work on mines there. Request granted, he made the short journey and proceeded to tackle an even dozen bombs. One night Glasgow's lord provost—a provost is the Scots equivalent of a mayor—gave a formal dinner for the bomb disposal squads complete with numerous speeches. "He sure can throw the bull," Kauffman commented. He "even borrowed Churchill's phrase 'never have so many people of Glasgow owed so much to so few.'" His name was Sir Patrick Dolan, and being "quite left wing," according to Draper, he was very pleased when the bomb disposal officers told him that they could not accept any official invitation unless their enlisted men were asked as well. That was a rule because in disposal work the enlisted men were indispensable. So each officer brought along one rating.

Not until March did Kauffman finally write a letter home telling of his January accident and his stay in Scotland, and that letter did not reach his family in Newport until the end of April. In March his mother became increasingly frantic for news about him, and his father was concerned as well. On 23 March Captain Kauffman wrote Capt. Charles Lockwood, who had taken Alan Kirk's place as U.S. naval attaché in London, asking if he could find any news of Draper.

In April Captain Lockwood sent Kauffman a dispatch: "Am informed by official sources Draper in good health doing well and that they are very proud of him." Draper, Lockwood went on, was up in Scotland, "very much alive and kicking." Lockwood's officers had told him that the younger Kauffman

> shows up here in the [London] office every now and then, and upon the next such occasion I shall, as you suggest, make him a Dutch uncle speech. As you know, many letters get sunk these days and I trust that young Draper will have a good alibi for not having corresponded more frequently with his aged parents. Best to you and I hope we see you over here with your tin cans [destroyers] soon. We need 'em.

And a P.S.: "Just saw the Captain who is head of that section [Llewellyn]. He says Draper is to be recommended for a decoration!"

Upon receipt of the letter from Captain Lockwood—who never mentioned Draper's accident, although undoubtedly he knew of it—Captain

Kauffman wrote his son again, from Newport, where he was on leave and "almost frozen . . . after spending all but six weeks of the past year in the tropics." Having been designated Commander, Destroyer Support Force, Atlantic Fleet, Kauffman had recently taken three of his destroyer squadrons into the North Atlantic for intensive antisubmarine training as well as for convoying troops to Iceland on their way to Murmansk to help the beleaguered Russians. It was an eventful period. Under a heavy veil of secrecy, his destroyers escorted Winston Churchill's ship through U-boat-infested waters to the Atlantic Conference in Argentia, Newfoundland, where Britain and the United States met as a gesture of solidarity and to clarify their objectives with respect to the war. Among other results of the conference, Roosevelt pledged that U.S. Navy ships would escort British merchant ships crossing the Atlantic as far as Iceland, where the United States had recently set up a base to relieve the British of the burden of manning this critical Atlantic outpost. During the conference, at chief of naval operations Adm. Ernest King's suggestion, Captain Kauffman spent several hours with President Roosevelt discussing the antisubmarine issue. In previous months the number of sinkings of British ships by German U-boats had risen alarmingly; Germany was gaining control of the Atlantic. One problem was the dearth of escort ships to protect Allied shipping. Another lay with sonar, the range- and direction-finding technology intended to locate the position of submerged enemy submarines. Sonar was not as dependable then as it would become later, and the Germans outfoxed it simply by having their U-boats attack at night from the surface, where sonar could not detect them. As a result of these submarine attacks, British shipyards had fallen far short of their capacity to replace the sunken tonnage. It was in this context that Captain Kauffman and Roosevelt discussed the desperate need of both the Royal Navy and the U.S. Navy for more destroyers.

Draper Kauffman's March letter finally arrived from Scotland, and in keeping with his penchant for withholding unpleasant details, he glossed over his accident:

> I have been hibernating in this lovely part of the world for a couple of months now. . . . The reason for this is that I had an accident back in January, which shook me up a bit. Right now I feel as fit as a fiddle, the only remaining effects are that I get tired a little

sooner than before and if very tired I sometimes have a bad night. In spite of this accident and the papers, this bomb disposal is not any more dangerous than crossing a New York street corner. . . . The one job I had in this period of two months was a most interesting one. Shortly afterwards I got a letter from the head of our department in the Admiralty in which he said, "It appears you and the Petty Officer and men working with you carried out a difficult task in a most satisfactory manner and I am taking steps to see that the action of all concerned is brought to the notice of the proper authorities." Captain Llewellyn is a real Welshman and not given to praise so I was very pleased with that.

By that time Kauffman had seen modern warfare from the standpoint of the soldier, the sailor, and the civilian. The most important thing to think about, he maintained, was how to keep the war out of the United States. Keeping the United States out of the war was unimportant by comparison. "To be absolutely selfish I think we should fight these Germans now while we can do the fighting on someone else's territory. . . . I can't tell you how wonderful it is for me to know that you all are not in danger of being blitzed some night." If the United States finally did declare war, he said, addressing his father's concerns, he would probably transfer to the U.S. Navy and take on some sort of liaison job, unappealing though that prospect might be. Seagoing duty was still an impossibility—he'd sent in a request three times to the U.S. Navy Department and been firmly rejected. And so he would remain in the line of work to which experience best suited him. That caused his parents no end of grief.

While pondering the fate of the West and his own future, Draper had time aplenty to be homesick. "I long for some American accent and slang!" he wrote longingly. "The other evening we went into a pub in Glasgow and saw a couple of Canadians who must have lived right near the [U.S.] border. I stayed there for about two hours just to listen to them talk."

His father answered this "most delightful letter" enthusiastically, commenting that Draper's mother was "a new person" since hearing from him, though of course she was worried about the extent of his injury. After his extended R&R in Scotland, Kauffman was ordered to report to Plymouth. He arrived, as he said, with his usual good-or-bad luck —it was 1 May 1941. That night started the infamous Plymouth blitz. Five out of the next eight nights the Germans pounded the city mercilessly. The aim of this and other hammering attacks launched throughout Britain during that month was no longer to soften up the island nation for invasion—Germany had given up on that idea. Rather, it was intended to distract attention from the megalomaniacal führer's upcoming invasion of Russia. For almost two straight weeks in Plymouth, Kauffman had virtually no sleep, which quickly silenced his complaints about not having enough bomb disposal work. The bombs were a varied series —some duds, some delayed action, and most with either antidisturbance or antiwithdrawal devices or both.

Kauffman was now a chief bomb disposal officer and had a squad of two sublieutenants, three chief petty officers, and twenty-four men. Unfortunately he had lost Petty Officer Martin, who had been his "staff and teacher" for six months, but not before Martin had made an impression on the Admiralty. A few weeks earlier, the king had commended Kauffman and Martin for a job done back in December. As Kauffman wrote home, "Martin, my whole squad and myself were commended by their Lordships (the Admiralty) for bravery and devotion. Then it [the commendation] says that the King has ordered that the names of Martin and myself be posted for bravery."

One Sunday Kauffman took off and was driven to Dartmouth to see the Royal Naval College. His driver was a WREN, the popular name for WRNS, or the Women's Royal Naval Service, who, as he wrote, took him for a "terrifying" ride through the tranquil English countryside, driving a contraption with bad brakes and bum steering over highly banked, curving roads wide enough for only one car. He concluded after barreling so fast down those narrow lanes that the most dangerous thing about bomb and mine disposal was the typical WREN driver. To foil the expected German invaders, street and village signs throughout Britain had been removed, a measure that ended up baffling only the average British motorist. The WRENS, however, were not average. Even without signs they found their way with the alacrity of bloodhounds after a scent, and they did not flinch when it came to lurching around bomb craters. They were nearly always in a hurry. As Draper said, "it was pure luck that you got where you were going when you were at the mercy of a WREN—never mind the bomb!"

These capable women did much more than just taxi bomb disposal squads around. They often took charge when the men came off a job, exhausted, mud-soaked, hungry, and cold. Many a WREN was known to seek out rare accommodations and dry clothes, and to make hot tea or cobble together a meal when it was too late in the night to find a pub or restaurant open. In a pinch, as Kauffman well knew, a WREN was an angel of mercy.

On 10 May 1941—exactly a year since Draper Kauffman had first seen action as an ambulance driver in France—the Germans brought this stage of their blitz to a virtual halt, thereafter dropping bombs and mines only sporadically. But the British would soon be faced with the terrifying prospect of attacks by the V-1, a jet-powered flying bomb, and the V-2, a liquid-fueled rocket. In the interim, the Germans pulled a nasty trick out of their bag that kept disposal officers guessing and on edge: the George mine, it was officially named. Draper Kauffman called it a "top hat," and in the summer of 1941 he had occasion to dispose of one. He went down to Bristol to make sketches of the weapon, then traveled back to London and told the UXB (unexploded bomb) Committee all the details. The guiding light of the committee was a navy lieutenant commander who had been the British amateur chess champion and whose mind was well equipped to puzzle out the design of Hitler's new threat. Kauffman explained as much as he could to him. They were not sure if it was a bomb or a mine. It had no parachute, and he had not found a fuse, but there was something resembling a top hat bolted on to the rear. Kauffman estimated that the weapon weighed about 2,200 pounds and had a circumference of about 36 inches.

He was sent back to Bristol with orders to dig down some thirty feet into the wet, sticky clay. Working that far down in mud and clay precluded any possibility of escape within the maximum window of seventeen seconds. He was to unscrew the top hat, lift it off carefully, and snip every wire he could find—in absolute darkness because, it was surmised, the Germans had installed a photoelectric booby trap that would set off the bomb or mine should the top hat be removed in daylight. Kauffman could then return during the day and defuse the thing.

At this time the U.S. Navy had three officers—Lt. Comdrs. Moe Archer, Muddy Waters, and Beatle Roach—who were shuttling back and forth between England and the United States in order to set up a mine-disposal school in the latter. They had been friends of Draper Kauffman's at the Naval Academy, though a couple of years senior to him, and Moe got permission to join this expedition provided that he did not venture near the weapon while Kauffman was working on it. "I was feeling around for the bolts in the darkness," Draper wrote later,

> when all of a sudden I heard a cough just above me. It was Moe Archer, coming down. So I climbed up. We were still working on the no-noise possibility of an acoustic mine, and I got him away from the hole and whispered "You have to go back!"
>
> Moe argued: "Now look, Draper, if it doesn't go off, we're perfectly all right and no one will know the difference. If it does go off, neither of us is going to get court-martialed."
>
> Well, I couldn't get him away so I let him come on down. (It was a very slight cough I had heard, and he was very quiet.) He had brought a wrench with him and helped me get the twelve bolts undone, which took forever in the dark. By very, very carefully and very gently feeling around, we would come across a wire and snip it. I distinctly remember that in at least two cases I cut a wire twice; since I couldn't see, I didn't realize I'd cut that one before. The top hat was a very heavy metal, and very awkward, particularly down in that hole. We had dug a sort of cave that we moved the top hat into.
>
> I have to admit it was far easier for two of us to do this than one. Of course, I should never have let Moe do it, but I could have spent the whole night arguing with Moe Archer, whom I'd known for many, many years. I will say that the 4 hours in that damp dark hole seemed like 40.

They managed to haul the weapon up two days later and proceeded to take a slew of pictures. They removed the fuses and brought the contraption back to London for the experts to have fun with. It turned out to be a mine implanted, as they had guessed, with a photoelectric booby trap. Had he fiddled with that top hat when the sun was shining, Draper Kauffman would have been blown to smithereens.

In June the British army, navy, and air force set up a joint committee to determine the reasons for various bomb and mine disposal casualties. Kauffman was asked to be on the committee because he was the only one who had a significant amount of experience in both bomb and mine disposal. It struck him as curious that he, an alien, had had more experience in both types of work than any native Britisher; many natives, however, had had much more experience with one or the other type of work. At any rate, the committee's conclusion was that the number one cause of casualties, other than a fuse going off, was carelessness, and the number two reason was fatigue. In many cases men were careless *because* they were tired.

At the end of June Kauffman's family received a cable saying that the BBC was going to broadcast a message from Draper on 3 and 4 July. No doubt the purpose of the broadcast was to nurture closer relations across the Atlantic as Britain strove to bring the United States into the war. And indeed the tide of American opinion was beginning to turn. The BBC ran a publicity photo with the comment, "Lieutenant Draper Kauffman, who until recently was the only American in the Royal Navy and who is the son of Captain J. L. Kauffman of the United States Navy, tells America of his impressions of wartime Britain from Trafalgar Square, London, on American Independence Day." On the third the family eagerly huddled around the radio to listen. The message aired that day was brief: "Hello Mother and Dad and Betty Lou! I'm feeling fine and not having too bad a time though I sure would like to get home for some leave, but that looks impossible. Everybody over here has been swell to us. Thanks a lot for the coffee, it was a Godsend. Give my love to the rest of the family and God bless you all." The next day he was given a little more time and spoke to a larger audience:

> Hello America,
>
> Believe it or not the British are celebrating the Fourth of July this year—but without fireworks. They have too much of that over here normally.
>
> These Limies are really a grand crowd. You have all read and heard how they can take it. Well, it honestly has to be seen to be believed. It is tragic yet terribly inspiring.
>
> Incidentally, they are all very grateful for the help coming over

> from home, and treat all of us who are serving over here like kings in spite of the very small part we are doing as yet.
>
> Their appreciation is amazing in a way, because it seems to me that it is we who should be grateful to them for the wonderful way they are mending the Anglo-American front line and keeping a barrier between the Huns and ourselves.

Draper's mother and father and sister were overjoyed to hear his voice—the first time since he'd gone to France sixteen months before.

Soon after the broadcast, the United States officially "borrowed" Draper Kauffman from the Admiralty, and he spent three weeks at the U.S. Embassy writing a thesis on bomb and mine disposal for the U.S. War and Navy Departments. He later could not find the report and presumed it must have been lost. During that period, the bombs and mines having slacked off, Kauffman also found some time for "extracurricular" activities, including of all things a bombing flight over Germany, which he took at the behest of a friend who was a Canadian pilot, very illegally and "just for the hell of it." As for his romantic life, he kept mum about that. His dad told him in a letter that a friend who had returned recently from England had asked if Draper was "still seeing that good-looking blonde barmaid." Draper never answered that question.

He occasionally got together with a group that had christened itself the Hornblowers. The Hornblowers were mine disposal officers who had come up with a clever idea: to trick land mines into thinking they were underwater and thereby render them inactive. Deciding to experiment with taxi horns, which had flexible rubber bulbs, they ventured into a London street, held up an entire row of taxis, and in the name of the Admiralty confiscated their horns. Each horn was affixed to a brass tube with a tap at one end. The mine disposal officer would attach a bicycle pump to the tube, pump the horn full of air, close the tap, then attach the tube to the fuse and open the tap back up. Air pressure would force the rubber seal and plunger down, "gagging" the fuse so that it could be removed. This contraption was partially effective, though it did not remove any of the other hazards associated with magnetic mines. Their success created a bond among the inventors, who in good British tradition celebrated their success with periodic dinners.

Kauffman wrote home saying he thought the war would be over by Christmas since "Hitler has at last overreached himself in this Russian thing." He had no way of knowing that the war would drag on for four more years. But he was right about Hitler stretching himself too far. In the latter half of May, Britain's shattered cities fell mostly silent as the Luftwaffe shifted its sights eastward to Stalin's front yard. On 22 June 1941, to the relief if not the joy of the beleaguered British, the führer launched his massive invasion up and down the long Russian front. Though not completely clear until much later, this was his greatest mistake.

At the time that Hitler made this fatal error, Kauffman had just heard he had been put up for the George Cross, Britain's highest award for bravery not in combat. However, as he wrote his family, "I have no thought of getting it, since what I have done is far less than what lots of fellows have done and got nothing for. In our crowd it is like a lottery—you take jobs in their turn and if it turns out to be a difficult and conspicuous one you get something, otherwise you don't." Mine disposal was indeed one of the conspicuous jobs—out of a total of nineteen George Crosses ultimately won by the Royal Navy, fourteen were awarded to men in mine disposal. But Draper never received the medal. According to Adm. Geoffrey Thistleton-Smith, former commanding officer of HMS Vernon, Kauffman—recognized as an "outstanding officer," someone with "courage, who thought things through"—probably did not get the medal "because he was American and the Americans weren't in the war yet. It might have been awkward."

Though Kauffman was driven by a deep sense of duty, occasionally he did think about the very practical issue of pay. As he pointed out, "The pay difference has often tempted me sorely—a lieutenant RNVR gets $90 a month, compared to $260 a month for a lieutenant in the U.S. Navy. And London is very expensive." But there were advantages to being in the disposal business. Disposal squads were ferried about in cars with distinctive red noses and sterns. "It's known by everybody to be a disposal car," he went on. "You can't possibly walk into a pub and pay for a drink. I start talking to people and they ask me why I'm here and so forth, and when I tell them—boy, the place is mine."

It was not just the average Brit who was intrigued by Draper Kauffman's presence in London. One day Winston Churchill reviewed the mine-disposal group. He came over to Kauffman and asked, "How did you happen to join our navy?"

"After I got out of prison camp, sir," Draper began, and gave a brief summary of his war story.

Churchill actually spent fifteen or twenty minutes with Kauffman, curious to know why he had joined the French army in the first place. And the prime minister did not forget him. Later Draper's father became head of the Allied Antisubmarine Warfare Board set up by Churchill and Roosevelt. After briefing Churchill the senior Kauffman had lunch with him and the latter said, "Tell me, Admiral, how did you feel about your son doing mine-disposal work over here in England?" Churchill held mine-disposal officers and ratings in high regard because of what he called their "cold-blooded heroism."

The admiration was mutual. "When Churchill gave a speech on the radio," Draper told his family, "I always went to a local pub to listen to it and to watch the expressions of the people while he was speaking, and . . . he had the people of that country in the palm of his hand the way Hitler did his people. . . . But so different, I mean night and day."

Not everyone was pleased that Kauffman was in England. One day he dropped in to see Captain Kirk, whose secretary told him that the young officer was in the outer room. Kirk opened the door and said, "Come on in." Captain Hillenkoetter, the U.S. naval attaché in Paris who had done so much for Kauffman when he got out of the German prison camp, happened to be there. Kirk said "Hilly, this is Reggie Kauffman's son."

Hillenkoetter replied, "Yes, I know him. Draper, what in hell are you doing in a Royal Navy uniform?"

"Well, sir," he said, "I'm a lieutenant in the RNVR."

Hillenkoetter said, "Do you remember that piece of paper you signed that you would never join any armed force against the German Reich?"

"Well, yes sir, I do," said Draper, "but it was signed under duress."

Hillenkoetter said, "That doesn't make any difference," and was quite stern with Kauffman. Alan Kirk thought that was very funny and sided with the young man.

In September 1941 Draper Kauffman got the great news that he was to be given a month's home leave. His ship left from Scotland, and the lord provost of Glasgow sent his mother a cable: "YOUR BRAVE SON HOMEWARD BOUND. GLASGOW THANKS HIM FOR HIS MANY LIFE-SAVING SERVICES AND CONGRATULATES YOU ON HIS DEVOTION TO DEMOCRACY."

3

Return to U.S. Shores

When Kauffman arrived home on what he thought would be a month's leave, the family was in Newport with his father's destroyer squadrons stationed at that time in the North Atlantic. Little did any of them know that wartime events would keep him at home for the next eight months, one of the rare periods during which he and his sister lived in the same household—or succession of households.

The family was extremely happy to have Draper at home. It had been at least two years since any of them had seen him. He had been in Europe for a year and a half, and for six months before that he was too busy in his job at the U.S. Lines to spend time with the family while they were living in California. His sister learned for the first time about the dangers of his job in Britain. Amazingly, their parents, wanting her to have a year of "fun," had been able to keep that information from her. To Betty Lou, Draper had been just a dashing Royal Navy officer who graced them with his rare presence. But for their parents, his return was a huge relief.

Not to mention, for his mother, a thrill. It was a year of fashionable parties in Newport and Washington, since people felt that, with events unfolding as they were, the good times would soon come to an end. Lieutenant Kauffman's mother took full advantage of that prevailing sentiment of carpe diem by taking him to an endless round of lunches, dinners, and teas, where she would introduce him to all her friends—in fact, it often seemed, to anybody who passed by. Because the introductions were so often made over meals, Draper would stand up, sit back down, and then have to stand up again. On one such occasion he winked at Betty Lou and said, "What I need is springs in my pants!" His ordeal stirred her sympathy and she objected to their mother, "He barely gets a mouthful to eat!"

While the young Royal Navy reserve officer found life much more relaxed at home, for those who had been living there, despite the parties, it was becoming more constrained. Gasoline was now hard to get, and the younger Kauffman was amused to find that a friend of his parents, Mrs. William Van Allen, sent her horse and carriage for them to dine with her and even occasionally to take his mother shopping. More shortages were on the way. Within a matter of months, meat was rationed, along with butter, sugar, coffee, and tobacco. But at that moment life in America looked pretty good, especially to someone who had just come from a country smashed by bombing raids and very nearly defeated by the Nazis. Deprivation was relative, as an episode with Lord Halifax illustrated. Lord Halifax was the British ambassador to the United States. Part of his ambassadorial role was to drum up U.S. support for the Allied war effort, and having heard about Draper Kauffman's heroic work in Britain, Halifax expressed his appreciation publicly. Around the time of Kauffman's return home, the ambassador spoke to an isolationist group and someone began pelting him with eggs. The ambassador reacted with delightful aplomb. "Isn't it wonderful," he proclaimed, "that in this country you have eggs enough to throw, whereas in mine people hardly have eggs to eat?" Kauffman basked in the luxuries of plentiful food, sleep, and family talk. He also very much welcomed opportunities to tell people about the valiant job the British were doing in holding off Hitler. A newspaper article about his commendation by the king had preceded him, so he was much more in demand as a speaker than he had been in the old days on the free lecture circuit.

The tide of public opinion was gradually turning in favor of the Allied effort. While in Britain, Draper had seen children being transported out of cities to safer rural climes; some thirty-two thousand of those young citizens were also shipped off to the United States, where they won over American hearts. The cultural landscape reflected changing opinion. Among the popular tunes of the day was "The Last Time I Saw Paris," composed after the fall of France. Another was "I Don't Want to Set the World on Fire," which Kauffman, because of his work in bomb disposal, jokingly claimed as his theme song. The movie *Mrs. Miniver,* in which Walter Pidgeon ventured out in a small boat to rescue survivors of Dunkirk, was drawing large crowds. And best-seller lists included a book called *The White Cliffs of Dover,* a long poem written by an American resident of England that ended:

> *I am American bred;*
> *I have seen much to hate here, much to forgive*
> *But in a world where Britain is finished and dead,*
> *I do not wish to live.*

Many people had committed the entire poem to memory and would quote verses with tears in their eyes.

The hints of change were everywhere. Admiral and Mrs. Nimitz, who were old friends of Kauffman's father and mother, came by for a drink one evening. The admiral, future commander in chief of the Pacific Fleet but at the time still chief of the Bureau of Personnel, asked Draper what he had been doing. When Draper told him, Nimitz wondered why he was not in the U.S. Navy. "Sir," said Draper, "each time I write applying to our naval reserve I get a letter back rejecting me because my eyes aren't good enough." "Well," replied Admiral Nimitz, "they are now."

After so much wishful thinking about Britain and the U.S. Navy, Draper had become convinced that the United States would never declare war, and he had no intention of joining up now, regardless of his father's feelings on the matter. He believed it was more important to be involved in a real effort against Germany. In any case, he thought no more of Admiral Nimitz's comment until a few weeks later, after the family had moved to Washington. At President Roosevelt's specific request, Reggie Kauffman had been appointed to the Navy's General Board and was now a rear admiral, by far that body's most junior member.

A few days after the Kauffmans arrived in Washington, Admiral Nimitz sent a memorandum to the Bureau of Ordnance (BuOrd) about the need to set up a bomb-disposal organization. Draper heard about the scenario third or fourth hand. Apparently at the Monday morning conference of department heads, Adm. W. H. P. Blandy, chief of BuOrd, produced Nimitz's memo and said, "By coincidence there is a U.S. Naval Academy graduate who is thoroughly trained in bomb disposal as a British naval officer, and he's in Washington. Furthermore, you know him—he's Reggie Kauffman's son."

The result was that Draper was asked to see Admiral Blandy. He arrived at Blandy's office in civilian clothes, and the admiral talked to him about transferring to the U.S. Navy. Draper told him that he felt he was doing a useful job in Britain, that the U.S. Navy was not at war and didn't look as though it would be, and therefore he would prefer to go back to England. That first interview was relaxed; Blandy invited Kauffman to sit down and chatted amicably with him. A few days later, on 1 November, a more official message came from Blandy's office saying that the admiral wished to see Draper that day at 1400 sharp. He threw on his British uniform, hurried over to the office, and spent the interview standing at attention before the admiral. "If you think the United States Navy is not at war," Blandy announced, "I suggest you consult your father. Our destroyer the *Reuben James* was torpedoed yesterday by a German submarine." It was true. On 31 October 1941 the *Reuben James* was escorting a British convoy eastbound across the Atlantic when it was torpedoed by a German U-boat and sunk. Casualties were high. This was the first loss of a U.S. ship in the Battle of the Atlantic, and there was no doubt in Blandy's mind that, despite lingering isolationist sentiment in Congress, President Roosevelt's campaign to get his country to take up arms would intensify.

Draper responded, "Admiral, the British navy has been pretty darned good to me about this leave situation and I have to go back there to resign decently, anyhow." Cutting him off, Blandy threw two messages across the desk. One was from the U.S. Navy Department to the Admiralty requesting Draper Kauffman's prompt release from the Royal Navy. The second was from the Admiralty, which, Kauffman noted regretfully, put up no argument about his transfer. His father claimed that he had not had a finger in this, but Draper always suspected him of it. "It's probably the only time I can think of where I have not been completely confident in what Dad told me," he remarked later.

On 7 November 1941 Kauffman was marched down to Admiral Nimitz's office and officially transferred to the U.S. Naval Reserve. Although he had lost his argument, it pleased him that at least on that day he received a paycheck from both the Royal Navy and the U.S. Navy.

Thus did Draper Kauffman acquire the job of launching the U.S. Navy Bomb Disposal School. Starting a navy organization as a lieutenant, and in the reserve at that, was a daunting task. Given permission to select someone junior to him as his executive officer, Kauffman chose Ens. Means Johnston, a very fortunate decision. Johnston, a tall, lean, engaging southerner and a top-notch officer, eventually became a four-star admiral. As it turned out, Draper's sister Betty Lou was responsible for this choice. She had a date with Johnston one night, and, running late, had kept him waiting downstairs in the company of her brother. When she finally breezed down ready to be whisked off by her date, all she got was a preoccupied nod. Draper spent at least another hour indoctrinating the ensign in the latest techniques of bomb and mine disposal, at which point Johnston promised to serve as his executive officer. Moreover, once Johnston hooked up with her brother he completely disappeared from Betty Lou's horizon.

Though it barely budged the isolationists in Congress, the *Reuben James* incident fanned prowar flames throughout the country. Slightly over five weeks later, on 7 December 1941, the Japanese fleet attacked Pearl Harbor. Admiral and Mrs. Kauffman were driving to the White House to leave cards for President and Mrs. Roosevelt when they heard the news on the radio. Reggie Kauffman slammed on the brakes, made a sharp U-turn, and came directly home, knowing the president would be swamped. Now there was no doubt about the path the country would follow. On 8 December the United States declared war on Japan. Three days later, Germany and Italy declared war on the United States. Draper Kauffman's wish had come true.

Within a few days President Roosevelt—who had at one time served as assistant secretary of the navy and, in a sense, ran his own personal Bureau of Naval Personnel—sent for Admiral Kauffman and asked him to go to Iceland, a pivotal staging point for U.S. convoys before they ran the gauntlet of German submarines en route to the Soviet Union. Kauffman was to establish and command a U.S. naval operating base in Iceland, sharing the area with Adm. Sir Frederick Dalyrimple-Hamilton of the Royal Navy. For a flagship President Roosevelt offered Admiral Kauffman his presidential yacht, the *Williamsburg,* which gave him added prestige, although a destroyer might have been better adapted to an Icelandic winter.

In organizing the bomb disposal school, Draper Kauffman knew that the fundamental challenge was choosing the right men. He got an unusual and, he felt, critical proviso from the Bureau of Personnel: he could personally select all the candidates for the school, drawing from the "midshipmen schools" at Northwestern in Chicago and Columbia in New York. In preparation for a war it felt was coming, the U.S. Navy had set up these schools to train college graduates as officers in the naval reserve. In spite of the isolationist tendency of the public and Congress, many young men were aware of the world situation and had volunteered for these schools. Kauffman went out to Northwestern on 10 December. He talked to the graduating class about bomb disposal and asked for volunteers. Out of a class of nine hundred, three hundred volunteered. Of course, that was only three days after Pearl Harbor, but during the remaining eighteen months that Draper was in U.S. bomb disposal, until May 1943, the proportion held steady: roughly one-third of every class he talked to volunteered. One of his arguments was that this work saved lives rather than destroying them. No daredevils, please, for bomb disposal, he said. You needed ingenuity and courage, or as they said in Britain, self-confidence, self-discipline, and self-reliance.

On 15 December Kauffman was just completing his selection of fifty out of the original three hundred volunteers when he got a phone call from BuOrd telling him to get to Pearl Harbor immediately. He was needed for bomb disposal work. Lieutenant Commander Archer—the Moe Archer who had worked with him in England on the George mine —went as well and also turned over to Draper an invaluable helper, a creative young chief gunner's mate by the name of Robert Eigell, who would later invent the long-handled wrench, which became an indispensable tool for bomb disposal crews. A bomb had dropped just outside the iron door of the ammunition depot at the army's Fort Scofield in Hawaii. "My imagination worked overtime the whole way out," Kauffman said later. "You know how you always think of the Japanese being very good with tricky things like booby traps. I had played as a child with some of those Japanese boxes where you try to open them and can't. . . . Of course we used the normal procedure, my wearing the mike, and Eigell, being at a safe distance, writing everything down. We sketched it carefully first. It was a 500-pounder. It turned out that I couldn't have set that bomb off if I'd had a sledgehammer. . . . The fuse was completely faulty. So the risk was absolutely zero, in spite of my imagination." He christened the bomb Suzabelle and had her parts shipped to his address in Washington.

Faulty fuse or not, Kauffman was awarded the Navy Cross for dismantling it. His sister later asked Tom Boardman, who was in her brother's first class of students and who would succeed him as officer in charge of the bomb disposal school, why, if the bomb were so simple, Draper had received the award. "Draper was simply being modest when he said there was no way he could have set off the Japanese bomb," Boardman replied. "Explosives are intended to detonate and will explode at unpredictable times and for uncertain reasons." Furthermore, he went on, "Draper had no idea until after the job was completed that it didn't pose an unusual hazard, and he didn't have information, which others did in subsequent operations, as to how the fuse operated. He thoroughly deserved the Navy Cross, despite his remarks to the contrary."

Kauffman's mother and sister were thrilled to be able to see him presented with the Navy Cross. His father, who had just been transferred to Florida, sent him a letter. After six paragraphs of careful instructions about the logistics of getting his wife and daughter to Miami, where they were going to join him, he finally commented, "I certainly want to congratulate you on getting your Navy Cross. You well deserve it, and to say I was personally delighted would be to put it very mildly." Draper later told his sister, "I think Dad really was proud of me, and I guess I knew it, in spite of him giving me the dickens all the time."

After dismantling Suzabelle, Kauffman was told to search the sunken battleships at Pearl for unexploded bombs. But none were to be found. The only thing he encountered was an occasional dead body that had not yet been retrieved. It was a grim business.

Draper Kauffman got back to Washington on 4 January, as his father was leaving for Iceland. He was beginning to get desperate because the first bomb disposal class was to arrive on 14 January and he still did not have a place to put the school. Above all, the location should lend itself to the digging of holes, since, as he pointed out, bomb disposal was "95 percent digging and 5 percent taking care of the bomb." He procured blackboards on the thirteenth and chalk on the morning of the fourteenth while still scrambling to produce a curriculum. Just before heading for Pearl Harbor he had sent for a British curriculum, which arrived at this propitious moment. He had also been firing off frantic messages to Britain in search of talent, a call to which Captain Llewellyn, his old boss in bomb disposal, eventually responded by sending over three experienced officers to teach advanced classes: Maj. J. D. Hudson, Capt. A. B. Waters, and a Captain Sharman. But for now Draper Kauffman was the only instructor, and that was a real problem—a fresh-caught lieutenant in the U.S. Naval Reserve with a very eccentric background and only one bomb to work with—Suzabelle.

Finally Means Johnston found a place for the school on the fifth floor of a building in the Navy Yard that was producing, as Kauffman recollected, 40-mm guns. It was a terrible place for a school, with no dormitory facilities—though it did have a washroom and a shower—and worse, no place for digging. Most of the students stayed in the yard's bachelor's officers quarters, as the first, most definite requirement for their acceptance into the school was that they be bachelors. That is, until Draper met Peggy Tuckerman, which eventually changed his rules and his life.

Because the Washington Navy Yard was so far from ideal, at the end of the first class Kauffman stopped school for a week and sent all the students out to scour the city for a place where they would have room to expand and to dig, and where there would be dormitory facilities. Preferably, it should be more than twenty but less than forty minutes from the Navy Department—that is, close enough for the staff to hopscotch over to the department but far enough to keep the senior officers from breathing down their necks.

A couple of the young ensigns came across American University, and it was just right. There was plenty of digging room in the fraternity area. So the Navy Bomb Disposal School cordoned off all the frat houses—all, that is, but one, which was situated outside the compound and which the bomb disposal staff rented from the university so they would still be eligible for their housing allowance. The university was suffering financially from a large wartime reduction in student enrollment and was delighted to have the new school. The negotiations went smoothly, except for some expected Navy Department red tape, and the staff and students settled in quickly.

Both Admiral Blandy and the Methodist bishop who was the head of American University were present for the dedication. Blandy talked for ten minutes; the bishop spoke for two hours and twenty-five minutes. As Draper later remembered, "It was the longest sermon or dedication I have ever heard, I think by at least twice, out in the hot sun. I'm not being critical of him because he couldn't have been more cooperative with us, but that was some dedicatory speech. I thought Blandy was going to have a fit because he was a very busy man."

Kauffman was able to recruit a Civil Engineering Corps officer to instruct the students in shoring up the sides of a bomb crater and two people from BuOrd to come down at different times to teach them about U.S. bombs and fuses. He had always thought the British method was deficient because it didn't teach what went on inside fuses—how they really worked. At the U.S. Bomb Disposal School, students were required to know how all fuses worked, not just German but also Allied fuses.

The course was unique in that the final exam took between twenty-five and twenty-nine straight hours to complete and included digging holes and other physical tasks. The purpose was to find out whether a candidate became careless when tired. As Draper had learned when he served on the ad hoc committee in England looking into the cause of casualties, carelessness and fatigue were the main culprits, after, of course, the primary one: the bomb blowing up before it was defused.

Eventually, once the U.S. Bomb Disposal School was in full swing, a new class would start every two weeks and graduate between ten and twenty apiece—some two thousand graduates in all. The first graduation took place in the summer of 1942. It was very hot, and after the marathon exam somebody filled a huge bowl with daiquiris and provided straws for communal sipping. The exhausted candidates sprawled out on the grass and sipped themselves into oblivion.

Nineteen naval officers graduated in that first class, along with four army officers who were to start an army bomb disposal school in Aberdeen, Maryland. Draper issued orders sending five of the young graduates to England; five others became part of the staff of the school; and the rest dispersed to various commands. Four were dispatched to North Africa to collect bombs and fuses. Those young men, brand-new ensigns and barely more than kids, started sending back "the darndest flood" of German bombs, fuses, and booby traps. Army Air Corps planes moving from the United States eastward were heavily laden, but returning west they were empty, so there was no objection to the ensigns shipping all this stuff back. Eventually somebody in the army found out that its planes were coming back full of German bombs, still with explosives in them, and the service raised "pluperfect hell" about it. But by that time there were enough bombs to stock the navy school and the army school at Aberdeen. Aberdeen had excellent facilities for "steaming out" bombs—steam injected into a bomb was condensed inside the fuse to discharge the condensers, making the weapon less sensitive to noise or vibration and therefore safer to handle. So all the bombs were sent to Aberdeen first. Subsequently the navy school would pick what it wanted and let Aberdeen have the rest. The two schools had an excellent relationship and the army unit was cooperative in every way.

Once Kauffman had the bomb disposal school well organized, his mother suggested to his sister that she get together with some of her friends and invite officers from the school over for buffet suppers on Sunday. Betty Lou took her up on the suggestion, enlisting the help of Peggy Tuckerman and several other close friends. The men loved the home cooking, and after supper they would play "The Game," a form of charades that was the rage in Washington at the time. Draper and Means Johnston showed up at the first event, but only to make sure they approved and to warn the women not to keep the students up late. Then they disappeared down the black hole of duty and responsibility. But the other officers never failed to appear and they all had fun.

The suppers turned out to be a nice break for Draper's sister because their mother had determined that she attend a business school to learn typing and shorthand. Betty Lou had been offered a job at the British embassy, where Lord Halifax wanted her as a receptionist. "But Betty Lou doesn't know how to do *anything*!" her mother objected when the ambassador made his offer. "I don't care," he replied, "as long as she promises not to use these dreadful new American tea bags." But their mother did care and insisted that her daughter learn enough skills to get a real job. Not all Betty Lou's days were spent pecking away at the typewriter and practicing shorthand. She also conducted interviews for radio station WWDC, talking with women close to wartime leaders, including Millie King, daughter of the chief of naval operations; Jean Wallace, the vice president's daughter; and the daughter of the prime minister of Iceland, who had been sent to live in Washington for the duration of the war. Mrs. Kauffman during this time devoted herself to Bundles for Britain and British relief, the wartime efforts to send British citizens hand-knit sweaters, scarves, gloves, and bandages.

The primary mission of the Navy Bomb Disposal School was to train officers and men in the subtle art of rendering bombs harmless. As it turned out, however, the army needed bomb disposal talent far more than the navy. The Bureau of Naval Personnel insisted there be a bomb disposal officer on every U.S. carrier, battleship, and cruiser, and eventually an officer was sent to each; later no one could recall a single bomb disposal incident aboard an American ship. There was little bombing activity off the coast of the United States or at sea. As a result, the navy school's secondary missions, intelligence, publications, and—one it fell into—assisting in fuse design, became more important. The British published very little, partly because as they jumped from one crisis to another they were far too busy to apply themselves to that time-consuming task. Draper Kauffman later remembered it as crisis management overseen "by the most marvelous crisis manager in history, Mr. Churchill."

The navy school started collecting intelligence from people in the field, and eventually it consolidated this information in the form of publications put out jointly with the army school at Aberdeen. With the army's help on drawings, the army and navy bomb disposal schools put out eight publications covering German, Japanese, British, and U.S. bombs and fuses as well as shells and fuses. By 1944 some ten thousand copies of the various books were in print. Typically, the navy school gathered the bombs and fuses and intelligence, while Aberdeen illustrated the fuses so they could be easily understood. The navy school would then publish the book, bypassing the army's lengthy six-month approval process for publication. Kauffman here again demonstrated his talent for cutting through bureaucratic red tape. The books were simply issued under his signature, which as it turned out was against regulations. He did not use the Government Printing Office or work through the Office of Naval Intelligence or even the Bureau of Ordnance. In fact, BuOrd, which always wanted many copies, asked no questions.

As Kauffman said later, "I would guess that that little organization was the most nonregulation outfit in the U.S. Navy at the time." (It was also, by design, scarcely known within the navy. When someone called the Navy Department one day and asked for bomb disposal, the navy operator responded, "blonde disposal?") Kauffman was known to lament the disadvantages of being a reservist and a junior officer. But he conceded that there were also some significant advantages. Nobody expected you to know anything about navy regulations. He'd say, "I'm sorry, sir, but you know I'm just a reserve," and people let him get away with whatever it was. He would never have dreamed of doing the things he did if he had been a regular naval officer—or so he said.

In November 1942, during the Battle of Guadalcanal, the navy school inadvertently got into the U.S. fuse design business. The Japanese were using a fuse that the navy called a daisy cutter, one that went off immediately on contact. Adm. William F. Halsey, Commander in Chief, South Pacific, wanted some daisy cutters and sent a long message to BuOrd on the subject. A young ensign, who happened to be one of the bomb disposal graduates, was at Guadalcanal and managed to get the U.S. Navy Bomb Disposal School added to the list of recipients of the Halsey request. The school started fiddling with the idea and a few officers went over to BuOrd to suggest that a one-foot-long pipe be added to their regular fuse to activate it as it hit the ground. The fuse design people at BuOrd, as Kauffman noted, just about "had a stroke" when confronted with a proposal for a new fuse by an outside organization, and a fledgling one at that. They found all sorts of things wrong with it, but the bomb disposal school manufactured 250 of them anyway at the navy gun factory, and the chief of BuOrd, Admiral Blandy, gave his stamp of approval. Halsey was very pleased with it, as was Admiral Blandy—who had the school set up a course for BuOrd's disgusted fuse design people and ordered every single one of them to take it. Kauffman did not blame them for being mad. They were real professionals and as his school was, he admitted, a bunch of amateurs, the course he set up for them was confined to describing Allied and enemy fuses without making suggestions about how to handle them. BuOrd's fuse design experts were never asked to dig, and whenever they could find an excuse to skip class, they did. In a move that almost seemed calculated to further humiliate them, Admiral Blandy ordered Draper Kauffman to give them exams. He managed to wriggle out of that assignment, fully aware that marking BuOrd fuse experts on their knowledge of fuses would be the ultimate blow. Gradually the two jurisdictions developed a much better rapport. By that time the Navy Bomb Disposal School had the best museum of foreign ordnance in the United States and Great Britain.

After Kauffman became head of the U.S. Navy bomb disposal group, he went back to England for a series of meetings with the Unexploded Bomb Committee. That body consisted of the committee chairman from the Royal Navy; a British army brigadier general; Kauffman's former boss, Captain Llewellyn; a Royal Air Force colonel, who had been a close friend and drinking buddy of Draper's; and Kauffman himself, representing both U.S. Army and Navy bomb disposal.

A problem concerning a new fuse came up, and the committee chairman, equivalent to an assistant secretary of the navy, asked the general his opinion. The general spoke at some length; what he said was all taken down by the secretary. The chairman then asked Captain Llewellyn for his views. When Kauffman turned to look at him, he found Llewellyn red faced and rigid. "First, Mr. Chairman," Llewellyn said loftily, "I insist that the general's remarks be expunged from the record. At these meetings I represent My Lords of the Admiralty—in fact I *am* My Lords of the Admiralty—and unless there has been a change very recently that I haven't heard of, the Royal Navy is still the senior service and will be heard from first!" A compromise was reached when the general suggested that "perhaps it would be wise if we merely moved my remarks, so that they come after Captain Llewellyn's in the record," and it was so agreed.

Kauffman and his air force friend, afraid they would burst out laughing, did not dare look at each other. Such protocol was a far cry from Draper's homespun bomb disposal school, which as he said was probably "the most nonregulation outfit in the U.S. Navy at that time."

By May 1942 Reggie Kauffman had been in Iceland for five months. German submarines had been deployed all the way to the shores of the United States and were concentrating on the southern coast and the Caribbean. Merchant ships were being torpedoed and sunk in full sight of U.S. beaches—in one month alone, forty-one ships went down in the Gulf Sea Frontier, which included waters from the Gulf of Mexico to the shores of the Carolinas. Miami's beautiful sand beaches were coated with oil and tar from these maritime disasters. In June the elder Kauffman, who had become known as Mr. Destroyer and the U.S. Navy's principal antisubmarine expert, was ordered to Miami as commandant of the Seventh Naval District and commander of the Gulf Sea Frontier. This prompted the wry comment from him that the navy was being especially considerate, sending him to winter in Iceland and summer in Miami. Though no additional forces could be spared for the Gulf Sea Frontier, Kauffman was under orders to put a stop to submarine losses there. He moved the navy headquarters from Key West to Miami, including the Subchaser Training Center, with which he worked closely. The center was headed by Capt. E. F. "Mac" McDaniel, a legendary figure who paid little attention to formalities, concentrating entirely on the job at hand and the welfare of his personnel, an approach Kauffman wholly approved of. A good many naval reserve officers experienced in small-boat sailing requested this duty, inspired by the prospect of commanding small subchasers.

Within days Admiral Kauffman had set up a major command post in the Dupont Building in Miami. A two-story-high command chart was immediately installed showing the position of all shipping, all suspected enemy submarines, and all U.S. forces. It stood opposite a large deep balcony fitted out like the flag bridge of a commander at sea with instant communications to all his forces, and with a small room containing a cot on which the commandant did what little sleeping was possible.

Before Mrs. Kauffman and Betty Lou left Washington to join the admiral in Miami, Draper's mother asked his sister's friend, Peggy Tuckerman, if she could possibly invite Draper out to her family's house in Bethesda, Maryland, and give him a square meal once in a while. She was afraid he would not eat, he was so busy. No one had any idea how conscientiously Peggy would honor the request. Before departing south, and without giving her comment a second thought, Draper's mother remarked to him, "I wish you'd get married to some wonderful girl like Peggy Tuckerman."

Thanks to sticking with the business school in Washington, when Betty Lou arrived in Miami she landed a job with T. E. "Tubby" Price, a naval reserve commander and top-notch lawyer whose professional expertise and familiarity with local politics were very helpful to Admiral Kauffman. Commander Price was the Navy Department's district civilian personnel officer in Miami, and he had been the college roommate of Gov. Spessard Holland. They set aside part of his office as a housing department so that Betty Lou could help the wives of the navy men who were flocking to Miami find places to live. At first that job was easy, since the Department of Transportation in Washington had requested that civilians not travel for recreation and because apartment owners in Miami were desperate for tenants. Soon enough tourists, realizing that the DOT directive was just a patriotic appeal and had no teeth, began arriving in hordes as if there were no war at all. The apartment owners preferred tourists, who were able to pay much more than navy families for apartments, and Betty Lou's job grew increasingly difficult. She was infuriated to see a picture on the front page of the *Miami Herald* of brown bodies vacationing on the beach, shading their eyes from the sun with newspapers whose headlines screamed "Bataan Death March" over an account of the Japanese attack on U.S. Army headquarters on Bataan in the Philippines, where many American survivors were literally marched to death.

Mrs. Kauffman meanwhile organized clubs that she called Navy Neighbors for the hundreds of young navy wives who came from all over the country to be with their husbands before they shipped out. Women would sign up to help cook, clean, and babysit for each other, especially when a baby was born. Since most of the arrivals knew no one, and many had young babies, the service proved invaluable and resulted in numerous fast friendships.

Reggie Kauffman went about the business of eliminating submarines with his typical concentration and ingenuity. During the following critical eight months German submarines were driven from the area, an accomplishment for which he received the Navy Legion of Merit and was decorated by the grateful Cuban and Brazilian governments.

Numerous prominent figures came through Miami during that period and many of them seemed to find their way to dinner at the Kauffman house on Pine Tree Drive. The family later had stories connected with people such as the Duke and Duchess of Windsor, movie star Clark Gable, boxer Gene Tunney, writer Philip Barry, and bandleader Eddie Duchin.

President Roosevelt, in order to get around the isolationists before Pearl Harbor, had negotiated the Lend-Lease agreement whereby the U.S. would "lend" fifty old four-stacker destroyers to the British in exchange for "leases" on bases on some of the Caribbean islands. Among Reggie Kauffman's jobs as commander of the Gulf Sea Frontier was to check on those bases, including the Bahamas, where the Duke of Windsor was living out his wartime exile with his wife, the former Wallis Simpson, but known to the Kauffmans earlier in Washington as Wallis Spencer. They were particularly hospitable to Kauffman, often inviting him to luncheons with golf in the afternoon.

Wallis was so desperately bored with Nassau that she used any excuse to escape to the United States. She did not like to fly and often wrote endearing letters to Reggie Kauffman, conjuring up good times once supposedly had by all of them together and imploring him to let her travel to the states by sea. Kauffman, however, was extremely short of ships in those submarine-infested waters and his plans did not include having the Duke and Duchess of Windsor sunk "on his watch." He therefore had to courteously decline.

On one occasion when they were on their way to New York via Miami Reggie persuaded Elsa to invite them to dinner in return for their hospitality to him. Elsa gave a small buffet supper. Betty Lou was especially interested to see them, finding the duke charming but the duchess intolerable, as she later remembered, in her insistence at being the center of attention and dominating every conversation. It finally became too much for Elsa, who had a knack for deflating self-important people. Betty Lou knew exactly what had happened as she stood in the hallway listening to a fascinating conversation between the duke and Paul Hammond, a famous sailor, when Wallis stomped in proclaiming in the middle of her husband's sentence, "I said it was time to go!"

Eddy Duchin, the popular bandleader and piano player, was a young naval reserve officer attached to the staff of the Subchaser Training Center. There was a rumor that Eddy, with his sensitive musical ear, helped to develop sonar, which was being tested in Key West. On off-hours he played the piano wherever one could be found, attracting crowds of admirers. At one point he approached Admiral Kauffman and begged to be sent to sea. The admiral said, "But Eddy, your musical entertainment here is so good for morale. The armed forces are always accused of putting round pegs in square holes, and here you are putting your great talents to work."

Duchin responded, "Admiral, I've got a baby son, and when he asks me later what I did during the war and I have to say, 'Peter, I played with a band,' I could never face him." Nobody understood that better than Reggie Kauffman who, as soon as the German subs had been driven from his area of responsibility, harassed every visiting senior officer with requests for seagoing duty. Eddy Duchin was sent to the Pacific where, using his musical ear to good advantage, he became sound officer aboard the USS *Bates,* engaged in antisubmarine warfare.

In January 1943 Reggie Kauffman was also sent to sea. He was appointed chairman of the Allied Antisubmarine Warfare Board, reporting directly to President Roosevelt and Prime Minister Churchill. In a six-month period he and other members of the board, which included three Americans and three Brits, traveled some forty-five thousand miles throughout the Atlantic, inspecting and evaluating each operational command and each training and support facility. The board's recommendations profoundly affected Allied conduct of the antisubmarine war.

One evening, toward the end of January, Betty Lou was giving a dinner party while her mother was upstairs in bed with a bad case of laryngitis. The telephone rang and it was Draper. Betty Lou called her mother to the phone, thinking her brother was going to tell them that he had been ordered to a new job. "I'm calling to say that Peggy and I are going to get married," he announced. A long silence followed on the Florida end of the phone.

"Peggy who?" his mother croaked.

Rather lamely—Peggy was sitting next to him—Draper responded, "Peggy Tuckerman."

Neither his mother nor sister had been given a hint that the two were seeing much of each other. In a state of shock, Mrs. Kauffman simply said, "I've got laryngitis." His sister's reaction was just as stunned. She told her brother that she was having a dinner party and began rattling off the names of the guests. As Draper remembered afterward, no phone call was ever so anticlimactic. "That's the last time I ever call you two when I have important news!" he said.

One reason for the surprise was that Peggy was Betty Lou's closest friend. The two had remained correspondents since the Kauffmans had left Washington, and Peggy had even visited them in Miami. It was obvious that she adored Draper, but then so did all his sister's friends, not only for his charming personality but also, in those days of swing bands and big parties, because he was a great dancer. But Draper had only dated women his own age, and Betty Lou always thought Peggy, like herself eleven years his junior, was just another kid sister to him. Moreover, Peggy was a brainy Bryn Mawr girl, not the glamorous sort his sister envisioned her idol, Draper, marrying—someone like Betty Furness from his Naval Academy days. Or another good friend, Beatrice Philips, whose father was an ambassador and who counted among her dates not just Draper Kauffman but also Otto, Duke of Hapsburg, who was living out his wartime exile in Washington. Or beautiful, amusing Nan Brereton, a navy junior (as children of naval officers are called) he had grown up with, who had a hundred male admirers at her beck and call.

In fact, it happened that the night of Kauffman's proposal to Peggy, he had a date with Nan. They were eating in a restaurant when he said, "Excuse me a minute," and left the room. Nan later recounted that the minute stretched on and on, and finally her date came back, apparently from a pay phone. "Guess what?" he said "Peggy says she'll marry me!" "Peggy who?" said Nan. "Peggy Tuckerman!" he said, with the biggest grin she had ever seen. "And on my date!" Nan commented in mock exasperation.

Betty Lou gathered that they had not really "dated" much, if at all—that Draper had mostly just seen Peg when she made him those dinners suggested by Elsa. So Peg may have been surprised by the proposal too.

Obviously, it had been percolating under the surface of his chaotic and busy life that Peg was more wonderful than all his glamorous dates put together. And she was more than just smart. She was marvelously practical, had a wonderful disposition with no affectations whatsoever, possessed great inner strength, and could face any challenge—the best possible match for a man like Betty Lou's brother who was too busy to be as attentive as most wives would like. On top of it all Peggy, like Draper, loved to dance.

They got engaged on Valentine's Day. Mrs. Tuckerman, Peggy's mother, said, "Now of course you can't get married during Lent," so Draper checked the calendar. As it turned out Easter came unusually late that year, which he took a very dim view of. The nuptials had to be delayed until the first of May.

The wedding was a grand affair. Mrs. Tuckerman's seating plan for the event in the National Cathedral was headed as follows: first section, relatives and godparents; second section, ambassadors, ministers, cabinet officers, other officials; third section, admirals and generals; and choir stalls, diplomats. While Peggy and her mother saw to the details, Peggy's fiancé remained oblivious to wedding plans except to cable his father in London: "Want best man to be best man!" He was preparing exams for what was by then the bomb disposal school's twenty-first class. A few days before the big day, however, Mrs. Tuckerman put a temporary stop to his preoccupation with work. She showed him the guest list and explained how important it was for his ushers to pay close attention to the seating plan and to follow protocol. He looked at the list and said, "Oh, Mrs. Tuckerman, that's awfully nice, but I do feel strongly that my enlisted men should sit up at the very front. I'd like the two front rows for them if you don't mind."

"Oh, but I certainly do mind, Draper," she replied graciously but very firmly. "If you look at the required protocol, you'll see that that's impossible."

Kauffman was equally gracious, and equally firm, and Peggy backed him all the way. The impasse was finally broken by the suggestion that the bluejackets sit in the choir stalls, which they did, ousting the diplomats.

Draper Kauffman, after a brief membership in the Catholic church, officially returned to the Episcopal church at the wedding. Peggy Tuckerman had been raised in the Episcopal faith and had attended the National

Cathedral all her life, but there was no pressure from her to convert. By this time Kauffman felt completely comfortable about switching back to the denomination of his childhood. As an ambulance driver in France he had seen and handled dead and horribly mangled bodies every day, and in desperate need of spiritual answers had sought out priests in village churches around the Saar region. But far from offering him answers, the priests simply informed him that he was a sinner for not going to confession often enough and not contributing enough to the church's coffers. Draper decided that his conversion to Catholicism had been primarily the result of Father Keller's charisma. Though Kauffman abandoned his recently found religion, the two remained good friends always.

The Washington papers covered Draper and Peggy's wedding in detail. "Society Throngs Cathedral for Marriage of Margaret Cary Tuckerman," said the *Washington Star.* The article went on in the flowery style of those days to describe the "pageantry" that unfolded "under the soaring Gothic arches of the Great Choir of the Washington Cathedral." Peggy, it was mentioned, had stood first in her class at National Cathedral School, had attended Bryn Mawr College and at present held a government war job. This was actually a job with the Office of Strategic Services, forerunner of the CIA—but for reasons of national security that was unmentionable. Peggy was also attending night classes at George Washington University.

Draper was given ten days' leave for the honeymoon. They went to New York, ate at a different restaurant every night, and attended the theater, the opera, and Barnum and Bailey's Circus, followed by dancing and supper. After four days of a glorious honeymoon, Draper got a telegram telling him to report at once to Capt. Jeffrey C. Metzel on Adm. Ernest J. King's staff in Washington. Captain Metzel headed a clearinghouse for special operations under Rear Adm. Walter S. Delaney, Admiral King's assistant chief of staff for readiness. Draper did what "anybody else would have done. I gave the young bellboy five bucks and said, 'Son, you can't find me. Come back tomorrow.'" So he was a day late.

Kauffman wondered what sort of trouble he was in this time. Given the sort of helter-skelter operation he was running, there was always somebody on his back about something. When he made it back to Washington, Captain Metzel said, "Have you ever seen pictures of the obstacles the Germans are building on the Normandy coast?" He was referring, of course, to the defensive works Hitler was installing to impede an Allied amphibious invasion.

"No sir."

"Well, they're putting obstacles up in six feet of water that will stop the landing craft there and the soldiers will have to get out in water six feet deep. Do you know how much an infantryman's pack weighs?"

"No sir."

"Well, neither do I, but they'll all drown." He waved his arms, hitting both sides of the old Navy Department corridor. "I want you to put a stop to that! You're to go around and see my WAVE yeoman who has orders for you to go any place you want to. Pick a place to train your people, probably an amphibious base, and you can have anybody you want, but don't forget speed is essential; speed is the core of the whole thing."

Kauffman began peppering him with questions. Captain Metzel, whose sobriquet was Thought-a-Minute Metzel, said, "Now look here, Draper, you know perfectly well that you're not supposed to ask the what, how, when, why questions of the commander in chief's staff. That's your job."

Then he vanished. Kauffman still couldn't puzzle out what in the world Captain Metzel was talking about. He went to see the WAVE and, sure enough, she had travel orders that would allow him to go to and from any place he wanted. Metzel had left him with a package crammed full of pictures of the so-called obstacles, which wasn't much help. How in the world was he going to get rid of obstacles on somebody else's beach? It was once said of Jeff Metzel that he had a hundred new ideas every day, ninety-nine of which were no good, but there wasn't another soul in the Navy Department who had a really good new idea every day—all you had to do was winnow out the good one. Apparently this was a good one.

Kauffman went back to the bomb disposal school in a state of shock and turned it over to Tom Boardman. The Bureau of Personnel agreed to that choice, but Draper asked to be kept on officially for about six weeks "in order to have some base to operate from," and, as Tom said, "a base from which to steal the best of the bomb disposal outfit."

4

Setting Up an Underwater Demolition School

In mid-May 1943 Peggy Kauffman had found a nice apartment in the McLean Gardens off Washington's Wisconsin Avenue, an attractive residential community created by the Defense Homes Corporation for some three thousand people involved in the war effort. By June, however, it became clear that Draper Kauffman would be setting up and running an organization elsewhere. In search of a place to train, he reconnoitered several amphibious bases, including Fort Pierce, Florida, just south of Vero Beach.

Capt. Clarence Gulbranson, the skipper of the base at Fort Pierce, offered Kauffman two offshore islands where he could blow things up to his heart's content. It all looked good to the young naval officer, and he returned to Washington and told his liaison in the office of the commander in chief of the U.S. fleet, Admiral King, that he would set up a naval combat demolition school at Fort Pierce. No one bothered to tell him that he ought to check with the amphibious force commander in

Norfolk. When the latter found out, he wanted to know who in the hell this damned reserve lieutenant commander thought he was, making decisions on the use of amphibious bases.

The problem of seniority would continue to dog Draper Kauffman. Though he was spot-promoted to lieutenant commander, this was still a junior rank, and there was always the question of whether it would be better to have a senior officer running the demolition school. What Kauffman had on his side was enthusiasm, stamina, and a willingness to accept the innovative and sometimes crazy ideas that the younger men proposed, all of which would turn out to be crucial as the school forged into the unknown area of amphibious operations against a ruthless and determined foe.

With regard to his staff officers, Kauffman, as he put it, was "shot with luck." His administrative officer was a former bomb-disposal man, Lt. (jg) Jim Warnock, who did a highly competent job of overseeing the school under difficult circumstances. Another valuable officer was Lt. (jg) Jim Wetzel, commissioned from a gunpowder company out of Wilmington, Delaware, called Hercules Powder. And there was Lt. Bill Flynn, a Seabee and in Kauffman's words "first class, an Irishman through and through." Easily the oldest man in the unit, Flynn had gone along on every long march at Camp Peary, a training center for Seabees near Williamsburg, Virginia, even on a dislocated ankle. Flynn's slogan was "Don't be last." Kauffman called him Mr. Morale because of his remarkable ability to build esprit de corps.

These four men—Kauffman, Warnock, Wetzel, and Flynn—made a solid administrative staff for one of the most innovative units in the navy. In a manuscript titled "Some Memories and Thoughts about Draper L. Kauffman," Jim Warnock recalls the birth of the underwater demolition school:

> While I was still at the Bomb Disposal School in Washington, Draper told me about the Allied concentration of troops in England, and the German defenses being prepared along the entire channel coast in France. He asked if I would be willing to help him develop the methods and force to penetrate those continental defenses. He said "I want you to be thoroughly convinced that you want to join me in this. Give me an answer . . . first thing tomorrow morning at the very latest."

> I said to him the next morning "Draper, I'm with you. I can't think of anything I can do to make a greater contribution, but—" He cut me off with "Fine." And handed me my orders, which were already written up. I was to report to the Commanding Officer, Amphibious Training Base, Fort Pierce, Florida, within four days. I flushed. "Draper, you're a son-of-a—" He cut me off with "Let's have a drink. Go on over to the lounge and I'll be there soon."
>
> He brought those staff members who were around and announced what was happening. . . . Funny thing, both Draper and I knew that the men in that room would be the first volunteers for and would form the nucleus of the underwater demolition operations.

They moved down to Fort Pierce on 6 June. Warnock was to set up the physical facilities and prepare a tentative training curriculum, while Kauffman was to select the personnel. Draper asked Warnock what positions were needed, and his friend rattled off a list, which included an explosives expert, a tough chief petty officer or master sergeant for physical fitness, bomb disposal officers versed in explosives, a civil engineer with hands-on building experience, and several officers who had been through amphibious training and knew landing craft and small boats. That was just a start.

Two days later, things started to happen. The officers began arriving, and within a week the basic staff was all on board. The men were extraordinarily compatible and motivated, a tribute to Kauffman's gift for selecting personnel. As Jim Warnock put it, they "began working even before they found a place to sleep." With the help of Captain Gulbranson and his staff, they created a tent village, requisitioned galley equipment, and brought in two fine navy cooks. Other necessities soon came pouring in—jeeps, latrines, command carriers, landing craft and rubber boats, explosives, and magazines in which to store them.

Kauffman now had to locate students, though he still had not figured out exactly what he was to teach them. Many questions needed to be answered: What kinds of explosives would demolish concrete-reinforced walls? How could steel tetrahedrons be destroyed *and* cleared out of the way before landing craft approached the shore? What was the best disposal method for coiled barbed wire that stretched for miles up and down a beach? How could they best deal with a barrier of closely spaced, pointed poles? How could they traverse mines that were buried under the sand, in the surf and on the beach?

The men from navy construction battalions—CBs, or Seabees—seemed fitted to the work of erecting obstacles, so Kauffman got permission to enroll some of them. He selected a number of Seabee officers, and then he raided the bomb disposal school for nineteen of its best officers. Seabee enlisted personnel were drawn from basic training at Camp Peary. Kauffman did not have a clue how many men he would eventually need.

As soon as he moved to Fort Pierce, Draper Kauffman set about drawing up the new school's initial objectives. Number one was the selection and screening of students—men who could think for themselves, absorb new techniques, and then apply them. The plan was to give them training in explosives and to emphasize physical training. Second to selection and screening was the development of an esprit de corps within the group. Goal number three was to find the best available minds for research.

Sometimes those minds came in different forms than Kauffman expected. The Bureau of Ordnance had received word that the navy combat demolition school was to be given top priority in personnel and the department was highly cooperative. When Draper Kauffman contacted them with a request for the most talented explosives people they could find, "they sent down," he later remembered, "a wild character named George Kistiakowsky. In spite of the fact that he was a professor of physical chemistry at Harvard, we used to call him the Mad Russian." Kistiakowsky, who later became scientific adviser to the president, was known for his impulsive behavior. When Kauffman borrowed some army tanks, the Russian—who said he had operated tanks back home—hopped into one and drove it around wildly, terrorizing everyone in his path. But the professor had excellent ideas about the types of explosives that should be used at Normandy.

One evening he had dinner with Kauffman and left early, about ten. They agreed to meet on the beach at five the next morning. When Kauffman showed up in the dark, he found the beach empty. "No George," he later stated. He waited patiently for several hours and then began to be afraid that the professor was sick. When he checked with the motel he found that his talented recruit had checked out the night before without a word. Draper called the Bureau of Ordnance to report this disgraceful behavior. "Calm down," he was told—and ordered not to breathe a word to anybody. "But lots of people already know about this," he complained. "What do you mean, not a word of it to anybody?" But his BuOrd contact was firm—no word to anyone, period.

BuOrd sent down another explosives expert and nothing was ever said about the loss of the eccentric genius. Not until much later, when Kauffman saw pictures of the first atomic explosion and glimpsed Kistiakowsky with his arm around Robert Oppenheimer, director of the atomic bomb program known as the Manhattan Project, did he realize where the man had been over the intervening years. "George probably relished the mystery of the thing no end!" Draper told friends.

Captain Metzel had stressed the importance of speed, always speed in the pioneer demolition work being undertaken at Fort Pierce. Draper Kauffman and his as-yet small staff struggled desperately to solve the problems entailed in removing enemy obstacles put on beaches to deter Allied landings. They obtained small rubber boats and explosives and searched for something to use the explosives on. With the requirement for speed paramount, Kauffman's staff had to borrow from other programs such as the army's Scouts and Raiders, who were also training at Fort Pierce. The Scouts and Raiders was actually a joint army-navy group formed in September 1942 for reconnaissance duty during the forthcoming landing at Morocco. They had an eight-week training course. With the idea of weeding out anybody who was not tough enough for the tremendous endurance that Kauffman envisioned would be required for underwater demolition work, he asked the Scouts and Raiders to condense their eight-week physical training course into one week for his trainees. The new students in the underwater demolition school were all to go through the week-long physical conditioning course, and shortly before they arrived the demolition school's commander realized that he could not put them through such a grueling initiation without participating in it himself. Hell Week—as the present-day Navy SEALs, the successors of the underwater demolition teams, still call it—began then and there at Fort Pierce.

With eight weeks of physical training telescoped into a single week,

40 percent of the class either quit or was injured. It was a grueling program—swimming four miles in rough surf, night swimming with heavy loads, ten-mile runs, tortuous obstacle courses, hand-to-hand combat training—with only brief respites for sleep and food. The program was completely volunteer, and the Bureau of Personnel agreed that a man could be dropped from the school with no stigma attached to his record. "Of course the story quickly went around that Hell Week separated the men from the boys," Kauffman noted wryly. "The men had sense enough to quit—leaving us with the boys!"

Captain Gulbranson sent for Kauffman the Monday after that first Hell Week. Just barely able to crawl out of bed, the commander of the underwater demolition school dragged himself over to the base commander's office.

"What's this about 40 percent of your class quitting or in sick bay?" Gulbranson snapped. Draper confirmed the statistic. "I don't think you have any idea what you're putting these men through, Draper."

For the first time Draper was glad he had gone through hell himself, because it put a stamp of approval on the process. The captain loosened up and agreed to keep Hell Week, which built an enormous esprit de corps among the survivors. It was the same situation with the twenty-nine-hour bomb-disposal exam: every student's objection to the exam was replaced upon graduation with a great deal of pride that he had passed it.

Dan Dillon was among those in the first underwater demolition class. In an interview with the author he told about leaving the New York City Police Department to join the navy in March 1943, exchanging pay of sixty dollars a week for navy enlisted pay of fifty-five dollars a month as a gunner's mate. He was assigned to Camp Peary. At the camp they were jammed in like sardines, the food was terrible, and worst of all they had nothing to do. Then, said Dillon,

> some naval officer comes along and tells us about this secret operation, so there was a good-size scramble for this duty. About two hundred of us volunteered for we knew not what. It was a way of getting out of Camp Peary . . . and we'd had a few beers. . . .
>
> After arriving at a clearing on a beach and setting up six-man tents . . . "This is your hotel, gentlemen," we're told . . . and after nine or

> ten days of physical training, I am peeved. "What did you get yourself into, stupid?" I asked.
>
> Then one day in walks an immaculate man with lieutenant commander's stripes on him. He introduces himself as Draper Kauffman and takes command.
>
> We find out his background through the scuttlebutt. . . . This is an Annapolis guy, regular Navy. We were testing him, all along, but my respect for him deepened because a lot of officers will tell you what to do, but they won't do it themselves. This man . . . asks for suggestions. If they're good, he uses them. . . . And he participates in everything . . . the dirtiest, rottenest jobs that we tackle, he is in there doing as well as the rest of us. How could you not respect him? You may be mad at him, but by God in a short time we all admired Draper Kauffman.

Kauffman later said that almost every good idea on the topic of demolition, whether it was practiced at Fort Pierce, in Europe, or in the Pacific, came from an enlisted man or junior officer.

It took a special touch to keep morale up in a place like Fort Pierce. In the 1990 winter issue of *Naval History* Capt. Frank Kaine, USNR Ret., who had reported for duty in June 1943, wrote: "Fort Pierce looked like the Gobi Desert . . . a big sandpile . . . the rangers and commandos—sadists, we called them—taught knife fighting, garroting, whatever. It was eight to ten weeks of extremely physical work, day and night. . . . And all this after Hell Week! . . . The thing that made it almost totally intolerable was the Florida water which was full of jellyfish and Portuguese Men o' War. It was pure guerrilla training—survival really. . . . The whole time you were wet, chafed with sand, completely miserable." In one particularly nerve-racking exercise, the men were given a section of beach to test their ingenuity with land mines. The mines were rigged with one-inch firecrackers, and students had to crawl over booby-trapped stretches of sand to locate and disconnect them. Woe to the person who made a mistake—the firecracker would explode and blast his face with sand, a rude reminder that in the future, he should be more cautious.

It did not help matters that, at first, Kauffman had put out an edict that wives were not permitted in Florida. Moreover, the training was classified, so no one could know what was going on. Needless to say, everybody suffered, including Draper himself. He wrote to Peggy, "I would give so much to see you for just one hour. . . . This week has been a tough one. It was necessary for me to take the whole course with the men . . . but that meant I had to do all business from 11 PM on, so you had a very tired husband for a week there . . . [but] even when I'm so tired I can't think . . . I still see your sweet face when I say my prayers at night." One of the officers' wives, who was pregnant, appeared on the scene and her husband hid her in town. Frank Kaine's wife heard about this and she made her debut too. "Next thing you know," wrote Kaine, "a whole gang of wives had to be hidden from Kauffman." On one occasion the officers stole his glasses, snuck off the island, and treated their wives to dinner and a movie. Without his glasses Kauffman walked right by them and didn't have the faintest idea who they were. As soon as Peggy arrived at Fort Pierce, however, the rule changed—from then on, wives were allowed.

The men may have pulled an occasional fast one on Kauffman, but there was no doubt that he was respected and admired. According to Captain Kaine, "Draper Kauffman was a good leader in more ways than one. . . . He was a slender guy, tall and thin with the original Coke bottle glasses . . . lousy vision. We all knew he was no athlete or anything, but he went through the training with us, every step of the way. We thought, 'Hell, if he can take it, we can too.'"

Fort Pierce was not all training, however. The demolitioneers and the Seabees competed in basketball games; the USO operated the Fort Pierce Recreation Hall; and there were USO clubs on Second and Tenth Streets, the latter of which boasted both indoor and outdoor dancing and, as a result, averaged twenty-two thousand visitors a month.

During the first class Kauffman and his staff did a lot of improvising, cobbling together a program that would bring results when the Allies finally launched their amphibious assault on European and Pacific shores. A small rubber boat was assigned to each six-man team, or naval combat demolition unit (NCDU), as they were originally called. The teams' task was to destroy replicas of the obstacles that would be encountered on German-held beaches. The NCDUs were eventually able to accomplish these objectives with devastating speed, in a matter of hours, at least at Fort Pierce. It was the Seabees' task to construct the elaborate defensive works. Seabees were in woefully short supply now that the United States was engaged in conflicts across half the globe, and Kauffman found himself shuttling back and forth to Washington on a borrowing mission. Eventually he was grudgingly given half a battalion of Seabees. They were godsends who performed a seemingly thankless task. It was difficult for them to see their painstaking constructions demolished within hours. In time, Kauffman and his staff allowed their precious Seabees to erect barriers as they saw fit, without such meticulous reproduction of the original. But from the time the Seabees arrived, a friendly rivalry developed between the two opposing groups. In the words of Jim Warnock, "The Seabees built and the UDTs destroyed. . . . The Seabees tried to build defenses and devices that the frogmen couldn't penetrate. How many times have I heard 'If you'd waited until the concrete set properly, you could never have taken it out!'"

With certain obstacles, it was difficult to determine where the navy's responsibility ended and the army's began. In six feet of water, for instance, the navy was responsible for objects up to the high water mark, while the army covered any above that. With the tide changing all the time, however, the demarcation line fluctuated. According to British intelligence, in the spring of 1944 the tides on the Normandy coast changed twenty-five feet twice a day.

The use of rubber boats for demolition operations was itself an innovation brought about by this first class of Draper Kauffman's. Under cover of darkness, NCDUs consisting of one officer and five enlisted men would approach the shore in landing craft, transfer to rubber boats, then swim the remaining stretch with their explosive charges attached to floats. When the men located obstacles, they would lash the charges to them, connect the charges, and detonate them by way of delayed fuse or electric leads connected to a "hell box" in one of the boats. More path-breaking ideas were to follow, especially after the National Defense Research Council sent in its contingent of scientists, physicists, and engineers to help. New types of explosives made their debut, such as long, sectioned tubes, called Bangalore torpedoes, which expedited the disposal of barbed wire. Jack Brown shallow-water diving gear—the forerunner of scuba equipment—replaced the simple snorkels. Communications made a leap forward with the advent of radio on landing craft. Primacord, a potent explosive, was found to be especially adaptable to demolition use. Eighty-seven hundred yards of primacord could detonate in a single second. It was 100 percent waterproof, and a thousand-foot reel weighed no more than twenty pounds, which made it exceedingly easy to handle.

Kauffman knew that fostering competition among the NCDUs would enhance performance, so he came up with the idea of allowing each team to invent its own wacky name. Soon Fort Pierce was home to the TNTeetotalers, Brooks' Brainy Blasters, Clayton's Deep-Sea Doodlers, and Andrews' Avengers. This promoted esprit de corps and injected a needed element of fun into the otherwise grueling business of training.

The NCDUs were too busy learning the minutiae of demolition to bother much with spit-and-polish navy regulations. "We were the despair of Snuffy Farnsworth, the executive officer of the base," Kauffman lamented. "It seemed as if he sent for me every day with some new incident of a demolitioneer who failed to salute or who had a sloppy-looking uniform. . . . Of course he was right, but I didn't have the time to indoctrinate these kids in navy regulations as well as teach them what needed to be taught. Captain Metzel's prime demand was never to forget the urgency of 'speed, speed, speed!'"

Of course, Hell Week, the attrition rate, and the top-secret nature of demolition work fanned the feeling among students that they were a special group, one that didn't need to bother with petty regulations. Elitism was an attitude that Kauffman and his staff fought from the first day of class to VJ Day, with mixed results. What they did succeed in doing was putting a "100 percent clamp on any demolition unit information until the end of the war. . . . We weren't sure ourselves what we'd be doing, and we certainly didn't want the enemy to know," he said.

Pride in their outfit, however, had its benefits. Kauffman started a custom with that first class. He would turn to the enlisted men on one side of a room and announce, "I will do everything in my power to ensure that no officer graduates from this school under whom I would not be happy to go into combat." Then turning to the officers on the other side of the room, he would say, "I will do everything in my power to ensure that no enlisted man graduates from this school whom I would not want to lead into combat." This exercise boosted morale—and in wartime, morale counted for a lot.

It was late in July 1943 that Draper finally asked Peggy to come to Florida. "I love you. Come down soonest possible," the telegram read. Peggy arrived the very next day. She plunged into navy life and enjoyed being there immensely, even if her husband's job took priority over her. And she had an unfailing sense of humor about that. At one point the two of them were scheduled to go to the wedding of another officer at the base. She put on her prettiest afternoon dress; Draper donned his dress uniform; and they got into the official car, the only one on the base. No sooner had he turned on the ignition, however, than Kauffman remembered a rule he had made, one inspired by his father, who was always meticulous about such matters: official cars were never to be used by spouses or for nonmilitary social occasions. "Sorry, Peg," he said. "Never mind," she replied good-naturedly, "I'll ride my bike," and off she went, chiffon dress nearly flying over her head in the wind, alongside her escort who was slowly driving the car. "There seems to be something not quite right here!" she called out, laughing. Draper Kauffman could never believe how lucky he was to have such a wife—when he had time to think about it.

Kauffman could be a hopeless case when it came to practical things. Jim Warnock recalled a time when he and his wife, Alene, witnessed their leader on his way out of Fort Pierce for a last-minute trip to Washington:

> We'd stopped by the apartment for some unremembered reason when Draper came crashing in. . . . He had picked up his airline tickets and some money and come home to take a quick shower, dress, and get to the airport. When he was presentable . . . he raced out of the bedroom and said good-bye. Peggy asked about his plane tickets. Draper felt in his coat pocket. No ticket. A hectic search began, and after about five minutes Alene found the tickets under the living room rug where Draper had put them to keep them from being lost. Then he couldn't find money. Together, we scraped up a few bucks and away he went. . . . Peggy had our sympathy. She was still paying florist bills for the beautiful flowers Draper had sent her during their courtship!

When Christmas 1943 came, Draper and Peg sent out a formal-looking Christmas card with the message "Merry Christmas from Lieutenant Commander and Mrs. Draper Kauffman."

But the unit's official card, designed by some of the men, showed a sailor rowing a boat for all he was worth, sweat pouring from his brow, the rest of the craft filled with explosives followed by the message:

A sailor, a boat, and ammunition
All together, that's demolition
So here's a note of Christmas Cheer
From a Naval Combat Demolitioneer!

That Christmas was a special time for Peggy and Draper. Despite the hectic pace of life at Fort Pierce, they were together, and Peggy was four months pregnant. It was the most thrilling experience of Draper Kauffman's life, even though it was occurring in the shadow of war.

Meanwhile, in September 1943 Reggie Kauffman and the Allied Antisubmarine Warfare Board had completed their work, and he was asked by Adm. Chester Nimitz, now commander in chief in the Pacific, to assume command of all cruisers and destroyers in the Pacific Fleet—38 cruisers, 339 destroyers and destroyer escorts, and 24 frigates. When his daughter wrote to say that with his love of destroyers he must now have the most wonderful job in the world, he responded that it was fine, but he would exchange it in a minute for "one little old tin can of my own."

In June 1944 Betty Lou became engaged to Prescott Bush Jr. In a letter to her father she mentioned that Pres's brother George was out in the Pacific, an ensign aboard the aircraft carrier USS *San Jacinto*. Deciding to check out the family, Admiral Kauffman located George Bush and invited him aboard his flagship for lunch. George wrote a very funny letter back to his parents in Connecticut, which they forwarded to Pres. According to George, he was told to report to the skipper of his carrier. "What have I done now?" he wondered. The skipper told him that Admiral Kauffman would be sending a boat for him if he were free to come aboard his flagship for lunch the next day. "Yes, sir!" said Ensign Bush, who went and polished his shoes and made sure his uniform was in perfect shape. After "a great lunch," Draper Kauffman's father escorted George back to the

San Jacinto in his admiral's barge. When the officer of the deck saw the admiral arriving, he immediately had the side boys lined up to pipe him aboard. Lo and behold, up the gangway came Ensign Bush, while the admiral waved goodbye and took off. Once the piping started, it couldn't be stopped. Ensign Bush was given the honors normally accorded only an admiral or other dignitary. George burst out laughing, whereupon the officer of the deck could not resist giving him a swift kick in the pants.

About the time Admiral Kauffman got his Pacific Fleet command, in the fall of 1943, his son began getting itchy feet. Here he was, sending men out to both oceans to fight the war while he was confined within the borders of the United States, training. In Washington on business, he made a point to see Admiral Delaney to request an "active" job. The admiral was firm. "No," he said, "you can contribute far more to the war effort at Fort Pierce than you can any place else." As luck would have it, that same day Kauffman went to lunch at the Roger Smith Hotel with friends and, seated at a nearby table, was Gen. William "Wild Bill" Donovan. Donovan, famed for his daring exploits in World War I, was the originator of the Office of Strategic Services, the precursor to the CIA. He was also—and this is what impressed Kauffman—author of the statement, "Physical endurance will give one control of one's nerves long after the breaking point seems to have been reached." Someone at Donovan's table knew Kauffman and told the general that the naval officer had been in the French army and the British navy, and had been involved in bomb disposal and underwater demolition. Donovan's antennae went up, and he asked his acquaintance to invite the young man over.

Draper Kauffman was not one to let an opportunity easily slip away. "General," he blurted out after being introduced, "would you have any useful job for me to do?" Donovan responded, "I was hoping you'd ask that, young man. The answer is yes. Furthermore, I can give you a spot promotion."

Kauffman immediately told Admiral Delaney about the conversation. The admiral listened quietly and politely. "I cannot stop you if General Donovan asks for you," Delaney said, but he pointed out that the Donovan organization had its detractors as well as its admirers, and in the end he succeeded in talking his subordinate out of the idea.

As always, however, Kauffman was determined to get into the action.

He ran into Adm. Milton E. Miles, who was running a top-secret operation behind Japanese lines in China that Draper could only characterize as "weird and wonderful." Miles decided to have his new people take a demolition course, and he dropped in at Fort Pierce when he was in Florida.

"Admiral," questioned Kauffman, "would you have use for a lieutenant commander—like me, maybe?" "Yes," replied Miles, "but you may not know much about what we're doing. There are an awful lot of disadvantages to it." And he began a litany of hardships that did not deter Kauffman at all. So the admiral produced an instruction book in Chinese that he happened to have with him, and Kauffman spent the next week slaving over Chinese characters. Peg found a Chinese truck farmer to help him. When Delaney found out about this latest venture, he blew up. "Hell, no!" he boomed, and Lieutenant Commander Kauffman went back and licked his wounds.

By this time Kauffman noticed something that disturbed him: a lack of interest on the part of senior officers in England in demolition. But it sparked an idea. He drafted a "message" from the U.S. amphibious commander in Britain to Admiral King in Washington asking that Lieutenant Commander Kauffman be sent to the United Kingdom immediately and citing the junior status of demolition people there. If he had stopped there, Kauffman might have gotten away with it and been packed off to England. But it happened that the day the message went to Britain, some navy demolition units were also being sent to Pearl Harbor. Thinking "what the heck, maybe I can double my chances," as he later explained, he wrote up an almost identical draft of the first message, but to be sent to Admiral King from Adm. Richmond Kelly Turner, Commander, Amphibious Forces Pacific. He then said to a young officer going to England, "If you can get this to Admiral Kirk or someone on his staff, maybe he'll send it back, or reword it and send it back." To another man headed west he repeated: "If you can get this to Admiral Turner, maybe he'll send it back."

As luck would have it the two messages arrived in Washington the same week, and they sounded suspiciously alike. Kauffman was immediately designated as the culprit and got called to Washington once again, and once again caught hell.

Reggie Kauffman, who had his headquarters at Pearl Harbor, apparently did not know what his son was up to, although through the grapevine he had heard a rumor that Draper was going to England. He wrote his son from sea in December:

> This is just to wish you and your bride a very Merry Christmas and a most successful New Year. I have written Peggy a little note too. . . . Before I left I heard you were going on Kirk's staff in England. I am not cognizant of the plans except in a general way but suppose you may go over anytime now.
>
> You know your own business but from my recent observations there is every reason for continuing in training along your line for sometime to come. These landings out here are tough and your opponents are just as tough. Landing on an atoll is entirely different from the shores of Sicily—and these little brown b— are not Italians in any way. Coral reefs are likewise one hell of a problem and much work can be done along that line. I have had nothing to do with that game, but the press apparently was surprised at the number of casualties. Landing operations never have been easy and against a determined foe they always will be tough. It simply boils down to, how badly do you want the place—and how much are you willing to pay for it?

His father too (who himself had pestered senior officers mercilessly to send him to sea from Miami after he had driven German subs from the region) was hoping to persuade Draper that he was more useful in the United States than in Britain. In the meantime the messages Draper had written requesting his services in England or the Pacific were, at least for the moment, shot down in Washington. In February 1944 his father wrote again, this time relating that Rear Adm. William "Spike" Blandy, soon to be Commander, Amphibious Forces, Fifth Fleet, had asked for Lieutenant Commander Kauffman to come to the Pacific as his flag lieutenant. Admiral Kauffman still hoped his son would stay a little longer at his school. There would be plenty of time left for him to see action. "It is a hell of a long way to the Emperor's Palace in Tokyo," he offered.

The growing intensity of the amphibious war in the Pacific, however, in particular the decimation at Tarawa, drove Admiral Turner to make a specific request for Admiral Kauffman's son, and in late March Draper Kauffman was summoned to the Pacific.

As he was leaving Fort Pierce for the Pacific, he wrote Peggy, who was back in Washington with her family: "I had a hectic last week. They gave me a whale of a farewell party Friday night. It was a corker (many corks) and left me in pretty bad shape to pack and finish up on Saturday night. I get to . . . Pearl Sunday morning. In the official order of detaching me, Captain G. added the phrase 'with regrets,' first time he had done that so I felt flattered. I almost hated to leave. . . . I sure missed you yesterday—it didn't seem right without you. I miss you more than I can tell my darling. Give my best to the family and lots of love to you both."

Kauffman departed three months before the Normandy landings, which had been the focus of his and his staff's attention for almost a year. The underwater demolition school sent thirty-two units to Britain to participate in the landings. Tragically, as only ensigns or junior lieutenants commanded those units, nobody in the upper echelons of command accorded them much attention. They were considered too junior to be given any intelligence on the enemy beaches.

Not until 15 April 1944 did somebody on the staff in Britain get five of these young officers together and start planning how to use their units. When one of the last rehearsals for the Normandy landing was being tied up in May, by which time the Germans had laid down more than five hundred thousand obstacles on the Channel coast, two lieutenant commanders who had never heard of demolition were assigned as demolition group commanders, one for Omaha Beach and one for Utah Beach.

Later, when this news filtered back to Draper Kauffman, the lack of attention on the part of top-level commanders surprised and distressed him, not least because his naval combat demolition units had originally been designed for Normandy.

According to Draper Kauffman, lack of leadership had much to do with the ensuing high casualties, even though he acknowledged that bad weather and high tides also were to blame. The underwater demolition groups suffered 52 percent casualties on Omaha. Fortunately there were fewer on Utah Beach where the underwater demolition groups were able to blast large gaps through the obstacles to make way for the troops. Those of the NCDUs at Omaha Beach who were not cut down did such an outstanding job that they were awarded seven Navy Crosses, numerous Silver and Bronze Stars, and one of the three Presidential Unit Citations given to the navy for the Normandy landing. But those events were still in the future. Kauffman left Fort Pierce in March 1944, and as he wrote, "from then on I was so preoccupied with the Pacific that I could not concentrate on anything else."

Draper Kauffman, about eighteen months, with his mother, Elizabeth Kelsey Draper Kauffman.
Author's collection.

Draper, age thirteen, with the author, age two. A Brazilian naval officer, seeing the picture on Comdr. Reggie Kauffman's desk, asked what the age difference was between the children. When told "eleven years," he replied, "They keep you that long at sea in your country!"
Author's collection.

Draper, age fourteen, at Kent School.
Kent School Yearbook.

Midshipman Kauffman, U.S. Naval Academy, 1929–33.
Author's collection.

Draper served with the French army as a member of the American Volunteer Ambulance Corps, March–August 1940.
Author's collection.

Draper joined England's Royal Navy Volunteer Reserve before the United States entered World War II.
Author's collection.

Sub-Lieut. Draper L. Kauffman, Royal Navy Reserve, and a rating (an enlisted man), with German delayed-action bomb they have dug out and Draper has defused.
Author's collection

Draper became a member of the U.S. Naval Reserve in November 1941.
Author's collection.

Fort Pierce, Florida, Underwater Demolition Training, Rubber Assault Boat Crews.
U.S. Navy photo.

a

b

c

d

Obstacles were erected by the enemy in an attempt to keep boats far enough from shore so that men getting out with heavy packs were likely to drown in deep water or be easy targets for snipers. At Normandy, Allied troops encountered multiple rows of obstacles; many had mines attached. At high tide the obstacles were underwater: (a) barbed wire with mines; (b) sharpened poles pointing seaward; (c) a series of cement triangles; (d) the "Belgian gate"(a huge construction popular with the Germans at Normandy). *U.S. Navy photo.*

Underwater demolition men attaching explosives to obstacles in the Pacific.
U.S. Navy photo.

Two demolitioneers in a boat; the one with flippers in the air has just dived backward into the boat. "Half fish and half nuts" was the term applied to these frogmen UDTs by troops waiting for them to clear the obstacles.
U.S. Navy photo.

Draper and Peggy (Tuckerman) Kauffman at their wedding at the National Cathedral, Washington, D.C., 1943.
Author's collection.

Lt. Comdr. Draper L. Kauffman, USNR, receives a Gold Star in lieu of a second Navy Cross from his father, Rear Adm. James L. Kauffman, USN, Commander, Cruisers and Destroyers, Pacific Fleet. When asked why he was laughing, Lieutenant Commander Kauffman replied, "Because, as Dad pinned it on, he said, 'Thank the Lord you found a clean shirt!'"
U.S. Navy photo.

Awards ceremony, 1 September 1944, recognizing gallantry under fire during Mariana Islands operation. First row (*left to right*): Lt. W. G. Carberry, USNR (Silver Star); Lt. Comdr. Draper L. Kauffman, USNR (Gold Star in lieu of second Navy Cross); Lt. T. C. Crist, USNR (Silver Star). The other men all received Bronze Stars: (*left to right*) Second row: Joe R. Reinheardt, SK1; J. D. Waters, BM2; R. E. Heil, CM1; J. E. Bagnall, GM2; Third row: A. D. Snyder, SK2; J. A. Schommer, CCM; R. B. McGinnis, CCM; J. D. Orr, CCM; E. K. Watson, CGM; J. C. Pipkin, EM2.
National Archives.

Comdr. Seymour D. Owens, killed at Tinian while commanding destroyer USS *Norman Scott*. He was married to Draper Kauffman's first cousin.
Author's collection.

Rear Adm. James Laurence Kauffman aboard the "Fighting Lady," the USS *Yorktown*. He gave the photo to his grandson James Laurence Bush with a note on the back: "To Jamie—Uniform worn at battle station. The knife is to cut lashings in case of sinking. The flashlight in case a bomb cuts electric power. I was watching some enemy planes circling."
Author's collection.

Rear Adm. James L. Kauffman, USN, outside his Quonset hut in the Philippines, with his son, Lt. Comdr. Draper L. Kauffman, USNR.
National Archives.

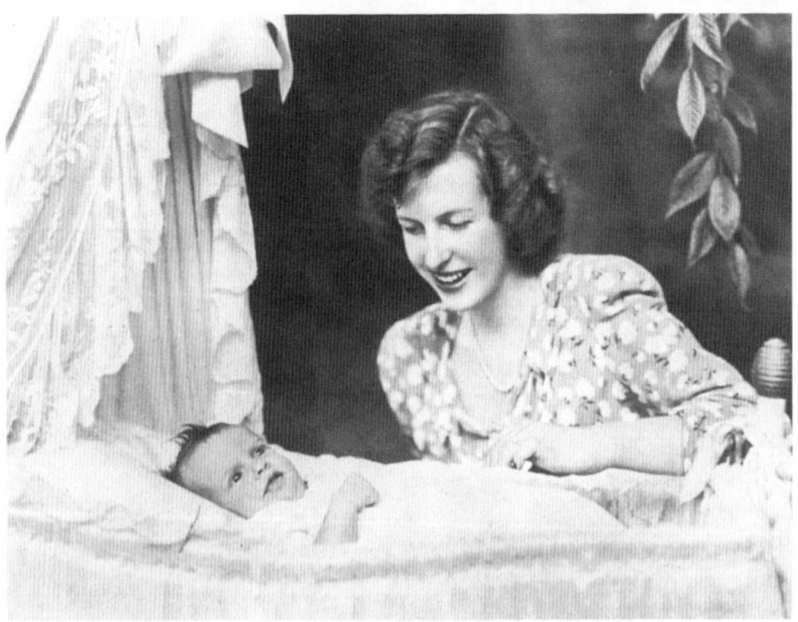

Peggy Kauffman with baby Cary. This was one of Draper's favorite pictures, which he carried everywhere with him.
Author's collection.

The Kauffman and Bush families, Christmas 1948 at commandant's quarters, Navy Yard, Philadelphia.
U.S. Navy photo, Ninth Naval District.

Peggy and Draper Kauffman with (*left to right*) Kelsey, Larry, and Cary, about 1948.
Author's collection.

The Kauffmans and Bushes at the home of Prescott and Elizabeth Bush, Greenwich, Connecticut, 1962. Front row (*left to right*): Prescott Bush Jr., Kelsey Bush, James L. Bush, Kelsey Kauffman, and Peggy (Mrs. Draper) Kauffman. Back row: Prescott Bush III, Elsa (Mrs. James L). Kauffman, Cary Kauffman, Elizabeth (Mrs. Prescott) Bush, Draper Kauffman, Larry Kauffman, and James L. Kauffman. Above the mantel is a portrait of Draper Kauffman's father, James Kauffman.
Greenwich Review, September 1962.

Elsa (Mrs. James Laurence) Kauffman, Draper's mother.
Author's collection.

Rear Adm. Draper L. Kauffman, USN, commanding officer, Cruiser/Destroyer Flotilla Three in his cabin with his father, Vice Adm. James L. Kauffman, USN, who was there on a visit.
U.S. Navy photo.

Portrait of Rear Adm. Draper L. Kauffman, USN, when he was superintendent of the U.S. Naval Academy, 1965–68. Painted by Alice V. Knight, it hangs in Luce Hall at the academy.
Photo by James Cheever, U.S. Naval Academy Museum.

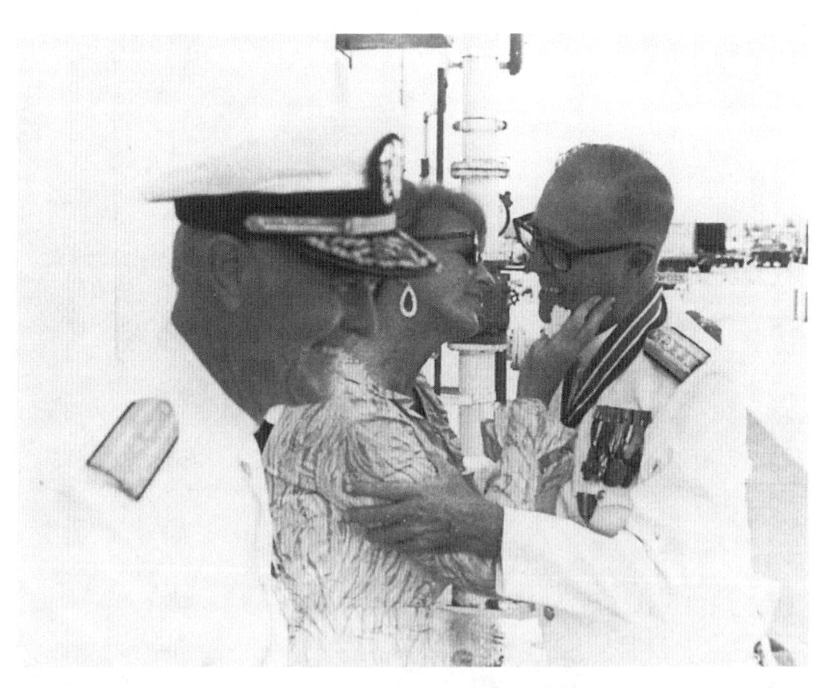

Draper receives a Philippine decoration—and a heart-warming homecoming from Peggy.
Author's collection.

Rear Adm. Draper L. Kauffman, superintendent of the Naval Academy, relaxes at his residence in Annapolis, where young midshipmen gathered frequently for dinner and conversation.
Author's collection.

Rear Adm. Draper Kauffman at his retirement ceremony June 1973, Great Lakes, Ninth Naval District, Chicago. On his left is Adm. Means Johnston, the principal speaker, who was Kauffman's executive officer when they set up the U.S. Navy Bomb Disposal School in 1941.
Author's collection.

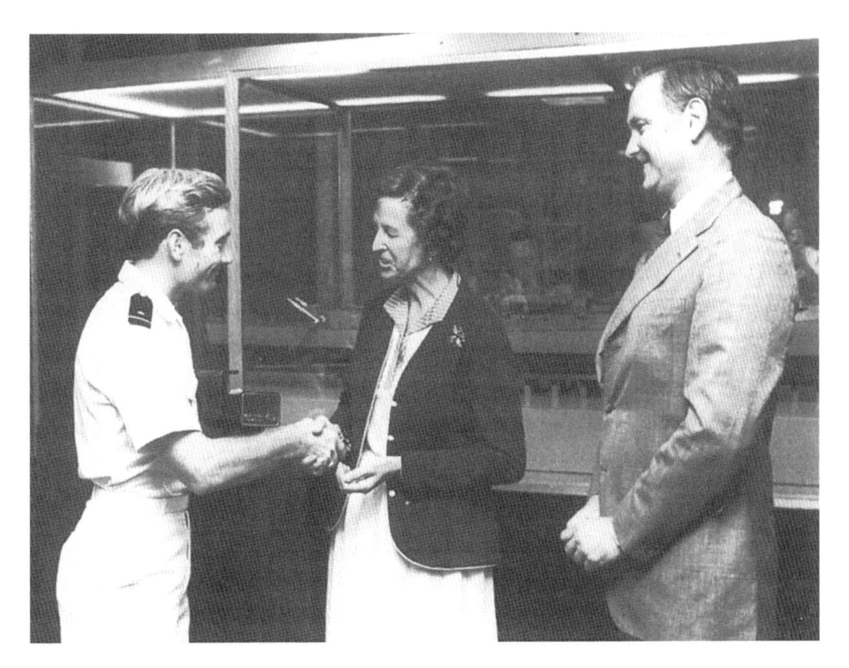

Peggy Kauffman presents the Draper Kauffman Leadership prize to Midshipman Lewis Cooper while Claude Hutchison watches. Hutchinson, formerly aide to Admiral Kauffman on the USS *Helena,* established the award. The prize winner is selected not by the faculty but by his fellow second classmen. (This is after Draper's death in 1979.)
U.S. Naval Academy.

A portrait of Draper Kauffman (Father of the Frogmen, sometimes called Granpappy Bullfrog) greets visitors as they enter the UDT / SEAL Museum. Portrait by Albert K. Murray, one of the four official navy artists in World War II.
Author's collection.

Statue of underwater demolition warrior at the UDT/SEAL Museum. The museum opened in November 1986 in Fort Pierce, Florida, where it all began. The life-size statue honors all NCDU, UDT, and SEAL personnel who have lost their lives in the line of duty. The pedestal depicts a tank trap, one of the many obstacles frogmen encountered as they cleared the approach for amphibious landings. Draper Kauffman Jr. unveiled the statue at the museum's third reunion on November 12, 1988. (NCDU were naval combat demolition units, the forebears of the UDT.)

U.S. Navy postcard.

Christening of the USS *Kauffman,* guided missile frigate, at Bath Iron Works, Bath, Maine, 29 March 1986. The principal speaker *(at podium)* was Vice President George H. W. Bush. Elizabeth Kauffman Bush christened the ship, which was named after her father, Vice Adm. James Laurence Kauffman, and her brother, Rear Adm. Draper Laurence Kauffman. Her niece Margaret Cary Kauffman was matron of honor. A frigate now is larger than a WWII destroyer, though somewhat smaller than a present-day destroyer. Vice Adm. William F. McCauley also spoke at the ceremony and called the USS *Kauffman*'s antisubmarine warfare capability "unmatched anywhere in the world."
Bath Iron Works photo.

Left to right: Cary Kauffman; Draper Kauffman Jr., Elizabeth Kauffman Bush, and Barbara Bush watch as the USS *Kauffman* slides into the water. (Kelsey Kauffman was in Australia.)
Author's collection.

The USS *Kauffman* is commissioned and goes to sea with a full crew and her first captain, Comdr. John Dranchak, USN. The speaker at the ceremony was Assistant Secretary of the Navy Chase Untermeyer, formerly Draper's aide in the Philippines.
Bath Iron Works photo.

5

On to the Pacific

Peggy was now in Washington with a baby coming in May and no husband. Despite the hardship of separation, she kept her sense of humor —even when she discovered some old letters from a girl Draper had met in Scotland while convalescing from his wounds. It was obviously a one-way romance; he had never written her back. In a letter to Draper's sister, Betty Lou, after Draper departed, Peggy wrote:

> So your dear brother has disappeared off to the wars, leaving his bride, six months pregnant, weeping on her mother's shoulder! At least I certainly was a couple of days ago. The doorbell rang and a special delivery letter came containing his last will and testament in which he left everything to his dearly beloved wife, and so on and so forth. . . .
>
> There I was totally dissolved in tears, at the dining room table, and the doorbell rang again. There were two enlisted men from the

> Bomb Disposal school, each holding the handle of a trunk between them. They didn't actually say, "Ma'am these are your husband's last earthly possessions," but they might just as well have because they said, "These are the things the Commander left at the Bomb Disposal school, and we thought you might like to have them." So I opened this trunk to see what was in store for me, and you know what was in it? Swiss lederhosen, 32 civilian ties and some of his old love letters.
>
> After I'd read these letters to "Bombs, darling, why haven't you written?" and looked at the Swiss lederhosen, and very moth-eaten ties (obviously all given to him by maiden aunts or ex-girls), my tears turned to slightly hysterical laughter!

Peggy kept every one of the letters Draper wrote home. They did not take up too much space in her scrapbook, but at least they kept her somewhat updated. He was sent to a secret demolition training base that Admiral Turner had set up on Maui, not far from Pearl Harbor where his father was based. He was designated commander of UDT (underwater demolition team) 5. One month before the landing on Saipan, he became senior UDT officer for that operation.

The camp on Maui, he wrote to his wife, was far from luxurious. Not only were they sleeping in tents and making half-mile treks to the "facilities," but there was no hot water and the food was terrible—something he raised hell about. Despite the shortcomings of the camp, Kauffman was determined to get in shape for the physical challenges that lay ahead:

> I'm off all liquor except beer, and down to 1 pack of cigarettes a day—next week 15 cigs a day, and the following week 10 a day. I am taking a good swim every morning so should be in shape soon. . . . I'll be over at Pearl tomorrow and can give this [letter] to Dad via his special pouch, which is much quicker than ordinary airmail. I have had a devil of a time getting paid as my accounts got lost but have been found again. A result of this is your anniversary present may be late. I am very ashamed not to have sent you a birthday present but couldn't have thought of a better one than Tchaikovsky's concerto. I congratulate you on my good taste. I guess you and Butch [his name for the unborn baby] are pretty big by now. . . . Thanks a million for sending flowers to Mother and Betty Lou for Easter.

> We had a mile race out in the ocean Saturday morning in a very choppy rough sea. I was very pleased to finish 6 out of 96—to be honest I was very pleased I finished. I'm in fine health. My only malady is missing You.

As the due date crept closer, he wrote more often: "I am being a typical pins and needles father-to-be. Oh darling if I could just be near you. I know I wouldn't be much help but I do love you so so much and I do feel so helpless while you are facing the music. My Dear, you can name the child anything you want . . . though I do hope you will name it Margaret Cary after you, if it is a girl. . . . I pray for you at night and many times during the day. May God bless you, my wonderful wife."

The big day arrived on 7 May. Peggy wrote her sister-in-law that she expected the baby to have a green nose, because a few days before the birth she had been down on her hands and knees at Tuxeden, the Tuckerman family's house in Washington, painting garden furniture green. "Stork Visits Kauffmans," one Washington newspaper reported. It was a girl, and her name was Margaret Cary Kauffman. Peggy's mother wrote Draper to report that the "Super Baby" had been considerate in arriving just after they'd come home from a wedding reception. She had driven her daughter to the Bethesda Suburban Hospital. "The baby is a dear little girl weighing 8 pounds and 3 ounces with dark and curly hair, a cunning nose, a beautiful little rosebud of a mouth, and I think has your dimple. Peg has a lovely room, full of flowers, and looks so well and happy. I . . . sent you a cable after wrangling with the telephone company and having to call on the Navy Department and some of your friends to help. Too much red tape!"

Draper's mother wrote his father saying, "It is a girl and I must say I am delighted as they are so satisfactory—girls so seldom want to make unsafe bombs safe or to blow up places and they don't want to become admirals and roam around the world making their wives miserable and lonely!"

A radiogram from the Pacific to Miss Margaret Cary Kauffman greeted the newest member of the family: YOUR FATHER AND GRANDFATHER WELCOME YOU ABOARD LOVE TO YOU AND YOUR SUPER MOTHER WE CELEBRATE—KAUFFMANS. And Draper's thrilled letter:

My darling Family,

Doesn't that sound wonderful? I still can't believe it though I had nine months' warning. . . . It would be futile to try to write how much I would love to be with you now and see *our baby* together. . . .

Darling, I will pray every night that I can be as good a father as your child deserves. It seems a terrific responsibility—so much will depend on us. I keep thinking though that the basic rules are all written down for us in the life of Christ.

Don't worry my sweet if you don't hear from me for a few weeks every so often. Though I won't be in a position to send mail I won't be in a danger area. I have a particularly swell gang with me and that counts for a lot.

Please send pictures of Cary—and the cradle—and of you with your new figure. How soon before we could dance if I were home? This is the first time in many many years that I've been homesick. Please send me all the details about Cary—weight, height, color of eyes (or aren't they open yet?). I am like a thirsty man in a desert with your letters like oases.

Well, my two wonderful girls, I will say goodnight and God bless you both.

While Draper and Peggy Kauffman's parental bliss blossomed, the war in the Pacific was intensifying. Kauffman's boss was Rear Admiral Turner, a crusty, demanding man who expected his subordinates to toil as tirelessly as he did. Amphibious warfare in the Pacific was a grueling business. It involved the landing of troops from transport ships—into the direct face of enemy gunfire. Typically, an island was first bombarded by sea and by air. Then transports approached to some six to eight thousand yards off the beach—often just a rock or coral ledge—to unload their troop-filled landing craft and amphibious tractors. These small vessels proceeded to a line of departure approximately four thousand yards from shore, formed into boat waves, and, in carefully timed sequence, forged ahead over reefs or shoaling water to designated points on the beach. Crossing from the line of departure to the beachhead line was especially treacherous. The boats struggled to pass through a hailstorm of enemy gunfire while simultaneously dodging a series of natural and man-made obstructions—reefs, barbed wire, pointed stakes, concrete blocks, and other impediments that were as difficult to maneuver past as they were ingeniously constructed.

In the early amphibious operations of World War II, the United States had no sure method of detecting and destroying underwater obstructions close inshore or of determining the depth of water there. Landing operations proceeded by a patchwork of educated, but often poor, guesses. The landing on Tarawa in November 1943 was a tragic case in point. Many hundreds of American lives were lost there because intelligence reports, based on aerial photographs, were inaccurate about the underwater geography between the line of departure and the beach. Marines heavily laden with packs had to wade ashore after their landing craft ran aground in an unexpectedly low tide, and they were sitting ducks for Japanese guns. A similar situation occurred on the beaches of Normandy, a turn of events that might have been prevented had underwater demolition teams been properly utilized there.

The tragic experience at Tarawa further kindled Admiral Turner's interest in reconnaissance and preinvasion demolition. In fact, Turner had already experimented with some underwater swimmers. Before arriving on Maui, Draper had sent some of his men from Fort Pierce to the Pacific, and Turner had ordered them out on reconnaissance missions in rubber boats at Kwajalein.

Turner now recognized the pressing need to plot the underwater terrain between the line of departure and the beach so that obstacles could be removed or avoided. And the best way of doing that, he decided, was to employ UDTs—as he said later in his foreword to Douglas Fane and Don Moore's *Naked Warriors*:

> [They were] the daring, skillful scouts of the underwater demolition teams, which, owing to the classified nature of their work, were unknown to the public. It became the task of these courageous volunteer teams to chart beach approaches and to seek and destroy underwater defenses. Their work greatly eased the landing of troops and cargo and reduced casualties, making them invaluable to the amphibious forces. And they never let us down" (xi–xii).

Admiral Turner decided that for the next operation, which was to take place in the Mariana Islands, he needed five full-blown underwater demolition teams—three for Saipan and Tinian and two for Guam. In early June, having been designated senior UDT officer for the landing on Saipan, Kauffman met with Turner in Pearl to discuss the impending operation. The admiral drew a rough outline of the island, indicating a reef about a mile off the beach with a lagoon in between the reef and the shore.

"Now, the first and most important thing is reconnaissance to determine the depth of water. I'm thinking of having you go in and reconnoiter around eight," said Turner.

Draper Kauffman had been in the navy long enough to know that "eight" meant eight in the morning, not eight in the evening. But it had never occurred to him that their operation would take place in daylight and so he automatically responded, "Well, Admiral, it depends on the phase of the moon."

"Moon?" Turner shot back. "What in the hell has that got to do with it? Obviously by eight o'clock I mean 0800."

"In broad daylight—onto somebody else's beach in broad daylight, Admiral?"

"Absolutely. We'll have lots of fire support to cover you."

Kauffman had great respect for Admiral Turner, but he believed daylight operations would be suicide, which is why they had done so much nighttime training at Fort Pierce. "I just don't see how you can do it in broad daylight," he said.

"The main reason is you can see in the daytime and you can't see at night."

So that was that. Kauffman gave the admiral an "aye, aye," but not a particularly cheery one. He went back to Maui haunted by this change. And he was not the only one disturbed by the prospect of daytime operations. As it turned out, several days earlier the elder Kauffman had attended a conference during which Turner gave Admiral Nimitz his opinion on daylight reconnaissance. Admiral Kauffman had listened in deep concern but was careful not to interfere.

An important part of the training would also have to be changed. At the base on Maui they had never contemplated swimming as far as a mile. Long-distance swimming had been part of Hell Week at Fort Pierce, but not one of the training requirements. (Some men at Fort Pierce were even taught swimming from scratch.) Now Kauffman announced to his men that no one would go on the upcoming operation who could not swim a mile. His team immediately picked up on the fact that if it was one mile out, it was also one mile back, and therefore they had to be able to swim two miles. He was asked about that right away. "Well," Kauffman replied, "I assumed that if you could swim the mile in, there would be a sense of urgency that would enable you to swim the mile back." Men did not necessarily have to be accomplished swimmers, but they did have to be unafraid of the open ocean. As Edward Higgins of Team 11 told it in *Web-Footed Warriors*, "Some men who were excellent swimmers close to shore became panicky far out at sea with nothing to cling to and no one to offer help. In windswept, choppy water, swimming from the rubber boats took a heavy toll, and man after man was checked out and returned to general Seabee service."

When they were not training, the men on Maui had ample spare time, and they were often asked to write up observations about their training. One Ensign Knorek recorded the following:

> With my lifebelt, greens, helmet, heavy shoes, slate, knife, canteen and a pack of powder I am marched to the beach where I am told to remove my lifebelt and swim to the pier where they will teach me to swim properly. Hours later the current finally bangs me up against the pier where two chief petty officers are in the process of breaking bones and drowning non-swimmers. I am asked how long I can hold my breath under water and how far I can swim underwater with 100 pounds of powder. I answer with 100 pounds of powder I could probably stay under water forever.
>
> After learning the proper strokes and being taught the proper way to breathe (20 years old and I never learned), I am led to a lecture hall where [a bos'n] attempts to convince me sharks won't bother me if I won't bother them. I assure him I'll not bother sharks. I am now completely unafraid of the water, I am fearless. I am a true demolition man. . . .
>
> In order to qualify for my fins I must swim one mile in less time than it takes the average demolition man to consume a case of beer—approximately 52 minutes and 18 seconds. . . . I tie 40 pounds of weights to my ankles . . . and plunge into the turbulent water.

> The swim proves I am not in the best of condition, but . . . I manage to finish 8 seconds under the qualifying time. . . . I've watched my muscles grow. In a week the results are amazing. By now I can hardly walk to the beach.
>
> Demolition training starts and safety precautions are very rigid. You aren't supposed to throw TNT more than 20 feet and you can crimp caps with your front teeth only. Yes, it is far different from the old fire cracker days.

In addition to intensifying swimming requirements and instituting rigid safety precautions, Kauffman addressed the issue of esprit de corps and morale. Before teams were put together, all the enlisted men went up on a stage to be questioned by the officers. Each officer, seeking five men for his boat, would write down the names of ten men he would like to have on his team. For their part, the enlisted men were given the chance to say, confidentially, if there was any officer with whom they did not wish to serve. Kauffman then would take all the names and make the assignments. After teams had served together, he requested that the officers do a meticulous evaluation of each enlisted man's performance in action, judging him not only for physical fitness and swimming ability but also for qualities such as initiative, leadership, and attitude about carrying out orders.

Among other new ideas that had taken shape on Maui was the expanded size of demolition units. Jack Koehler, executive officer of the base (and later, assistant secretary of the navy), was a very capable man and a great stabilizing influence during a difficult period. While Fort Pierce was still organizing six-man NCDUs (naval combat demolition units), Koehler arranged for hundred-man teams with thirteen officers and eighty-seven enlisted men and renamed them underwater demolition teams (UDTs). He realized the central importance of the swimmer and gave priority to developing equipment for him.

Kauffman decided to use two of the hundred-man teams for reconnaissance on Saipan and keep one team in reserve. He got permission to pass on the intelligence he received from Admiral Turner to Dick Burke, the commanding officer of UDT 6, the other team heading for Saipan. Though they collaborated, the teams still trained on their own and employed different techniques, which might not have seemed efficient but, as Kauffman asserted, was useful because they were able to test more ideas that way.

Their training techniques could be ambitious. One morning Kauffman did something that, in his words, "only a reserve would have dreamed of doing." He knocked on Admiral Turner's door.

"What do you want now, Draper?"

"Well, sir, what I would really like is to borrow—just for a weekend—a couple of battleships and cruisers and destroyers."

"You want to do what?" Turner roared. Lieutenant Commander Kauffman repeated his request. "I heard you, and what in hell would you like to borrow my battleships and cruisers and destroyers for? Or perhaps I should say your father's cruisers and destroyers."

"Well, sir, you speak of this very heavy fire support, these guns firing directly over us, and I guess that this would be a very unusual experience, to be swimming in with 6- and 8-inch guns firing almost a flat trajectory right over your head."

"As a matter of fact," said Turner, "it would be good training for the ships too. Okay."

The admiral sent over two battleships, three cruisers, and a squadron of destroyers for the weekend. "We swam in to the barren island, Kahoolawe," Kauffman later recalled, "while the ships fired over our heads, and I must say it was an extraordinary experience to actually see the 12-inch shells from the USS *Pennsylvania* arching over our heads. And a really necessary one, to get people used to it before they had to worry about shells coming the other way."

That weekend also gave them a chance to rehearse communications. Capt. Peter H. Horn, Admiral Turner's communications officer, listened in on the UDT circuits and afterward declared that easily the first prize for bad communications in the navy went to the UDTs. With only a couple of weeks before the landing at Saipan and with the clock ticking, Horn sent two of his people to Maui to try to train the UDTs in communications discipline.

Everybody was talking at once, clogging the airways and using slang. Among other things, Horn told Kauffman that he should use official call signs, not make them up. Kauffman's official call was Blow Gun, and so he had told his exec, John DeBold, "All right then, you're Blow Pistol."

But Blow Pistol was not an official call sign and, in fact, there was no official call sign for the exec. Though Kauffman knew Horn was right, the captain, he decided, was too much of a purist. In the absence of an official call sign for his executive officer, he used Blow Pistol anyway.

The improvised training continued all the way into the last weeks before the operation, which was risky, but Kauffman felt that flexibility was more important than orderliness. For example, the Fourth Marine Division commander said that he wanted accurate plots of water depth because he would be conveying his tanks in LCMs (landing craft, medium). The tanks would leave the landing craft at the reef, and unless they had a path from the reef to the beach that was three and a half feet deep or less, their operators would drown. From the looks of the aerial charts, there appeared to be a shallow area off the northern beach where the tanks could get in. The division commander had drawn up his tank plan accordingly but wanted to make sure there was no mistake.

The prospect of plotting a lagoon two thousand yards wide by two thousand yards long with accuracy worried Draper Kauffman and his UDT cohorts. At the last minute—one week before the operation—they developed what is called string reconnaissance, a method that was still being used by navy SEALs in Vietnam. They obtained two empty condensed milk cans about four inches in diameter and welded them together, end to end. They then affixed two large round wooden flanges to the ends of the cans, and around the cans wound eighteen hundred yards of fishing line. One end of the line was attached to a buoy anchored just outside the reef. They knotted the fishing line every twenty-five yards with a distinctive knot so that the swimmers, who swam in pairs, always knew exactly how far they were from the buoy, that is, how far in they had gone. Each swimmer had four plexiglass slates and two pencils that could write underwater on which to record water depth and other information every twenty-five yards, or wherever there was a significant change such as a pothole. Meanwhile, the APD (attack personnel, destroyer) took radar bearings on each buoy so that the notes on the slates could be properly plotted.

When the UDTs sent a message to the supply officer in Pearl saying they had to have fifty-five miles of a certain type of fishing line by the following Tuesday, a day was lost because the supply officer asked for amplification. He was sure the request was an error because he could not imagine why they would need that much fishing line. But the need was emphasized and the precious line was supplied by the deadline. (A supply officer at Saipan had a similar reaction when one of the UDTs requested five hundred rubber prophylactics just prior to a night reconnaissance of Tinian. They were used to waterproof the swimmers' penlight flashlights.) The fishing line's distinctive knotting had to be performed on the fly, when the UDTs, en route to Saipan, had a day in Eniwetok. Each unit of two men put up posts in the sand twenty-five yards apart, wrapped the line around the posts, and got the job done.

Also at the last minute, Kauffman had his men marked up with ship's paint. He had complained because people would come back from an exercise and report "the water is knee deep" or "it comes up to my chin" or "it's halfway between my elbow and my shoulder." As a result he had the bulkhead on an APD measured for height and marked, then made everybody stand against the bulkhead and be measured. For every foot of height above the deck, a solid black line was painted around each man's legs, arms, or torso; half feet were marked with dashes. The men hated the paint, which took forever to get off—but it did make their reports of water depth more accurate. Most of these innovative ideas, as Kauffman later claimed, came not from him but from junior officers or enlisted men.

During the last weeks before the UDTs left for Saipan, Kauffman had been shuttling back and forth to Pearl Harbor working with Admiral Turner's planning staff. Only two days before they departed for the mission, Admiral Turner placed Draper Kauffman in command of all three teams assigned to the operation.

6

The UDTs Come of Age in the Marianas

THE CLOSER THE AMERICANS GOT TO JAPAN, THE FIERCER THE FIGHTING grew. By the time the UDTs set off for the Marianas, the naval battles at Coral Sea and Midway and the determined U.S. assault on Guadalcanal had changed Japan's strategy. Instead of advancing farther, now the Japanese had to reinforce their far-flung island garrisons to form successive rings of defense against attacks on the homeland. The defenses presented a formidable set of obstacles in the path of the American forces. U.S. strategy took the form of a dual thrust: army general Douglas MacArthur would push up through the islands of the southwest Pacific while Adm. Chester Nimitz led his naval forces on an island-hopping drive westward across the Pacific. When Nimitz's offensive finally reached the Marianas, Tokyo lay 1,270 miles away. Though the Americans were closing in on Japan's jugular from two directions, it was by no means clear that the upcoming amphibious assaults would ensure a U.S. victory.

Many thousands of American lives were yet to be lost in the terrible struggle. Capture of the Marianas would breach the Japanese inner ring of defense, something that they had long dreaded. In response to that deep-seated fear, they had constructed formidably elaborate defenses. In the name of the homeland, the Japanese were determined to fight to the death. It was a grim prospect for American fighting men, including the underwater warriors.

Nimitz and his planners had targeted the Mariana Islands of Saipan, Tinian, and Guam for amphibious assault, the latter a U.S. protectorate until the Japanese had invaded. Unlike other islands that U.S. forces had encountered on their island-hopping journey, the Marianas were not coral atolls or thick jungle. They were mountainous and studded with caves, which gave their defenders a great deal of comfort and protection. Saipan was a heavily cultivated, densely populated island of eighty-one square miles, and dug into its mountainous spine were more than twenty-nine thousand defenders, many of them civilians. The natives of Saipan and Tinian were fiercely loyal to the Japanese emperor Hirohito, while the natives of Guam, most of whom had been herded into Japanese concentration camps, were intensely partisan to the United States.

In late May 1944 the UDTs, by now often referred to as "frogmen," boarded high-speed transports for Saipan. These APDs were World War I–vintage destroyers, "four-stackers" converted to personnel carriers, and they were small and cramped. The *Gilmer* and the *Humphreys* had been pressed into service to transport the UDTs. On each vessel some twenty UDT officers were quartered with the ship's officers in what was already limited space, while eighty UDT enlisted men were jammed into the forward fire room from which boilers had been removed. In addition to being intensely hot and uncomfortable, the enlisted quarters were crammed with tons of high explosives. A hit by an enemy shell—in fact, a simple dropped match—could blow the ship to smithereens. In these quarters the navy's freshly trained swimming scouts were fated to spend eight months.

Admiral Kauffman saw the APDs depart Pearl and later sent a letter to his son: "I trust all goes well with you and that the battle cruiser *Gilmer* rides along pleasantly. . . . I was wondering how many of your gang took kindly to life on an APD, particularly down in the fore hold, where they were quartered. Lots of love, lots and lots of good luck, and God bless you, Dad."

The APDs joined the task force on 6 June, which happened to be D-day in Normandy. The men aboard the ships cheered exuberantly when early news of the Normandy invasion was optimistic. However, as Draper Kauffman would later learn to his dismay, the underwater demolition men encountered terrible difficulties off the shores of France. In addition to high tides, a major concern for the high command was the overarching need for tactical surprise. Nevertheless, the demolitioneers did not agree with their commanding officers' orders that in order to maintain secrecy the demolition teams at Normandy were to go in *with* the troops rather than ahead of them—a problem that the young officers with their junior rank lacked the clout to remedy. Moreover, because of confusion in the order that ships arrived on the coast, many of the demolition units did not even get to the beaches in the first wave, and when they finally did disembark, they found troops clinging for protection to the very obstacles that were supposed to be blown up.

Omaha Beach proved the most difficult. As Stephen Ambrose points out in *D-Day,* "The beach obstacles proved to be more dangerous than the German infantry or artillery. German snipers concentrated their fire on the U.D. teams so that almost no lanes" were opened (520). The approaches to Omaha's four-mile-long beach were heavily planted with impediments such as ten-foot steel gates, posts deeply buried in the sand, and "hedgehogs" capped with mines. Above the beach was a man-made sea wall covered in barbed wire, beyond which lay a grassy open area peppered with mines. Any GI fortunate enough to make it that far found himself exposed to fortifications embedded in the sandy bluffs overlooking the beach. Much to the chagrin of the UDTs, these formidable defensive works had barely been touched before D-day. Within hours of the launch of the invasion, the waters off Omaha were so clogged with bodies and debris that the commander of the U.S. contingent, Lt. Gen. Omar Bradley, debated whether to transfer his follow-up troops to other, more accessible landing sites. Soon, however, local commanders managed to rally their stunned troops, and eventually the GIs took the beach, albeit at a high price: three thousand men were lost on Omaha, a third of total Allied casualties that day.

Draper Kauffman at that point knew none of the details about Normandy; he was concentrating on the UDTs' first real landing in the Pacific. U.S. forces were now set for the initial landing in the Marianas. The operation came under the command of Adm. Harry Wilbur Hill, Commander, Amphibious Group 2, who answered to Adm. Richmond Kelly Turner, head of the Fifth Amphibious Force of Adm. Raymond Spruance's Fifth Fleet. Marine lieutenant general Holland "Howlin' Mad" Smith was in charge of the Fifth Amphibious Corps, while Maj. Gen. Thomas Watson was chief of the Second Marine Division participating in the landings.

Kauffman was still chief instructor at the underwater demolition school on Maui; he had gone to the Marianas to gain real-life experience, which would bear directly on future training. Three teams totaling three hundred officers and men were to take part in the Saipan operation. Draper Kauffman was in command of all three. En route to their destination, he drilled the men in the fundamentals of the operation plan. These included above all the concept of independent action. As much as possible, UDTs were to operate without depending on other UDTs or radio or other communications signals. An order for a team to retire would be given only by the commanding officer or his successor, and until that order was given, the men were to continue their job regardless of enemy fire. In addition to serving as commander of all three teams, Kauffman personally commanded the hundred-man UDT 5—the team he would go in with, the one he knew firsthand, and the one whose actions he was therefore best able to describe.

Saipan, some fourteen miles long and five miles wide, was a tropical island of sugar plantations, terraced hillsides, and a large Japanese civilian population. Running down the island's center was a mountainous spine that gave way, in the southwest corner, to a long coastal plain. The Second and Fourth Marine Divisions were to land on the southwest beaches and make a northward sweep, pushing the enemy into the island's northeastern tip.

D-day was set for 15 June. On D-minus-1 the UDTs went in to

Saipan's southwestern beaches. It was a clear sunny day, with a mild breeze that sent two- to three-foot waves lapping at the edge of the reef. The men wore swim trunks and sneakers and carried equipment that included plexiglass slates, waterproof pencils, knives, diving masks, life belts, first aid kits, knee pads, and gloves. Reconnaissance men used the buddy system, always swimming in pairs. One, the lineman, unreeled the fishing line and took regular soundings, while the other, the searcher, set off on a zigzagging course to find mines or coral heads and mark them with balsa floats. Draper Kauffman's swim buddy was a young man named Page whom he called his seeing eye. Page was color-blind, and as Kauffman loved to say later, Page would tell him what they were looking at and he would tell his subordinate what color it was.

Team 5 was assigned four beaches to clear, which were contiguous and ran north to south: Red 2, Red 3, Green 1, and Green 2. Each was seven hundred yards long. Aerial surveys indicated that enemy defenses consisted of a series of five trenches about ten yards from the waterline, with machine-gun positions every forty to fifty yards. A barrier reef and a lagoon lay off the beach. Water depths at the reef and in the lagoon were not known.

The Marines were keen to know more about other possible emplacements, such as blockhouses back of the beaches as well as possible exits from the beaches. They assigned a young marine lieutenant, Gordon Leslie, to teach the navy swimmers what to look for in those areas. The teams would get two and a half hours of fire support, from 0900 to 1130—no additional time because of a limited ammunition supply—and thirty minutes of carrier air support from 1000 to 1030, during which the swimmers were to close in from three hundred to one hundred yards. The carrier aircraft would strafe parallel to the waterline and about ten yards inland.

At exactly 0900 Kauffman and his team left their APD in four LCPRs (landing craft, personnel, ramped), each of which carried a platoon of swimmers. Each pair had its string reconnaissance reel, buoy, and anchor. The APD guided each landing craft to the point at the north end of its seven hundred yards of beach, whereupon it paralleled the reef and dropped the first reconnaissance pair off. Every hundred yards farther, the landing craft dropped another pair.

Kauffman earlier had had what he thought was a brilliant idea. Events proved him mostly wrong. He decided that platoon and assistant platoon leaders, with their buddies, should ride on rubber mattresses outfitted with small electric motors. This, he believed, would enable them to keep track of the swimmers and exert a measure of control over reconnaissance and demolition operations. But the mattresses were easy targets. Fane and Moore write about the ill-fated craft in *The Naked Warriors*:

> Flying mattresses carrying two swimmers apiece with radios and binoculars headed into the lagoon. Ens. R. P. Marshall's mattress was overturned on the reef by a near mortar burst. Unable to right it, he started the mile swim across the lagoon. "Red" Davenport got well into the lagoon when a Jap sniper punctured his mattress and he took to the comparative safety of swimming.
>
> Following the harried mattress teams, pairs of swimmers swam steadily toward the beach, the lineman unreeling his fish line and taking a sounding every 25 yards while the "searcher" zigzagged. . . . Draper, nearing the reef on his flying mattress, headed for swimmer "Red" Davenport to offer him a tow.
>
> "Get the damned thing out of here!" yelled the normally courteous UDT man. . . . "Red" had already had one mattress shot out from under him. (96, 98)

The units had been divided into odd and even numbers. At three hundred yards the odd-numbered units were to take the slates from the even-numbered ones and return to the landing craft, while the even-numbered units would continue on and scout out the approaches to the beach. In that way, if the men closing on the beach were killed, their information would be saved. Each time a swimmer returned to the reef, the landing craft would brave mortar fire to pick him up. To retrieve swimmers, the craft had to reverse its engines and come to a dead stop, which made it a virtual sitting duck while the exhausted man crawled aboard or was yanked up by helping hands.

At three hundred yards from the beach, Kauffman turned over command to his executive officer John DeBold in the lead landing craft while he and Page, an even-numbered unit, anchored their flying mattress and proceeded to swim the rest of the way in. Remarkably, all the men heading for the beach closed to within fifty yards under heavy mortar fire.

Mortar shells were exploding underwater; six men suffered internal injuries as a result —Harold Eng, N. A. Renbarger, R. LaForest, S. J. Morell, D. W. Henry, and Harold Hall, who was thrown completely clear of the water by the force. Despite injuries, nearly all the men made it back to their landing craft. Team 7's landing craft was sunk, but her men were retrieved by another.

One man on Team 5 was killed—Bob Christianson—and two others, R. E. Heil and A. H. Root, were missing. Concerned about saving the reconnaissance information, and fully aware that all fire support was to stop at 1130 while enemy mortar fire continued unabated, Kauffman ordered the remaining landing craft back to the ship, a very unpopular decision with two men missing.

Back on the APD, Kauffman asked the fire support ships to keep a lookout for the missing men, then joined the others as they began collating their reconnaissance material. A cruiser reported sighting what were thought to be two men in the water at a position well inside the reef. After recording everything he had learned during the morning mission, Kauffman gathered three fresh men and some LCPR crewmen to go in search of the lost sheep. Apparently he was not the only one with bad eyes that day. The others with him thought they spotted two men in the lagoon, too. The team's commanding officer then told the men to "cruise around outside the reef and I'll swim in." Approaching under heavy enemy mortar fire, Kauffman got to within fifty yards of the sighted objects when he found they were not human at all, but coral. Discouraged, he made his way back to the reef. The landing craft was on a zigzagging course, and as he approached it he saw two men waving from its stern. He was so thankful that upon reaching the reef, Kauffman leaped up and began waving his hands in the air like a prizefighter—until some sniper's bullets reminded him where he was.

Apparently Heil's leg had been injured on the way in. His buddy Root bandaged him up and then departed for the beach to complete his reconnaissance mission. On the way back Root picked Heil up, and they crossed over the reef to get beyond the line of fire, which is why the LCPR had lost track of them. Not until after Draper Kauffman started in toward the shore for the second time that day were they spotted and retrieved.

The man that Team 5 had lost, Bob Christianson, was one of the most highly regarded and popular men on the team. Kauffman wrote Christianson's mother in Minnesota and sent her his own Navy Cross, saying, "He deserves it far more than I do."

Draper Kauffman would later be awarded a second Navy Cross for his actions off Saipan that day. The commanding officer of the *California,* H. P. Barnett, praised the demolition team's leader in a letter to his superiors: "Learning that two of his men had been left on the reef, [he] returned to the beach and personally rescued his men under extremely heavy rifle and machine gun fire. This officer was not under my command, but I consider that his conduct merits especial recognition."

Kauffman and his staff sent a preliminary recon report to the task force, then spent all night drawing up laboriously detailed charts containing the string-reconnaissance information. When Turner's amphibious force arrived the next morning, fifteen copies of the report were ready for them. Kauffman sent Ensign Marshall over to Admiral Turner and General Smith's joint flagship, the *Rocky Mount,* expecting that he would turn his charts over to some lieutenant. The young man arrived aboard and was immediately whisked off to Turner's cabin. Kauffman personally delivered charts to Admiral Hill on his flagship. Other charts were taken by Ensigns J. C. Adams, R. G. Adams, and L. G. Suhrland to General Watson, the marine division commander, as well as to the tank battalion, LVT (landing vehicle, tracked) companies, and LCM groups.

The only route the UDTs could find that would safely convey the tank battalions to the beach went from Red 3 diagonally down to the middle of Green 2. That was a considerable distance from where General Watson had planned to land. After Kauffman had talked to Admiral Hill, General Watson, who was on the same ship, came in and thundered, "What in hell is this I hear about your changing the route for my tanks?" Draper explained, and the general cut him off. "I know, I know, all this has been explained to me, but I want them to go in across Red 2."

"General," said Kauffman, "they'll never, ever get through there."

Watson responded, "Well, all right," then turned to his operations officer and started dictating a lengthy message to his tank commander.

"Sir," Kauffman offered, "you don't have to send that. Just tell your tank commander to follow Demolition Plan Baker."

Once again Watson flared up. "Who the hell's tanks do you think these are?" Draper Kauffman apologized, but to no avail. "Young man," said the general, "you're going to lead that first tank in, and you'd better be damned sure that every one of them gets in safely, without drowning out."

So the leader of the underwater demolition teams borrowed an LVT and on D-day, starting at H-hour-plus-thirty minutes, he and the marine observer, Gordon Leslie, led the first tank in. Watson had given Kauffman a harrowing task, for the invasion did not get off to a smooth start. Shore bombardment from battleships that was intended to soften up defenses prior to the landing had not been very effective against the enemy's numerous and widely dispersed gun positions, and the invaders were delivered a hefty, bitter dose of mortar and artillery fire as they approached the beaches. But Kauffman's LVT kept forging ahead through the heavy fire, marking a shallow lane to the beach for the tank to his rear. The ocean bottom was devilishly irregular—anywhere from three to eight feet parallel to the shoreline and of course varying in depth toward the beach. As soon as the LVT reached shallow waters, Kauffman turned it around and went back. "Thank heavens for my skin," he said, "none of the tanks drowned out."

He had suggested to General Watson and Admiral Hill that the UDTs blow a channel through the reef deep enough for landing craft. They decided to wait and see how resupply went with the LVTs. At about 1130, just when Kauffman and Gordon Leslie returned from the tank operation, the UDT commander received a message from Admiral Hill telling him to go in and ask the shore party commander where he would like a channel blown through the reef. So they turned the LVT around and headed back in, this time all the way to the beach. As Kauffman later described the scene:

> We were huddled down in the LVT with a piece of stub pencil and scratch paper, trying to figure out how much explosive we needed to use on a channel about 300 feet long, 40 feet wide and 6 feet deep, when the LVT touched down on the beach, and we jumped out. It wasn't until then that we realized how we looked. We had on our swim shoes (for the coral reefs), which had originally been white and

we'd dyed blue, but they'd ended up sort of baby blue. We had on swim trunks, a facemask around our necks, and that's all; no helmet, nothing like that. Of course there on the beach were the Marines, carrying on as they normally do, digging holes in the ground and shooting at people and people shooting at them, and the damnedest racket.

And, boy, let me tell you, Gordon and I started digging fast. I ended up between two Marines. One Marine gave a startled look at this character dressed in this fashion and called across to the other Marine (in very colorful language I won't repeat), "For heavens sakes, we don't even have the beachhead yet, and the so-and-so tourists have already arrived!"

The hour and a half it took us to find that damned shore party commander, hopping from hole to hole, . . . extremely conspicuous in those weird uniforms, was one of the scariest times I have ever spent. But we found him and he indicated where he wanted the channel blown through the reef, and added, "Furthermore, I want it very, very badly and very, very quickly."

That night the UDTs started laying their explosive. They ultimately needed 105,000 pounds of tetrytol in 20-pound packages—some 5,000 packs—and it was extremely difficult to lay. Each pack had to be secured firmly to the coral reef, which was difficult to do with the constantly pounding surf. The packs then all had to be connected by primacord in order to fire simultaneously. The primacord was laid in triplicate so it would not be cut by the combination of sea action and coral. This all had to be done under cover of darkness—at least, it was supposed to be. The UDTs were under orders to complete the task by dawn but in fact were not ready to fire until about 1000. The Japanese finally realized that something was happening on the reef, and they sent mortars raining down during that last hour—a terrible danger because any one of the shells that hit a pack or a section of primacord would blow up the entire explosive charge, along with all the men.

They finally finished wiring the complicated maze together. Kauffman then pulled the nine fuses, three for each of three circuits, and the teams swam for their lives. The fuses were set for ten minutes, but a premature explosion was always a dread possibility. They soon reached the relative safety of the landing craft. The immediate area had been cleared of other vessels, and it was a good thing, for nobody had any idea how powerful the explosion would be. When detonation took place it produced a base surge of a type Kauffman said was comparable only to what he later saw when he witnessed the nuclear underwater test at Bikini. He had neglected to tell Admiral Hill exactly when the fuse would be pulled. Thus Hill was unprepared when suddenly, from his flagship, he saw a wall of black water shoot for a quarter of a mile straight up then spread outward. After enveloping four or five LSTs (landing ship, tank), the water engulfed his flagship, depositing a filthy residue of tetrytol. Kauffman was called for immediately. He shuffled into Admiral Hill's cabin and stood there, dripping black water on the rug, as they discussed the advisability of letting the task force commander know when any future explosion like that was set to go off.

It took the demolition teams another twelve hours to make the channel navigable, because the initial blast had failed to dredge out all the shallow areas. Their work received positive comments from Admiral Hill in his action report and from Admiral Turner.

Once the channel was prepared, Kauffman got his introduction to Squeaky Anderson, the legendary beachmaster for whom he and his men worked the rest of their time on Saipan. Anderson was both an exceptional person to work with and a true character. Though he wore the insignia of a navy captain, his uniform was completely nonregulation—black socks held up by garters, marine trousers ripped off halfway above the knee, and an open shirt that revealed the better part of his broad chest. He had been seen thus striding up and down the beach under heavy fire without showing any concern for the enemy—behavior that he would repeat, under even heavier fire, at Iwo Jima. Never once was Squeaky Anderson seen digging himself into a foxhole for protection. If someone came along, he would bellow, "Here, young man, I'm Squeaky Anderson—I'm the beachmaster." An amazing stream of profanities flowed from his mouth, delivered in a strong Scandinavian accent. Those who thought he was merely a funny old man were very much mistaken. He was exceedingly capable and upbeat and Admiral Hill treasured him.

Something Kauffman did not appreciate until some time later was how very conspicuous his demolition teams were, and not just because of their odd uniforms. As the three hundred frogmen participating in the Saipan operation swam back and forth, they had a built-in audience on some four battleships, six cruisers, and sixteen destroyers, all circling around, watching them, and listening to their communications. Each of those support ships had a copy of Admiral Turner's op order against which to scrutinize the UDTs' progress, and to make matters worse, they all knew that their leader, Draper Kauffman, was the son of the Commander, Cruisers and Destroyers, Pacific.

Kauffman did not give this any thought until he ran into crew members from the ships who quoted lines from his communications. He was most often ribbed for mistakenly thinking that shells that were landing in the lagoon were coming from U.S. fire-support ships. He had had a little cracker-box radio on which he called John DeBold, his exec:

"Blow Pistol, this is Blow Gun! For God's sake tell the support ships they're firing short!"

In a slow, calm voice DeBold responded, "Skipper, those aren't shorts, they're *overs*. They're not ours!"

To which Blow Gun replied, in a deflated voice, "Oh!"

Kauffman wrote his father from Saipan on D-day plus one, when he was aboard the *Gilmer*:

> Yesterday AM we went in as planned at 0900. The fire support ships however could not get in as close as we had hoped because they were still being shelled. We got our first taste of fire going in to the reef in our landing craft. It was estimated 3", 5", and 88 mortar.
>
> The boys did a beautiful job. They all kept their heads and got their survey parties off at the regular 100-yard intervals along the reef edge. (We just went to general quarters for an air raid—16 planes. My station is down below with my men—hope we don't get hit as we have 40 tons of explosive aboard.) It became obvious right away that the Japs had the edge of the reef registered perfectly for range so landing craft stayed off about 50 yards while dropping men. We sent most of the men in swimming except for eleven flying mattresses. (I'm now talking only of Team 5 on Green and Red beaches.) It soon became apparent that the mattresses were main targets but we did not dare leave them as we needed their speed and mobility. Four of the mattresses were sunk by fire without scratching the men on them, although one man on another mattress was

killed—one of my very best men. I anchored my mattress at 300 yards from the beach and started in at 1000 expecting heavy air support as promised . . . while we were attempting to get in to the waterline. Not one plane appeared. I got to about 100 yards from the beach and even with my bad eyes could see the Japs. . . . I set up my radio and called for the damned aviators, but the aerial was shot away while I was using it. . . . How we got back with the loss of only one man and seven injured, I don't know. (I sure wish we didn't have our explosives aboard here—all hell is breaking loose topside. This has been quite a raid. We have been firing constantly. The scuttlebutt now is that we are firing at boats—just had two of them hit—lots of cheering topside!)

Reggie Kauffman wrote Draper the same day, and their letters crossed. He was shaken because he had read a dispatch from UDT 6 about the Saipan operation and he was not sure that Draper had pulled through. "I hope you are okay," he wrote. "Incidentally at the conference today Admiral Nimitz congratulated me on having such a son as you and the fine work you and your gang did. I also noted the casualties. Captain Tom Hill told the conference what a grand job you all did. I hope and pray all goes well with you."

Despite the huge difficulties of getting ashore, by the end of D-day twenty thousand Marines had landed on Saipan. A little over three weeks later, on 9 July, the island was declared secure, but not before horrendous sacrifice on both sides. As American forces swept northward up the island's mountainous spine, the desperate defenders staged a suicidal banzai attack. The commander of the Japanese army on Saipan, Lt. Gen. Yoshitsugu Saito, sliced his stomach open with his samurai sword. The final horror occurred after the fighting ended. On Marpi Point, the island's northernmost tip, hundreds of civilian Japanese including wives and children joined the few remaining Japanese troops and, despite promises from the American victors that they would be treated well, flung themselves off the jagged coral cliffs to their deaths. When it was all over, the battle for Saipan had claimed twenty-nine thousand Japanese dead and more than sixteen thousand American dead or wounded. Though it was a heavy price for U.S. forces to pay, finally Japan's inner ring of defense had been breached. The United States was now in possession of a base from which aircraft could launch strikes against the homeland.

The UDTs were already gearing up for the next operation at Tinian. That island, just south of Saipan across a two-mile channel, was fifteen miles long by two to three miles wide, and the Japanese had built three airfields that the Americans were eager to get hold of. The one town, Tinian Town, in the southwest, had a valuable anchorage, Saharan Harbor, and three excellent beaches—in navy terms, the Red, Green, and Blue beaches. From the naval point of view, these southwestern beaches were desirable because they were partially protected from the sea. High ground abutting the beaches, however, made them relatively easy to defend. They had two other distinct disadvantages: they lay out of range of marine artillery on Saipan, and the island commander had concentrated his defenses there, so that amphibious troops would be plunged into fierce street fighting almost as soon as they landed. The houses in Tinian Town, even if they were shelled, would provide important cover for the defenders.

On the northwestern side of the island lay two other beaches, White 1 and White 2, merely thin gaps of sand between jagged coral cliffs. One of those beaches was 120 yards wide, the other half that width—both woefully narrower than the one thousand yards considered the minimum size for a division landing. Moreover, the White beaches were vulnerable to inclement weather coming from the west. Nevertheless, they were well within range of the marine artillery on Saipan, and with no high ground to speak of, they had no defenses. Clearly the Japanese assumed those beaches were too small to land on and were concentrating their defenses around Tinian Town.

The Tinian operation was under the command of Admiral Hill but, subject to the concurrence of Admiral Spruance, the final selection of landing beaches was made by Richmond Kelly Turner. The UDTs almost immediately got caught between Admiral Turner, who strongly favored the southwestern beaches, and General Smith, who wanted to land on the northwestern (White) beaches. "To be caught between those two distinguished gentlemen," Kauffman later remembered, "was very interesting, because whenever they were together—and Dad said this was also true at parties—the sparks flew all over the place." At one conference he heard Admiral Turner say, "All right, we'll send Draper with his teams in to the White beaches and see just how good they are." To which Smith replied, "The hell we will. What you'll do is tell Draper to come back and say they're impossible to land on. What we'll do is send in an impartial group, my Marine Reconnaissance Company."

The conversation went on in this vein until finally a decision was made to perform joint reconnaissance with both the Marines and the navy. Kauffman gathered from what he heard after the war that Admiral Hill was actually on the side of General Smith. Hill believed the risk involved in landing on the White beaches was considerably outweighed by the advantages. Ever the navy loyalist, he never openly sided with Smith in their conferences, but he was said to have strongly pressed Smith's case with Turner.

Draper then got together with Jimmy Jones, commanding officer of the Marine Reconnaissance Company. Though not under direct orders to come back with a specific opinion, they gathered that their respective bosses would each like a certain conclusion, and that those conclusions were mutually exclusive. Jones and Draper had no choice: they decided to come up with a joint report that they were both happy with and let the chips fall where they might.

They were both well aware of the requirement to keep their reconnaissance mission under wraps. They had to remain invisible when crawling onto the beaches and to smooth the sand over before disappearing back into the sea. The need for secrecy meant that at Tinian, unlike the Saipan operation, underwater demolition work would be done at night, the way it had originally been planned.

They divided into two groups. Jimmy Jones was not a good swimmer, so his executive officer had to be the senior Marine on the mission. Group Able, consisting of six Marines and six navy swimmers under the marine lieutenant, would reconnoiter the northernmost White beach; Group Baker, led by Draper Kauffman, also with six Marines and six underwater demolition men, would cover the beach farthest south.

The White beaches were about a thousand yards apart. Conveyed in separate landing craft, the two surveillance teams were to go within two thousand yards of the beaches, switch to rubber boats, proceed another four hundred yards, and then swim the rest of the way in order to remain undetected.

They started off with a rocky rehearsal in Magicienne Bay, Saipan, during which, among other glitches, the radar on their ship, the *Gilmer,* went out. Despite the problems that caused, they went in to their assigned beaches on Tinian on the following night, JIG-minus-14 (JIG was the designation for D-day at Tinian). It was a clear, dark night. The *Gilmer's* radar had been repaired but when the teams were halfway in it malfunctioned again. Compounding their problems was a faulty intelligence report indicating a one-knot current moving south off the beaches when in fact the current was flowing faster than that and in the opposite direction. The two groups thus ended up well north of their respective beaches, though in the blackness, with no landmarks visible, both thought they had landed on the mark. As a result of the confusion, Group Able missed its beach completely. Kauffman's Group Baker finally located White 1, although its objective had been White 2.

Kauffman realized the mistake when his team arrived but made the decision to reconnoiter White 1 since they were there. The marine and navy contingents performed the land and water reconnaissance together, since neither group had complete confidence in the other. Their first mission was to find out the condition of the approaches to the waterline. About twenty yards of the sixty-yard beach was obstructed with heavy coral, which was hard on the shins. The second objective had two parts: one, to see if the exits behind the beaches were usable (because of thick foliage showing in aerial photographs it was impossible to tell) and two, to check what appeared in intelligence photos to be a line of dots halfway up the beach, which everyone assumed were mines. A close reconnaissance of the beach revealed the existence of usable exits to the rear of the beach and, surprisingly, no mines. The Japanese commander clearly was not expecting an amphibious invasion by this route.

After reconnoitering the beach, the men of Group Baker were faced with the need to painstakingly obliterate all their tracks. When they were finished they needed to locate their rubber boat. Because of the mistaken reading of the current, they failed to find the boat or even their landing craft, and they all ended up swimming back to the *Gilmer* some four and a half miles out. They arrived on board at 0430 exhausted, but with enhanced respect for Admiral Hill.

Hill had a heavy weight on his shoulders that night as he checked and coordinated myriads of details that were all part of the upcoming landing. Yet every half hour until the UDTs returned, he called them on the radio. His call sign was Pinup.

"This is Pinup himself. Is Blow Gun himself there?" he would say. He then would ask Kauffman how many blondes the swimmers had picked up and how many brunettes. A blonde translated as a swimmer whose fate was known; a brunette was a missing swimmer. The men were impressed. As Kauffman later explained, "Here was a very, very senior officer with a tremendous amount to think about, all night long calling us to find out how we were doing, and making plans for a reconnaissance in the morning to pick up the swimmers if they weren't all back. After I got to know that man, I realized this was typical of him."

The next night, guided by the radar of the APD *Stringham,* Group Baker went back in and found its original objective, White 2. This time Kauffman nearly blew it. As his team was swimming from the northern end of the beach to the southern end, he heard a conversation in progress —this after every man had been warned repeatedly to maintain absolute silence. He was about to yell out "Shhhh!" when he realized that he was hearing Japanese, not English. He had no idea what these Japanese soldiers were doing—whether they were working or were on patrol and had just stopped to chat—but they remained in place for the full hour that the team was reconnoitering, and several close calls occurred. At one point, Kauffman shed his trunks and rolled in the sand to camouflage himself. Eventually, the team covered all the approaches from north to south, as well as the northern half of the shore. They found no mines.

Armed with information from the reconnaissance missions, the high command in the morning decided to land on the two White beaches. UDT 5, Draper Kauffman's team, would go in late on the night of J-minus-1 to blow up the heavy coral at the northern end of White 1. In addition, under an order from Admiral Hill, they were to return to that beach to find and destroy what was suspected to be a line of mines some twenty yards up the beach, terrain that the earlier recon units had not had a chance to inspect. Though Kauffman expressed his fears that such a move might be suicidal, Hill insisted. The mission would take place only a few hours before H-hour; thus even if the mines exploded, the Japanese would not have much advance notice of the coming landing.

Team 7—the other unit that had been active at Saipan—would make a thorough daylight reconnaissance on the southern beaches of Saharan Harbor and look for something to blow up, regardless of what it was, in order to deceive the Japanese into thinking that American forces would be landing on the beaches near Tinian Town.

Kauffman's team estimated that two thousand pounds of tetrytol would be needed to clear out the coral on the northern flank of White 1. How could they swim that much explosive in without being seen? Their solution was to lash a thousand pounds onto a long section of rubber hose from an oiler and to load the rest of the material in and around a heavily reinforced rubber boat, which would remain just barely afloat. The two loads were to be towed by Kauffman's landing craft to two thousand yards, then pulled to five hundred yards by another rubber boat. The swimmers would carry lines in to the beach, then haul the two loads in. They were counting on not being seen by the Japanese and knew that if they were spotted the results could be disastrous. Two ensigns suggested dressing in camouflage white and searching for mines by working from opposite ends of the beach. If mines were found, they would put half a pound of tetrytol on the mine horns, wire the horns together, and then fire them.

Several rehearsals for the mission took place. The last one went very well and buoyed the team's spirits. Had they remembered the rule from theatrical circles that a good dress rehearsal means a bad performance, they might have reacted differently. The night of J-minus-1 was miserable. The seas were moderate, but for a rubber boat anything other than a calm sea is a problem, and heavy squalls were coming from ashore.

With great effort the team got their landing craft to two thousand yards from the shore—this time the radar was working—and transferred to their rubber boats, only to be blown repeatedly off course beyond the line of the landing craft. After continued unsuccessful attempts to rectify the situation, Kauffman, at about 0230 hours, reluctantly ordered all the explosives jettisoned in deep water. He then jumped into the water and led six men in. This was the unit chosen to dispose of the suspected mines, but again no mines were found. Dumping the explosives was a huge disappointment to the UDTs.

The quiet, clandestine work of the demolition teams had been invaluable to the Tinian operation by proving it might be possible to land on the White beaches without tipping off the Japanese. On 24 July the Americans staged a giant ruse to fool the enemy into thinking they were about to land at Tinian Town. After carpeting the town with what appeared to be a preinvasion bombardment, a large fleet appeared offshore and began unloading landing boats. Those craft approached the shore, then retreated several hours later, which the Japanese attributed to the success of their shore batteries. In the meantime, following artillery bombardment from Saipan and attacks by American P-47s, Marines started landing on White 1 and 2, those narrow gaps in the cliffs on Tinian's northwest coast that many had believed could not be used for an amphibious invasion. By nightfall, fifteen thousand Marines had made it onto shore, encountering only light resistance. Total casualties for the Marines numbered only five. The deception had worked. By the time the Japanese realized what had happened and rushed north, the Americans were able to repulse their counterattack.

But as if to prove Admiral Turner right in wanting to use the other end of the island, the wind blew up and became increasingly heavy, and by JIG-day-plus-4 the White beaches, planned for use to supply troops ashore, were useless. No one who was involved in the action on Tinian ever trusted weather forecasts again. Thanks to the landings on the White beaches, though, the Marines managed to capture Saharan Harbor from the land. Supplies could then be sent in through the harbor and across the beaches that Richmond Kelly Turner had been so eager to use.

Despite that success, a tragedy occurred at Tinian for the Kauffman family. Draper Kauffman had a first cousin, Patricia Donavin Owens, whose husband, Comdr. Seymour Dunlop Owens, was skipper of the destroyer *Norman Scott*. Owens had been awarded a Bronze Star at Saipan "for heroic achievement as Commanding Officer of a close-in fire support ship in the face of repeated enemy fire." The *Norman Scott* (named for another friend of the family killed in action) had covered the landings on Saipan, and on 25 July the ship was part of the feint attack near Tinian Town intended to mislead the Japanese about where the U.S. landing would take place. The enemy, however, had its own surprise in store. The placement of three heavy Japanese guns was not revealed until the battleship *Colorado* and the *Norman Scott* moved in close to shore to cover the landings that supposedly were coming. Certain that this was the actual invasion, the enemy let go with the hidden guns, killing forty-three men on the *Colorado* and nineteen on the *Norman Scott,* including Seymour Owens. Among the many messages sent to the ship was one from Draper Kauffman aboard the *Gilmer*: "My condolences to you who have lost an excellent and kind man." A tribute sent from Adm. Reggie Kauffman read: "In the battle for the capture of the Marianas no vessel of the fleet has been assigned more hazardous duty or has performed that duty more eagerly than the *Norman Scott*. . . . All of us mourn with you for your courageous dead and sympathize with your wounded. To your gallant ships' company the Force Commander says 'Well Done and God Bless You.'" Commander Owens was awarded the Navy Cross posthumously for his heroism at Tinian. Destroyer no. 767, commissioned in April 1945, was named the *Seymour D. Owens*.

Tinian fell with relative ease within a week of the invasion, followed soon thereafter by the more bitterly contested Guam, to the south. With the Marianas now in American hands, Japan's inner ring of defense had been breached. By November 1944 American B-29 bombers would begin launching raids against Japan using air bases in the Marianas.

In spite of the UDT disappointments on Tinian—the explosives jettisoned, the fruitless search for nonexistent mines—Draper Kauffman characterized the landings on Saipan and Tinian as a considerable success. His demolition teams' accomplishments—finding the path for the tanks across the lagoon on Saipan, blowing the channel through the reef there, and playing a role in the choice of beaches at Tinian—were substantial. The teams learned a tremendous amount from the actions at Saipan and Tinian, and the experience would have a marked bearing on future operations.

At the same time, Kauffman was fighting several minor battles about how much recognition his men deserved, and who would get it. The first, he recalled, "was an argument between Admiral Turner and myself—guess who won." Turner insisted that the UDT leader put in citations for the Silver Star for all his officers and a Bronze Star for every man who had swum in to the Saipan beach. Kauffman took strong exception to that. As he tried to argue, the enlisted men had gone in just as far as the officers. In fact, the person who went in first at Saipan, almost to the waterline, was a chief petty officer. He suggested either Bronze Stars for everybody or no individual awards but a unit citation. But to no avail.

The other skirmish concerned pay. Kauffman was called to the flagship to talk to a flag officer who had come out from Washington. The officer, whose name he could not remember, told him that papers had been prepared and advance approval received for UDT personnel to receive pay and a half. Kauffman had two objections. First, he said, "although I had in the UDTs . . . the finest bunch of guys in the navy, I had one serious problem with them and that was keeping their egos down." In addition, extra pay, with the prestige that it brought, would make it harder to keep the teams secret. Kauffman asked the admiral's permission to go back and discuss it with his men.

"Well, fine," the admiral replied, "but I must say I had not expected to run into opposition from this quarter!"

Kauffman gathered UDTs 5 and 7 together and put the question to them. "I've got to go back to the flagship tomorrow, so I have to have your answer by ten o'clock tomorrow morning."

They brought it to him in writing, and the answer was unanimous: "We want hazardous-duty pay only when Marine infantrymen get it."

Kauffman took the document over to the flagship.

"You say this is unanimous?" said the admiral.

"Yes, sir."

"Well, the first person I'm going to make sure sees this is General Holland Smith!"

"From that moment on," Kauffman observed, "the UDTs could do no wrong in the eyes of the Marines! The kids who wrote this . . . couldn't have dreamed up a better public relations stunt. Of course they had seen the Marines in action."

The pay-and-a-half plan was killed, and the scuttlebutt blamed Draper Kauffman, who, some of the men suspected, thought a pay raise would attract the wrong kind of people. "We cursed him up and down for a long time," Dan Dillon told the author, "because we could have used that extra money. But I have to say—whenever there was a difficult job to be done, Draper would volunteer for it. . . . Even though at times we hated him, we respected him. As a matter of fact, after the war, I bragged everywhere: 'I served under Kauffman. He's number one, the golden boy of the Navy. If there's an impossible job, who do they ask for? Kauffman!'"

Kauffman, though he didn't see the other UDTs in operation first-hand, was extremely proud of their performance on Guam. From 14 to 20 July, during the invasion of Tinian, UDTs 3 and 4 were doing "a magnificent job" prior to and during the landings on Guam. Under the leadership of Lts. Tom Crist and W. Gordon Carberry, they made several daylight reconnaissance missions north and south of Agat Bay, then blasted a mile of natural obstacles and more than three hundred artificial barriers. The latter consisted of six-by-seven-foot palm log cribs filled with coral and connected by thick steel wire hawsers and, landward, barbed wire posted in the coral. On W-day (D-day for Guam), UDT members acted as pilots for the first wave of landing craft and supplemented the beach masters. One of their very finest officers, Ens. Tom Nixon, was killed in that engagement; he was later honored when a camp city in Guam was named Camp Nixon Underwater Advance Base.

When UDT 4 returned to the fleet, Adm. Walden L. Ainsworth hoisted a flag salute on the *Honolulu*: "UDT-4 well done." Both teams' officers and men were given a citation by Admiral Turner; Lieutenants Carberry and Crist were awarded Silver Stars, presented to them by Admiral Kauffman.

During training for the invasion on Guam, UDTs 3 and 4 had engaged in friendly arguments with the Marines about which of them would get to the beach first. The day of the landing the Marines were greeted by a neatly lettered sign:

WELCOME MARINES
AGAT USO—2 blocks Courtesy UDT 4

Lieutenant Carberry chewed out the men and their officer for the irresponsible prank. That night, when he submitted a detailed chart of the landing beaches to Adm. Richard Connolly, commander of Task Force 53, aboard his command ship, the *Appalachian*, he concluded with strict military formality by recounting the matter of the sign. The admiral dressed him down brusquely for permitting this to happen. When Carberry reached the door, however, Connolly added, "Lieutenant, that's one hell of a story—wait till I tell Turner; he'll have those Marine generals eating crow!"

Kauffman, still anxious to keep egos under control and UDT operations secret, and to maintain a good relationship with the Marines, was not amused. He disciplined the men who posted the sign by giving them a choice: they could get out of underwater demolition or they could spend four days on burial duty with the Marines. They chose the latter, but it was such grim duty that after three days they told Draper they could not take it any more; since he needed them and they were good men, he relented. The story of the sign became everyone's favorite, and in time similar signs popped up on other beaches, or so it was said. Whether those signs were actually posted, or the teams involved simply could not resist saying so, no one now knows for sure.

7

Three Stripes, Three Stars

DRAPER KAUFFMAN LEFT FOR THE MARIANAS OPERATION WITH ALL HIS clothes and two new pairs of glasses and returned to Hawaii dead tired, with only the shirt on his back and a single pair of broken specs. His father begged him to get some rest. He kept promising to but never had time. Finally he was ordered to a rest camp. His dad drove him there and bought him a case of beer. It was time for a break, and time to write Peggy. At the end of July 1944, he sent her the first real letter in some time:

> Here I am, at last, back in a comparatively civilized area. . . . I am not at all sorry because I was tired, though I have a lot I should do. It is grand here. I put on swimming trunks before breakfast and stay in them all day. I have a nice cabin to myself with a very comfortable bedroom, living room, bath, and icebox for beer and ice. I dropped about 19 pounds on the show but drank at least three pounds yesterday evening so should be back to normal soon.

> Now that the show is over I can give you some of the story. I am, as I told you, chief instructor at the school. It soon became apparent that it was impossible to do the job properly until I had been on at least one operation so I went along on the Marianas one and learned a lot. In light of that I am going to completely change the school around when I get back next week. Our gang did a magnificent job and I was terribly proud of them. Of course, we lost some and I have never been able to school myself to take such losses calmly even though we knew it would have to be.

He mentioned that Admiral Turner—notoriously tough on recommendations—had recommended more than sixty UDT members for Silver Stars and more than three hundred for Bronze Stars for their actions in the Marianas operation, the largest mass recommendation for navy or marine personnel so far in the war.

Meanwhile, Kauffman had got hold of some liquor from the States, a real treat since, according to him, only three kinds of booze were sold on Maui—"whiskey scotch-flavor," "whiskey bourbon-flavor," and "whiskey gin-flavor." Cracking open the rare bottles of manna, the men toasted their victory in the Marianas with raucous delight. Then Kauffman shared with them the recent news about the demolitioneers who had participated in the Normandy landing, whereupon their joy turned to sorrow. More than 50 percent of their Fort Pierce buddies who were on Omaha Beach had died, as well as others of them who saw action at Utah Beach. The UDTs' accomplishments at Normandy were nonetheless impressive, especially in light of the fact that the teams were operating at a huge disadvantage, many having been sent in *with* the landing troops instead of ahead of them. As Draper acknowledged to Peggy,

> I have been told that our gang did a wonderful job at Normandy also, so it seems that all that effort down at Fort Pierce has paid a lot of dividends. Remember how discouraged I got sometimes, particularly when Washington seemed so cold to the whole idea?
>
> Dad just came out and showed me a letter from you in which you were very worried over a story told you about me at Saipan. There is nothing to worry about at all, dear. I got through without a scratch though I must confess there were times out there when I

> was scared as Hell. I must now return to earth and the sedentary though important job of teaching.
>
> I am thrilled with the pictures of you and the baby. I carry the three-picture frame with me every day and everyone I meet says (1) how did you ever persuade such a beautiful dame (my equals in rank) or lady (my juniors' and seniors' description) to marry you and (2) what a tremendous amount of personality Cary has for her age. My God, what I wouldn't give to see you both. I never hear a waltz without getting homesick.
>
> I am thrilled with Betty Lou's engagement. I hope Prescott is everything she should have—he had better be. . . .
>
> Save as much as you can so that if I do get home you can come to whatever port or place I land in and we can have a big spree. I am trying to save up for that too and have $100 set aside for it already.

As planned, Draper Kauffman was relieved as commanding officer of UDT 5. In September he became head of the experimental and development unit on Maui as well as training officer. He set up an advanced training course for Fort Pierce graduates and combined a basic and advanced course for UDTs recruited from the fleet. Lt. J. K. DeBold took over Team 5 with Lt. (jg) R. P. Marshall as his executive officer. According to Kauffman, this worked out beautifully because in the process of getting an organization started, he had stretched himself thin and left behind a good deal of chaos. That was the disadvantage of being both team and group commander. He had also been spending a great deal of time on the flagship planning, or working with Admirals Turner and Hill, and as he said, not paying nearly enough attention to the organization of the team, even though he was going in on operations. Within a month or so, John DeBold had UDT 5 well organized and everything flowing through official channels.

Now that the Mariana Islands were secured, the United States turned its attention to the final fierce drive toward the enemy's homeland. It was time for the dual thrust—General MacArthur's push up through the islands of the southwest Pacific and Admiral Nimitz's westward drive across the Pacific—to converge in the Philippines. For MacArthur, it was a long awaited passage. In January 1942, pushed back by the Japanese invasion of the Philippines, American and Filipino forces under his command had withdrawn to the Bataan Peninsula on Luzon. In spring of that year MacArthur went to Australia to take command of allied Southwest Pacific forces, leaving his army behind to surrender to the Japanese. MacArthur vowed to return and liberate the Philippines.

Kauffman was fully aware of how momentous coming events would be. In addition to being the UDT training officer at Maui, he was now on Admiral Turner's staff working out UDT plans for landings on the Palau Islands and the Philippines. As plans officer he got an inkling of where the war was headed, including the possibility of a landing in Japan—which, if everything went right, could come in the following year, 1945.

For such a landing, he believed, at least thirty UDTs would be needed, which would mean at least tripling the output of the training base at Fort Pierce. He asked Admiral Turner to send urgent messages alerting Washington to this expanded need, and he dispatched some demolition people back to Fort Pierce to pass on the lessons they had learned.

Then he went to Capt. John M. Taylor, who had been assigned to Admiral Turner's staff to monitor the UDTs. Taylor always said that was the worst job he ever had in the navy—that the UDTs were his problem children—and yet he had a real understanding and appreciation of underwater demolition work. Kauffman told Taylor that what he thought the underwater demolition group should have, as the war progressed and operations got bigger, was a regular navy captain as its head. During operations that person could command close-in fire support. It had to be a captain, he reasoned, because no destroyer commander was going to take orders from a lowly reserve lieutenant commander.

Captain Taylor agreed. He and Admiral Nimitz's gunnery officer got together and picked the perfect man, a great big ruddy Irishman by the name of B. Hall Hanlon, who was called—what else?—"Red." When he heard of his appointment as Commander, UDTs, Amphibious Forces, U.S. Pacific Fleet, Captain Hanlon was on his way to take command of a large ship. "To say he was disappointed must have been putting it mildly," Kauffman said, "but you would never have known. He embraced his new job with tremendous enthusiasm, commanding the loyalty of team personnel right off the bat and proving to be a top-notch administrator." In fact, after Hanlon's six-month duty with the demolitioneers, one tough old chief petty officer was heard to say, "That's the only guy who didn't take Hell Week that I will buy as a true UDT man." Hanlon's new designation, ComUDTPhibsPac, was quickly shortened—thanks to the UDTs' desire for secrecy and love of informality—to MudPac.

A number of UDT missions took place before Hanlon started his new job. From his station on Maui, Kauffman kept a close eye on continuing operations in the Pacific. The Palau operation, undertaken to secure a staging point for aircraft and ships heading to Leyte in the Philippines, began with an initial naval bombardment of Peleliu Island on 12 September 1944. UDTs fanned out over the coral reefs off the selected beachheads, searching for natural and man-made obstacles. They blew up a series of wooden antiboat obstacles and placed explosives at strategic spots in the reef to open a path for the LVTs and make berths for the LSTs that would be participating in the invasion. The operation went well from the point of view of the demolitioneers.

Thirteen men from two of the teams at Peleliu accomplished an outstanding feat. These intrepid scouts, after enduring a three-mile swim in very shallow water within close range of Japanese snipers on shore, managed to locate a safe route for the tanks to travel during the invasion.

By the evening of D-day, American casualties at Peleliu amounted to 210 killed and 900 wounded. This initial toll would have been heavier had it not been for a new tactic being tried by the defenders, one that would be repeated later at Iwo Jima and most devastatingly at Okinawa. Instead of a wholesale attempt to push the attackers back into the water, the Japanese commander put up only token defense at the beachhead and concentrated his defenses inland in an interlocking network of caves excavated from the coral rock and almost impervious to bombardment by sea or air. On 15 September 1944 the First, Fifth, and Seventh Marine Divisions came ashore and secured the beachhead. But their work had just begun. One by one, the caves had to be emptied out or sealed off with flame-throwers, a slow, painstaking effort that would take until the end of November and beyond.

By mid-October, though not thoroughly mopped up, Peleliu was effectively secured as a staging point, and it was time to begin the invasion of the Philippine Islands. The eastern shore of Leyte, the eighth largest island in that chain, was the place chosen to gain a foothold.

Elements of Adm. Thomas Kinkaid's Seventh Fleet would support the landings. A typhoon on 16 October sank some of the small minesweepers set to clear the entrance to Leyte Gulf, but this didn't delay the operation, which got under way on 18 October. That day a fire support unit under Adm. Jesse Oldendorf moved into Leyte Gulf to bombard the southernmost of the planned beachheads and to bring in the UDTs. It was a nerve-racking business, for the units came close on the heels of the minesweepers and no one could be sure that all mines had been cleared from the gulf. In the aftermath of the storm the UDT landing craft were pitching madly, and it was difficult to locate mines in the murky, churning water.

In the afternoon UDTs disembarked from their transports and headed toward the shore in their landing craft, covered by destroyer guns. For some fifteen minutes, the beach was still as a desert save for incoming fire. Then at 1515 the landing craft met with a pelting rain of defensive fire from mortars, machine guns, and a 75-mm gun. Oldendorf's destroyers tried to target the sources, but they were well hidden in brush to the rear of the beach.

Events that day showed that the enemy had finally become aware of the UDTs and their methods of operating. Though UDTs 3, 6, and 10 came through the operation unscathed, other teams suffered casualties. On the eighteenth, three UDT men were killed (one each from Teams 4, 5, and 8) and fourteen were wounded in ninety minutes. The next day Team 9 had one killed and numerous wounded. One man from Lieutenant DeBold's UDT 5 was killed, and UDT 8, under the senior demolition officer at Leyte, Lt. Comdr. Donald Young, had one man killed and five wounded. The hardest hit was fledgling UDT 9 under Lt. Comdr. James Eaton. Facing the enemy for the first time, those men took a fatal hit that sank their boat; one swimmer was killed and eleven were wounded. Determined to complete their mission, the crew of UDT 9 returned to their transports and after some hasty reorganization, headed back to the shore.

As the ranks of wounded grew, landing craft zigzagged about, picking them up and returning them to their destroyer transports. Had it not been for the nature of their mission, which required that they glide through the water widely dispersed, the UDTs would have suffered a worse fate off the shores of Leyte.

The next day, 19 October, more UDTs combed the northernmost of the projected beachheads, and though Japanese defenders delivered some sharp fire, the mission was accomplished without major incident.

On 20 October the landings at Leyte, supported by Admiral Kinkaid's seven hundred fighting ships, proceeded relatively smoothly. In a theatrical gesture destined to go down in the history books, General MacArthur waded ashore and announced to the Filipinos and the world, "I have returned." The landing owed its success partly to the weakening of Japan's air power, partly to Leyte's eastern beaches, ideal for amphibious invasion, and partly to the Japanese commander's decision not to fully contest the landings. Later the Japanese would try to reinforce Leyte, but to no avail, and by the end of the year the Allies would have it firmly in hand.

The Leyte operation was a mere prelude to the larger and much more challenging task of clearing the Japanese from dozens of other southern Philippine Islands, including the Allies' main objective, Luzon, and its capital, Manila. By now Draper Kauffman had been appointed chief of staff to Captain Hanlon. The UDT commander in chief flew to the Philippines as an observer, leaving Kauffman to his new desk job in Hawaii, though he would have much preferred taking off with Hanlon.

Having been briefed by the UDTs that had participated at Leyte, Hanlon was well aware of the need for close fire support from destroyers. Admiral Oldendorf was in command of the fire support unit for Luzon. And since Hanlon would be observing the action from Oldendorf's flagship, the battleship *California,* he was in a position to persuade the fire support commander to push his destroyers in close to the initial beachheads on Lingayen Gulf, on the island's west coast.

On 6 January 1945, following two days of heavy kamikaze attacks, the *California* led Oldendorf's ships into Lingayen Gulf for the preliminary bombardment. The UDTs were primed and ready to go, when suddenly a cloud of kamikaze planes came buzzing in low over the hills to avoid radar detection. The lead plane smashed into the *California*'s control tower, and soon the scheduled bombardment turned into a struggle for sheer survival. A score of ships were hit, including three cruisers, and many small ships went down before Admiral Oldendorf finally took his fleet limping out of the gulf. That night, he assigned the destroyers and the UDT transports to screening duty.

The morning of 7 January dawned clear and bright, without any sign of kamikazes. Oldendorf returned with his ships and commenced the bombardment, after which the UDTs took off in their landing craft. Captain Hanlon had arranged for them to approach the shore in staggered units and on roundabout courses, so they would not resemble an assault wave. UDTs 5, 9, and 15 covered Lingayen's southern beaches; UDTs 8, 10, and 14, the northern ones. Thanks to superb fire support, the swimming scouts did not suffer a single casualty.

On 9 January the largest amphibious landing yet in the Pacific war got under way on twelve separate beaches. Again the invasion went without a hitch, because the Japanese commander, who was not in a position to waste his dwindling resources by opposing it, concentrated them inland. But in the coming months, the island of Luzon would have to be dearly bought from the fierce Japanese resisters.

A kamikaze plane hit the transport *Belknap* on 10 June, resulting in dozens of casualties, including eleven dead and fifteen wounded from UDT 9. In ten landings on enemy-held islands, the UDTs had lost only eight men; now in a single stroke, aboard a transport, eleven were killed.

Save for that tragedy, operations proceeded smoothly at Lingayen, as they would elsewhere in the Philippines in the days to come. Kauffman had reason to be proud of the UDTs. While the various battles for the Philippines raged, Admiral Kinkaid's amphibious commander, Adm. Daniel Barbey, made the following report:

> The results achieved by these UDTs are far above anything anyone might imagine. It seems incredible that men in small boats and men swimming should be able to close a heavily defended, hostile beach in broad daylight to almost the high-water mark without receiving such severe damage as to make their operations a failure. That they are able to do so is due not only to the gunfire and flame barrage, but to the skill and intrepidity of these men themselves. When one watches them perform under the gunfire of the enemy, one cannot fail to be

impressed by their boundless courage. The nation's future is safe when defended by such men as these.

Before the Allies began storming the Philippines, Admiral Turner recommended Draper Kauffman for a second Navy Cross, for his performance at Saipan and Tinian. Kauffman's father was chairman of the awards board in the Pacific, and when Draper's name came up he left the room so he would not be part of the discussion. When others decided in favor of the recommendation, however, the elder Kauffman was delighted to accept the job of pinning the Gold Star on his son (a star was awarded instead of a second Navy Cross). A picture of the ceremony shows Draper laughing. When asked what was so funny, he replied, "Because, as Dad pinned it on, he said, 'Thank the Lord you found a clean shirt!'"

Draper Kauffman was not the only member of the family with good news. His sister Betty Lou and Pres Bush had decided to set their wedding date. It was to be a small wedding at a little church on Belle Isle, not far from Miami Beach, with just family and close friends coming to the house afterward. In February Pres and Betty Lou would be moving to Brazil. There he would be pursuing his career with Pan American Airways as part of that company's airport development program, which built airports in Brazil under the auspices of the U.S. Navy. Brazil would furnish the land for airstrips that the United States would build and use during the war, and which afterward would be given to the host country. Pres had even worse vision than Draper and that, in addition to a knee injury, had prevented his being in the armed forces, though he was working with the navy. Betty Lou wrote to her father and Draper asking them what would be the best time for them to get back to Florida so that the wedding date could be set. Her father responded that since they had no way of knowing what their plans would be she should pick a date, and they would just hope to get there. They decided on 30 December 1944, so that if father, brother, or both could come, the timing would overlap with Christmas. Moreover, Pres's brother George had a month's leave in December, during which time he and Barbara Pierce planned to be married as well. The brothers could thus serve as each other's best man.

Draper's wife, Peggy, and their baby daughter, Cary, left Washington for Miami to spend the winter with his mother and sister. Betty Lou had traveled north to ski, to christen the submarine *Atule,* and to meet Pres Bush's family. When her bridesmaids were unable to get train tickets (not an easy task in wartime) to come south for the wedding, Sam Pryor, vice president of Pan American Airways and a friend of the Bushes, offered to fly them all down with the family. Pres was having problems of his own with the wedding party. Many of his classmates from Andover and Yale, as well as other friends, had turned up in Miami at the Subchaser Training Center. He would ask them to be ushers; they would accept with alacrity; and then they would disappear without a trace, ship movements naturally being secret.

Betty Lou said that Pres reminded her of both her father and Draper. "Maybe that's what started me loving him—a *gentle-man,* and *funny,*" she wrote to them. She thanked them both for writing to Pres (even Draper managed to put pen to paper in that instance) and welcoming him into the family. But it was a worrisome Christmas season for the family at home. News dribbling in from the Pacific during the previous summer and fall—from Saipan, Tinian, and Guam—had been grim indeed. Then Draper's mother broke her leg and was in considerable pain and unable to devote much time to the wedding. A pitiful Australian pine, the only Christmas tree Betty Lou could find to decorate the house, had sagging branches that would not support the weight of ornaments. It seemed a fitting symbol for a less than ideal Christmas.

To top it off, in December Admiral Kauffman sent the unwelcome news that he would not be able to come home for the wedding. He had moved to a new job, which he could not explain at the time. Unable to make the trip himself, he started campaigning to enlist Draper's services as substitute father of the bride—and he managed to throw in more fatherly advice while he was at it. "I noted," he wrote to his son,

> that there was to be a conference on underwater demolition back in the States, and also that Fort Pierce wanted some hot information. . . . As you know, your sister is to be married on December 30 and I was very much in hopes that you could be there to give her away. My inability to be present is very distressing to me and I know I shall always feel very badly about it. . . .

In addition to my Sea Frontier job, I took over the SOPA [senior officer present ashore] duties in this area, and I am now an operator as well as an administrator. . . . I have been living aboard ship and will continue to do so through the next few operations. They have built our headquarters ashore, and I am moving part of my staff there today. However, I do not expect to move to my hut for some time. I might add that this is one of the hottest, rainiest, and muddiest places I have ever been in.

I have had very nice letters from your mother and sister. Your mother says that your baby girl is one of the best children she has ever seen and apparently is in excellent health. Subject letter brings forth some very uncomplimentary comments regarding your failure to write to Peggy. I have told you my opinion of your failing many times. When you were young, there was some slight excuse, but for a man in your position, with a wife and child, frankly, I can see no excuse whatsoever.

I hope you are getting over to Pearl Harbor occasionally and relaxing a bit, when the opportunity affords. Don't forget that anything that interferes with your health, whether it is your teeth [Draper was plagued by dental problems] or relaxation, should be corrected immediately. . . .

I know you have no time to write me, but if you should see anyone coming this way, let me know how you are getting on.

His wayward son was not completely remiss in letter writing. Shortly thereafter the younger Kauffman wrote his mother to say he had settled down to teaching again and he did not like the job, though it did have some compensations. It had given him the freedom, for instance, to get over to Pearl Harbor that morning. The purpose of his trip was the opening of a big recreation center that his dad had had built for his men when he was Commander, Destroyers and Cruisers, Pacific, and that Admiral Nimitz had insisted be named in his honor. Capt. "Sol" Phillips presided over the ceremony, since, at the last minute, Admiral Nimitz could not come. The event took place at a magnificent site overlooking the bay. Phillips's speech was very complimentary of Admiral Kauffman and also made clear to Draper the nature of his father's new job. "Admiral Kauffman," Phillips said, "has been ordered to command the Philippine Sea Frontier, a tough assignment since the Philippines have not yet been captured." After mentioning Kauffman's forty-one years of service, during which "the welfare of his men was constantly in his mind and in his heart," Phillips noted that in conceiving the recreation center, Kauffman "was forced to use considerable tact, a touch of diplomacy, and, occasionally, a neat axe. He can use any one of the three."

Draper was delighted by Phillips's speech and by the big sign that he unveiled with a flourish: Kauffman Recreation Center. "Dad," his letter went on, "made a few remarks, passing the credit on to his staff as he always does, whereupon Captain Phillips proposed three cheers and everyone let loose. I was very proud."

Draper went on to say that he was eager to give his sister away at the wedding, though "I am not presuming that Betty Lou would want me to substitute for Dad. . . . I will let you all know in a week or so what my chances are of getting home for the wedding. I did not try to swing it before when I had a combatant job, but now that I am just a schoolteacher again I don't feel guilty about trying."

Unfortunately, because of the demands of his job as chief of staff to Captain Hanlon, he could not get leave. "I haven't been as disappointed in many years as I am now about this trip home," he wrote his mother. "I did so want to give Betty Lou away and meet Pres. Also, I would give my right arm to be with Peggy just for a day or two. If I have to be on a staff I sure wish it was somewhere that she and Cary could be. Gosh I will be glad when this damned war ends. How are the wedding plans going? I'll bet it is a cracker jack with you at the helm and Betty Lou as the star."

Betty Lou was extremely disappointed that neither her father nor her brother would be at her wedding and sad, too, at the prospect of not seeing either of them for a long time, since she and Pres expected to leave for Brazil soon and be away for three or four years. She had given Draper a Saint Christopher medal to keep him safe, and now she wrote a letter asking him to make sure he wore it and telling him how much all of them—his mother, wife, and sister—missed him. Pres wrote too, saying "I loved your sentiments about Beth because they are mine also. . . . I'll do my best to see that your precious sister will always be the happiest girl on earth."

Reggie and Draper Kauffman were sorely missed at Betty Lou and

Pres's wedding, but the ceremony was a very happy one and helped brighten the gray Christmas that had just passed. Peggy served as her sister-in-law's matron of honor; Pres's sister Nancy was maid of honor; and Pres's brother George was best man. Adm. Walter Anderson gave away the bride and offered toasts that Reggie and Draper had written for him. The newlyweds honeymooned in New York City and spent a week with Pres's parents in Greenwich, Connecticut, which allowed them to attend the wedding of Pres's brother George and Barbara Pierce in nearby Rye, New York, where Pres was able to return the favor as best man.

Draper Kauffman was champing at the bit in his new desk job and complained to his father about not being allowed to continue as commander of UDT 5. He still harbored hope that he would be assigned a job at sea. Meanwhile, the selection board for reserves was meeting, and he awaited news of whether he would be promoted. His hope was tempered by the prospect of the seventy-five hundred lieutenant commanders up for promotion, of which only six hundred would be selected. "I feel certain there must be a hell of a lot of officers who have been to sea since the war began who would and should probably be given first choice," he remarked. In the end, happily for him, he was promoted to commander. News of his three stripes reached his father, who wrote a congratulatory letter: "Will you please do me a great favor. Will you go down and buy yourself a new brass hat, shoulder marks, and silver oak leaves, and send me the bill. I can't think of anything that I would rather get you than the above."

As always, Reggie Kauffman's remarks to his son mingled pride with a hefty dose of wise counsel:

> I would keep several things in mind regarding the immediate postwar period. You naturally will want to get back to the States and find yourself a job, but do not overlook the fact that you are at present drawing not a bad salary and that there are such things as transportation of household gear, and medical attention for yourself and family which will cost you plenty in civilian life. In other words, I suggest you "keep your shirt on" and not quit the Navy until you have something very definite lined up. I appreciate the fact that there are several million men in your same position, and that you will prefer to get as much head start as possible. At the end of the

last war, there was a great rush by young officers to be released from the Navy and after a few months outside, [they] tried to get back in, as the jobs they had been promised failed to materialize or at least were not up to their expectations and did not provide sufficient funds for them to live the way they had as officers of the U.S. Navy.

I know of course, that as usual, you are very busy but I would like to suggest that you make it your business to visit Pearl Harbor at least *twice* each month. . . . I have observed many officers during this war and there is no doubt about it, many of them "go stale" when they confine their activities entirely to the small group with whom they work daily. . . .

Take a few minutes off and write me a letter as soon as you can, as I do not expect the mail service to my future base to be very reliable.

In answer to Draper's complaint that he should be with his UDTs and not in an administrative job, his dad commented bluntly, "Your remarks about not being cut out for a staff officer are just a lot of bunk. Any man who thoroughly knows the job is a good staff officer." And he gave his opinion about the ideal chief of staff. That person had four characteristics, his father said: first, knowing what you were talking about; second, when you did not know the answer to a problem, saying so; third, when your boss was raising hell about the personnel of your unit, listening carefully, if painfully, and not passing on the cussing to subordinates; and finally, anticipating the boss's ideas and having a plan of your own for any future operations or contingencies.

He offered one more suggestion: "Keep in mind that most of your subordinates are *also* thinking and that they are not quite as dumb as you think they are! . . . The sooner you realize that you are now a Director and not a Doer, the happier you will be and the better things will run. . . . Again, my congratulations, Commander! Lots of love and lots of good luck, Dad."

It is remarkable that Reggie Kauffman had time to pen such a long letter to Draper, considering his job as Commander, Philippine Sea Frontier. It was a very trying time for him. He had told Admiral Kinkaid, his old roommate at the Naval Academy, that he would take over as SOPA, and this added quite a few additional duties to his existing ones. He had recently moved ashore to set up a workable sea frontier operations center. During all that, he had to deal diplomatically with "the big boss," as he called Gen. Douglas MacArthur, Supreme Allied Commander in the Pacific. "We get along very well together," he wrote Draper, "although . . . the opinions of the Army and Navy are rather far apart. Many of the Army here have done nothing but . . . plan . . . a way to get back to the Philippines and avenge Bataan, which I can well understand; but the Navy looks on this whole operation as merely a stepping-stone. This job of mine is an important one, but under the command set up, it is one of the most difficult I have ever had, as I have only one idea, and that is to get on to Tokyo, get this damn show over, and go back to Miamisburg [his native town in Ohio], where I can turn in my plane for a horse and buggy." Of course he was just letting off steam. He was already cooperating with the army, relying on what Sol Phillips had described as his "considerable tact, a touch of diplomacy," and occasional "neat axe."

Draper Kauffman's mother wondered why her husband, who had been at sea for the better part of five years, with only two short periods at home, and had held positions of great responsibility, had not been given three stars. Reggie Kauffman took a philosophical view of that. As he said to his son, with all the officers and enlisted men dying around him, "to worry about high rank and honors just doesn't seem right. . . . When the war is over, regardless of the rank and decorations you may have, the real test will be whether you . . . feel that you have always done your damnedest and if you have, what the hell difference does it make what the world thinks."

Like Draper Kauffman and so many other officers and men stuck in the Pacific that Christmas of 1944, his father was tired of the long, grueling war, and he was a bit blue. He wrote his family letters reporting on the men he worked with, saying what a great job most of them were doing. Now that he had a headquarters—a Quonset hut—he took to inviting people in for meals, not only his peers but many young officers as well. Dinner companions fresh from the States were especially welcome; admirals could be just as hungry for news and faces from home as the youngest bluejacket. It cheered him up greatly when Peggy sent him a special Christmas present, a leather wallet with pictures of her wedding with Draper and of the baby. He put it alongside his bunk. On Christmas

Day, Viray, his steward, whipped up some eggnog out of brandy, rum, powdered milk, and real eggs, a wartime rarity. Reg's old friend and Naval Academy roommate Tom Kinkaid joined him for a holiday swim, and afterward, with the eggnog, as he wrote to Draper, "we toasted all of our numerous kinfolk, including of course your family, and Pres and Betty Lou."

Shortly after that Rear Admiral Kauffman received a vice admiral's three stars, pinned on by Admiral Kinkaid. Draper Kauffman, along with the rest of the family, had fresh reason to be proud.

8

The Final Stretch: Iwo Jima and Okinawa

THE HIGH COMMAND'S NEXT OBJECTIVE WAS AN EIGHT-SQUARE-MILE chunk of rock and ash called Iwo Jima, an island whose southern tip was dominated by a dormant volcano, Mount Suribachi. Iwo Jima—Japanese for Sulfur Island—was so called because of its unearthly terrain of steaming sulfur pits and caves. U.S. forces coveted this godforsaken speck in the vast western Pacific because it lay halfway between the Marianas and Tokyo, roughly 650 miles from each. Without Iwo Jima, the B-29 Superfortresses flying from Saipan to drop bombs on Japan would have a treacherously long round-trip flight menaced by enemy fighter planes and with no refueling facilities. Iwo Jima would give the B-29s and their P-51 fighter escorts a badly needed forward base and emergency landing strip, and it was a vital acquisition in the stepped-up air war against Japan. The capture of Iwo was likely to prove another critical breach in Japan's inner ring of defenses.

But taking Sulfur Island would be a monumental task. It was home to a labyrinth of caves, bunkers, and pillboxes interconnected by eleven miles of tunnels. Within this meandering underground fortification twenty-one thousand defenders were holed up and determined never to surrender.

The only alternative to Iwo Jima was the island of Chichi Jima in the Bonin Islands to the north, but its terrain was too rugged for rapid construction of an airfield. Moreover, intelligence showed that it was more heavily fortified than Iwo because it harbored a crucial Japanese communications center. The radio towers, which rose two hundred feet in the air and sprouted numerous antennae, were guarded by radar and fighter planes.

It was at Chichi Jima that George Bush, a torpedo bomber pilot and the brother of Pres Bush, Betty Lou's fiancé, had a narrow escape slightly more than four months before the Iwo Jima landings. Lieutenant Bush was part of a mission to destroy the towers. As he approached them, his Avenger was hit by intense fire from Japanese antiaircraft gunners and it erupted in flames. He continued flying toward his targets, delivered the payload of bombs, and headed back out to sea. But it was soon clear that Bush's plane would not make it back to his carrier, the *San Jacinto,* and he parachuted into the ocean. His head was bleeding profusely after striking the fuselage, but he managed to inflate his rubber raft and propel himself away from Chichi Jima as fast as he could paddle with his cupped hands (the raft's paddles and drinking water had been lost). Pilots from his squadron were able to stave off the enemy at first but soon had to head back to the carrier to refuel. After several hours in the open sea, Bush was rescued by a submarine, the *Finback*. He was extremely thankful for his luck—but he was devastated because he lost both his crewmen. No trace of either of them was ever found. As an intermediate base for emergency bomber landings and fighter planes, Iwo Jima, if it could be captured, would prove a godsend to pilots like George Bush who were flying sorties against the enemy's inner defense ring and homeland.

In mid-February 1945 Rear Adm. William Blandy readied his task force for the intensive preinvasion bombardment of Iwo. His force included four heavy cruisers, a light cruiser, sixteen destroyers, and six battleships, among them the *Nevada, Texas,* and *Arkansas,* all of which eight months earlier had supported the landings at Normandy half a world away.

In anticipation of the Iwo operation, Captain Hanlon had reorganized the UDTs. In addition to commanding a team himself, he would be in charge of four other units: the destroyers under the senior destroyer commander, Rear Adm. Bertram J. Rodgers; twelve LCI(G)s (landing craft, infantry, gunboats) under their squadron commander, Michael Malanaphy; six APDs under Capt. Jack Horner on the *Gilmer*; and five UDTs under Draper Kauffman, whose prayers for an operational job had been answered. He was still serving as Hanlon's chief of staff. Although the *Gilmer* remained the flagship for Hanlon and his staff, Kauffman was given a gunboat as a command post from which to run the beach operation.

The UDTs en route to Iwo Jima were deeply indebted to Admiral Turner for a change he had instituted. Prior to the Marianas operations, when the first APDs were departing Hawaii with their greenhorn demolitioneers, Turner had inspected their sleeping quarters on one of the old four-stack destroyers—the ex–fire room with ninety-five bunks sitting five high over a double layer of tetrytol explosive. It was bunkroom-cum-magazine, and as Kauffman put it, "hotter than the hinges of hell." For eight months UDTs setting off for the war zone had been supremely uncomfortable on the old destroyers.

Admiral Turner happened to go aboard on a very hot day. "This will have to be fixed," he said immediately, and he made the decision then and there to add troop space topside to some new destroyer escorts. The first five of the new APDs were available at Iwo, and they were vastly more comfortable than the nearly uninhabitable fire rooms of the old destroyers. Kauffman said that every demolition man who had slept on an old APD "blessed Admiral Kelly Turner up one side and down the other!" upon transferring to the newly outfitted quarters.

The four underwater demolition teams slated for action in the Iwo operation were transported on the *Barr,* the *Bates,* the *Blessman,* and the *Bull.* Upon their arrival off Iwo Jima early on the morning of 16 February, D-day-minus-3, the UDTs scrambled topside to scrutinize the island in the distance. It looked peaceful, but nerves were on edge. As J. W. Spence recalled in an unpublished collection of memoirs from members of UDT 12, "The first question that entered each swimmer's head was . . . what was the water temperature. Right off we could see that we were in for a chilly swim the next morning." It was cold on the morning of the seventeenth when they began loading their personnel reconnaissance boats. Tied to them were the small rubber boats used to approach the beach. The men slathered themselves with silver camouflage grease and cocoa butter, which would help them keep warm in the sixty-five-degree water. As they greased up, they feebly tried "to knock off the tension with humorous remarks that went over like lead balloons." Spence continued: "We were rigged in just swim trunks, swim fins, a face mask, knife, several mine detonators, and a lead weight with line for determining depth, but beads of sweat took the place of goosebumps. And instead of having choppy water as we had expected and wished for, we had a sea as calm as a mill pond." The calmer the water, the more exposed they were to enemy fire.

All of Iwo's beaches lay on the southern half of the island. The beaches of that triangular piece of the island that the UDTs hoped they would not have to use were on the west coast. The more desirable series of landing beaches was situated along a thirty-five-hundred-yard stretch running toward the northeast from Mount Suribachi on Iwo's southern tip. An airfield was located near the east coast that it was imperative for the landing forces to secure as quickly as possible. But aerial photographs made clear that those beaches fell off sharply into deep water. On beaches with a near-vertical drop, it was almost impossible to land a boat because it would swing around and veer broadside to the waves and wind. The UDTs had to know how steep the slope was. Should it prove too much of an incline, they would be forced to use the less desirable beaches to the west. Almost all the beaches were overlooked by Suribachi, where the defenders were perched. The preferred beaches had particularly bad flanks, with Suribachi on the left and high broken cliffs on the right.

Among the puzzles raised by intelligence photos was a line of about forty sizable holes along the eastern beaches. The holes appeared to be lined with concrete and extended almost to the waterline. Intelligence people raised the unpleasant possibility that they contained fuel-oil lines that the Japanese would ignite, sending a wall of flame down the beaches as the first waves of Marines landed.

Draper Kauffman found that most planners for amphibious operations, with the notable exception of people like Admirals Turner and Hill, tended to seize on the worst possible scenarios. Still, the thought of that wall of flame had him worried because the Marines wanted one or more UDT men to peer down one of the holes and find out what was in it. That, of course, was only one of a myriad of questions the Marines wanted the UDTs to answer. Among others: What type of gun emplacements would they encounter? Would the beach sand take wheeled vehicles? (That question, Kauffman lamented, was one the UDTs weren't knowledgeable enough to answer.) And, of course, what was the terrain like? They could answer that query, but in naval terms that did not translate easily into Marine Corps lingo.

Once the men finished greasing up on D-minus-3, they moved ahead to complete their tasks. One demolition team performed a feat that earned them great respect in the fleet. Those men were assigned the job of sneaking a heavy, battery-powered directional navigation light onto Hagashi Rock, about a half mile offshore. During the mission they were discovered by the Japanese and fired on, but they managed to install the light and escape without injury. The spot they picked for the light was protected by the rock formation and could not be hit from shore. It remained operational for a least a week, shining directly out to sea and greatly aiding U.S. forces involved in the Iwo Jima operation.

The following day, 17 February, the UDTs were to conduct reconnaissance of the eastern beaches in the morning and of the alternate western beaches in the afternoon. The battleships were out at 5,000 yards, the cruisers at 3,000, and the destroyers at 2,000; in addition, there were some LCI(G)s that were to go in to 1,000 yards for close-in fire support. The LCI(G)s were the sort of infantry landing craft that had been used in Europe, but they had been outfitted in the Pacific with 4.5-mm mortars, 4.5-mm rockets, and 40- and 20-mm guns.

The Japanese knew that LCIs had been designed to carry infantry companies of roughly 120 men. What they did not yet know was that some of those vessels had been outfitted as gunboats. The first wave of the reconnaissance operation consisted of seven LCI(G)s advancing in line abreast. Draper Kauffman, who was controlling the UDTs, was in the center boat in the wave, accompanied by a radioman. Five reserve LCI(G)s came in just behind the first group and, following those, twelve regular LCIs carrying the lion's share of the demolitioneers. The Japanese, Kauffman said, were certain that the LCI(G)s were

> the first wave of the real landing. They had hidden in the caves in Mount Suribachi and in the high broken cliffs on the right flank of the beach a murderous series of 5- and 6-inch batteries, designed to be used for the first time to enfilade the beaches when the regular landing started. Our intelligence hadn't found them and we had not seen them. . . . Unfortunately for the LCI(G)s, . . . all hell broke loose when they got to about 1,500 yards. I . . . was on the center LCI(G) with my radioman and my radio to control the teams, and within ten minutes my LCI(G) was sinking and had to turn around. I had a small landing craft along with me which had taken me to the LCI(G), and I transferred with radioman and radio into that and then transferred to the LCI(G) that came in to take its place. Well, this one lasted only eight minutes, and during the eight minutes my radioman was killed and my radio was destroyed, and the skipper of the LCI(G) was very badly wounded.

All twelve LCI(G)s involved in the mission were badly hit and one was sunk. The crew of the crippled craft that carried Kauffman reversed course and hightailed it back to the destroyer *Twiggs,* whose skipper, Lt. Comdr. George Philip, had been a Naval Academy classmate of the UDT commander. Philip had been keeping close watch over the scene, and as they hoisted his friend aboard he belted out, "My Lord, Jonah, why did you have to pick *us*?"

During all this, as Kauffman later recalled, "the heroism . . . of the LCI(G) skippers and their crews was extraordinary. As long as they had a gun to fire, they kept coming back onto the line, no matter how beaten up they were. It was a darned impressive thing to see." In the end, the demolitioneers found no underwater obstacles or mines. That good news came with a heavy price in casualties. One UDT casualty, Ens. Frank Jirka, was wearing a pair of borrowed shoes when he set off on his mission that fateful morning. After he had both his feet blown off, the ensign's first reaction to the man who had lent him the footwear was a stoic "sorry about losing your shoes." For their brave performance at Iwo Jima, the LCI(G)s would later receive the Presidential Unit Citation.

During the frantic action, Captain Hanlon had pushed the destroyers in much closer to shore so they could make better use of their guns. As a result several destroyers were damaged, but according to Kauffman, Hanlon saved the UDTs by giving that command—and did considerable damage to Japanese gun emplacements.

As had been planned, forty-five minutes after the landing craft had put their swimmers in the water, Captain Hanlon ordered the destroyers to illuminate both the right and the left flanks with white phosphorus and lay a smokescreen close to the shoreline—in fact, at the water's edge. The idea was to camouflage any particularly brave soul who might seize the chance to crawl onto the beach and look down one of the potentially deadly wells.

"I finally got on the *Twiggs* and the reconnaissance went smoothly," Draper related. "The day before, we had raided the ship's stores to get empty tobacco sacks, and we gave them to the men to tie to their swim trunks and bring sand back from the shore." A few men managed to get samples of sand, and three men actually ventured far enough onto the beach to inspect the wells. There was no sign whatsoever of pipes; the wells apparently were to be used as snipers' stations. The other good news was that while the beach gradient was sharp, it was not steep enough to keep the Marines from landing.

Back on the landing craft, en route to their transports, the UDT men got a slug of brandy and a pair of dry long johns to warm up. When everybody assembled back on the flagship after the morning's frantic action, they counted their losses, which were heavy: more than two hundred casualties including fifty-plus killed on the LCI(G)s. Of the UDT men who had gone in on LCI(G)s, there were four casualties—two wounded and two killed. "My luck was with me, for sure, that day," Kauffman said.

As the participants were writing up reports in the *Gilmer*'s wardroom, the men with the sand brought it in and dumped it on the wardroom table. Kauffman gathered the Marines who had taken part in the operation and said, "I'm darned if I know what kind of sand wheeled vehicles can go on." The Marines said the sand was sufficiently coarse to take wheeled vehicles. Kauffman immediately shot off a message for Captain Hanlon to relay to the troops heading for Iwo that the sand would accommodate wheeled vehicles. He would live to regret that hasty note. "If I had only added a phrase such as 'Marine observers state that the sand is coarse enough so that wheeled vehicles will move on it,' it would have been all right," he lamented, "because somebody would have known that coarse sand does not accommodate wheeled vehicles." He also regretted not sending a sample of the sand: "I could have sent back some of the sand. I didn't . . . realize what a very important question this was." It was one of some fifty questions the Marines had asked, and as the minutes ticked by and the questions were ticked off, Draper became preoccupied with the prospect of the afternoon reconnaissance, which was pressing in on them. If this afternoon's reconnaissance is anything like this morning's, he kept thinking, this will be one hell of a day.

"I've always felt very bad about the business with the sand—giving the Marines the go-ahead on using wheeled vehicles," Kauffman later said. He took full responsibility for his message. As it turned out, however, senior officers had been well informed about the matter. Adm. Harry Hill, commander of the attack force at Iwo, stated in his oral history, later quoted in the book *The Pacific War Remembered,* that the Americans had received superb advance information about Iwo Jima, both from surveillance photographs and from Japanese documents captured on Saipan. It was known well ahead of time, said Hill, that the beaches on Iwo were

> of black volcanic ash or sand and steep terraces which might cause early trouble for wheeled vehicles. . . . From the start of planning we were concerned about the soft volcanic sand . . . behind the shallow beaches. We [made] a series of tests on a very soft beach [on] Oahu, [where] we beached . . . tracked and wheeled vehicles and found [that they] stalled. . . . Successive photos indicated a beach much softer than normal—this meant real trouble. [Beachmaster] Squeaky Anderson came up with a solution: . . . steel matting. [By the time we left Hawaii] we had over eight miles of matting with tractors and [sand] sleds ready for use. This proved to be invaluable. (291, 294)

The afternoon reconnaissance of the beaches to the west, undertaken without the LCI(G)s, all twelve of which were out of action, was nowhere near as eventful as the morning's episode. The UDTs did draw fire, but they suffered no casualties. By midnight all the UDT charts were completed, and three hundred copies were made of each one. Two of the APDs were peeled off and sent back to the flagship with the charts and with representatives from each UDT.

As a result, on D-minus-1 morning every marine commanding officer had in his hands charts of the beaches on Iwo Jima, information about any gun emplacements found, and a description of the lay of the land to the rear of the beaches. Not only was this highly useful information for the Marines, but it helped calm nerves. As Kauffman was told later by many Marines, they were always apprehensive before a landing, and it comforted young Marines in particular—those new to amphibious landings—to know that other people had gone in before and come out alive. It also helped that the UDTs were able to kill fearful scuttlebutt about petroleum tanks and apocalyptic walls of fire.

That night a tragic incident occurred. The ships were retiring from Iwo with the intention of coming back first thing in the morning. One of the APDs, the *Blessman,* headquarters for UDT 15, was heading out to sea under the command of her very able skipper, Lt. Philip LeBoutillier. The sea was calm and there was a great deal of phosphorescence, which illuminated the ship and made it a clear target. Suddenly a Japanese Betty swarmed in and dropped a 500-pound bomb through the *Blessman*'s steel superstructure; it exploded in the starboard mess hall, killing almost everyone on the spot. As Kauffman recounted it,

> She was about twenty minutes astern of us . . . and she sent out word, fortunately before her radio went out, which it did very quickly. We turned around, in the *Gilmer,* to go back to her aid. . . . She just looked like a torch. She had lost all power and all communications; and of course she had 50 tons of explosives on board, which made us all a little nervous.
>
> Captain Hanlon had the *Gilmer* make a pass very close to her and dropped a landing craft with me aboard. I went over to the *Blessman.* After I'd been aboard enough to see what the story was, I reported back by my hand-carried radio to Captain Hanlon, ending with the stupid statement, "Fire has not reached the explosives yet." Captain Hanlon wryly answered, "I gathered that!"
>
> They had not abandoned ship. Captain Hanlon then had the *Gilmer*

put right smack alongside and used the *Gilmer*'s fire-fighting equipment to get the fires under control. Our primary job was putting out the fires and getting the badly wounded off. . . .

Of course I was horrified to find the wreckage . . . and the terrible losses, killed and wounded. . . . It was the closest I can think of to the early days of my work as an ambulance driver in France, seeing these terribly mangled men.

Gunners Mate First Class Dan Dillon was aboard the *Blessman* that fateful night:

We were off duty. I had gone into the mess hall . . . and the place was packed. I said to some guys, "Move over."

"Come on. Where are we going to move over? There's no place for you."

So I walk out of there, and I go over to the other side of the ship. Then this thing comes in over my head, and it's got a delayed fuse on it. It goes through the steel deck up there and explodes right in the mess hall, killing them all. The lights go out; the engine room is blown out; the whole side of the ship is blown out. A wall of fire meets me. Some guys were blinded, and I get them on my belt and we go up on top. My buddy, Bob May, who swam in with me to Iwo Jima that day, is horribly wounded. . . . We get him comfortable, we lay our wounded out on the deck. We try to start our hand-billy auxiliary fire-fighting equipment with like an outboard motor; they won't start. So we start a human fire chain, a bucket brigade. We're losing ground. The fire is getting closer and closer to the explosives. Nobody will come near us. We are on our own, and we are doomed.

Now a voice comes out of the darkness. I recognize it as Draper. He says, "Have you thrown the explosives over?"

We look at each other. We know we don't have much time. We know that he has the power to put the fire out, so we tell a lie, and we say, "Yes, Commander, we've thrown them over."

He says, "Stand by. I'm coming alongside." And by God, he brought his boat alongside, they brought that water in on the hose like a fireboat; they smothered that fire and saved the rest of us. . . . When he heard the explosives weren't off, he looked at me. But I will say, knowing Draper Kauffman, that where things were the worst, that's where he would be.

Unbeknownst to Dan Dillon, Ens. E. F. "Andy" Andrews and another UDT 15 officer, Ens. Bob McCullum, grabbed one of the hoses and went into the hold. The fire had already taken hold in the ammunition locker, right next to thirty tons of tetrytol and other high explosives. Desperately they fought the fire until they were able to put it out and prevent the *Blessman* from blowing up. Warrant Officer Steve Stright methodically moved explosives away from the bulkhead, which had become very hot.

Unfortunately for UDT 15, it was on the *Blessman* that night. Nineteen of its men were killed and twenty-three wounded. More than 40 percent of the team were casualties, the heaviest loss sustained by any UDT during the Pacific war. The ship's crew lost twenty-two.

By 19 February the UDTs had cleared the beaches sufficiently to allow seventy thousand Marines to begin landing. D-day morning was sunny with a ten-knot breeze, but by afternoon the wind whipped up, causing a sharp breaking surf on the steep beach. Based on the UDTs' reports, it had been decided that the Marines should land on the eastern beaches. At H-hour Kauffman met the beachmaster, Squeaky Anderson, aboard a gunboat and observed the first wave of the amphibious landing. The Marines of Maj. Gen. Harry Schmidt's Fourth and Fifth Divisions were "catching pluperfect hell," in Kauffman's words, wading through a hailstorm of enemy fire and dropping like flies; he assumed the beachmaster would not go in for a couple of days. But at H-plus-90-minutes, Anderson said, "I think they've secured the beach now. Let's go." Kauffman went along to take notes dictated by Squeaky Anderson, and he witnessed firsthand the beachmaster's legendary derring-do. Most of the Marines were belly down in the sand, digging their foxholes for dear life, but not the beachmaster. He just walked up and down that beach in his perfectly shined shoes, black socks, and garters, his unbuttoned shirt flapping in the breeze, as though he were immortal. Meanwhile, Draper Kauffman had his pad and pencil and was struggling to keep up: "The difference between the fact that he was walking sedately along the beach while I was diving from one hole to another made it a rather unequal proposition. A perfectly extraordinary man—I loved him." Fourteen loudspeakers were carried ashore, and eventually the voices of Squeaky Anderson and his assistants were booming up and down the beach.

Nothing could have prepared the Marines for what they found when they hit the shore. First, there were the steep terraces of soft volcanic ash, which initially stymied their advance. In addition to the maddeningly shifting ground, there was what the Fifth Marine Division's second lieutenant Walter Curley—who was a friend of Pres's at Yale—described as Iwo's "unearthly terrain . . . , an area of mammoth sulfur caves . . . with dead lying about indiscriminately." In days to come, the men would bathe in sulfur springs and use the "hot sulfur pits above the airfield . . . as cooking ranges."

As it turned out, in another way Kauffman's misgivings about not providing sufficient warning in regard to the soft sand's inability to accommodate tracked vehicles were misplaced. The steel matting came in very handy and in some ways the volcanic ash/sand actually proved to be a blessing. According to Jim O'Dell in *The Water Is Never Cold,* "It was easily dug, bagged, and retained behind any type of bunker support," and it "absorb[ed] the concussion and lessen[ed] the shrapnel burst of the enemy's mortars and artillery" (199).

Despite the severe preinvasion pounding from Admiral Blandy's task force, Iwo Jima's twenty-one thousand defenders were still holed up in their underground labyrinth, and it would take some two months of fierce struggle and more than twenty thousand U.S. casualties to root them out. The fighting was so intense that the beach was temporarily abandoned. By the fifth day, the Marines had battled their way to the summit of Mount Suribachi and planted the American flag.

While the Marines were occupied, the UDTs' demolition work continued. They were to start clearing the chaotic wreckage of the invasion from the eastern beaches, but they could not demolish anything except the wooden landing craft because blowing up metal amtracs and amphibious trucks would have scattered more lethal shrapnel than a Japanese barrage. At Squeaky Anderson's request the demolition teams also surveyed a western beach to see if it could serve as a supply route. Captain Hanlon's MudPac staff viewed the prospective area in a couple of ramped landing craft. Kauffman and other beach reconnaissance veterans went along. When the two craft approached the shore in the face of heavy sniper fire, it was clear that many Japanese were still dug in. The MudPac patrol beat a hasty retreat when mortar shells hit near the stern of one boat and lifted its propellers out of the water. But they were able to determine that the western beach could be used as a supply route once it was secured.

For a week and a half, in the face of storms and enemy fire, the UDTs toiled to clear wrecked vehicles and disarm enemy land mines and booby traps. Within nine days, the beaches were clear enough to evacuate casualties and move in more troops and supplies.

The value of Iwo Jima quickly proved itself. Even before the island was entirely won—thanks in part to the Seabees, who rapidly transformed the smoldering battlefield into an airfield—the first of many B-29s to come made an emergency landing there instead of plunging into the cold Pacific. Before the war ended, some twenty-four hundred B-29s carrying more than twenty-seven thousand crewmen would land on Iwo.

For their outstanding work at Iwo Jima, the UDTs received a stream of congratulatory messages. Secretary of the Navy James Forrestal spoke of "their gallant and effective part in making the landing on D-day possible." Admiral Turner applauded them for courageously gathering reconnaissance information that "contributed greatly to the success of the landing." Admiral Hill expressed his appreciation for a fine job carried out "under difficult and hazardous conditions. Your group is making naval tradition of a fine order." Captain Hanlon sent the following message to the UDTs: "This command can add nothing to these statements except to heartily concur with them. It is a high honor to command you." As for Draper Kauffman, once his work was done at Iwo, he left the godforsaken chunk of volcanic rock and ash and never wanted to look back.

The press of events was sweeping them all forward, this time to Okinawa. Okinawa was one of the Ryukyu Islands, which included Kerama Retto, Ie Shima, and various lesser islands. A poor, densely populated farming community whose natives were treated by the Japanese as an inferior race, the lowly island of Okinawa drew to its shores a U.S. armada of thirteen hundred vessels, and for one good reason—its proximity to the enemy. The island lay only 340 miles from Japan. If the United States could gain this final stepping-stone, it would likely launch an invasion of the Japanese homeland.

Toward the end of March 1945, an amphibious support force under

Admiral Blandy and an additional bombardment group of cruisers and battleships commanded by Adm. Morton L. Deyo set out for Okinawa. Despite heavy seas and gale winds Blandy's force arrived in the Rykukyus on 25 March, Palm Sunday. The first landing on Okinawa, Love-day, was set for 1 April, which that year happened to be Easter.

For the UDTs Okinawa was to be the last real operation, and much the biggest, of the war. There were twelve teams, each with a hundred men and a small staff. Fourteen APDs and a varying number of regular destroyers, LCIs, and other vessels were set to join in the operation.

The American forces concentrated first on Kerama Retto. A fine anchorage surrounded by eight islands, Kerama Retto lay about fourteen miles west of Okinawa and would serve as an advance naval base for fueling and ammunition replenishment. Minesweepers—the unsung workhorses that always paved the way for amphibious assaults—had found such a heavy concentration of Japanese mines off Kerama Retto that the UDT mission was delayed. But at 0600 on Palm Sunday, five destroyer transports carrying UDTs arrived off Kerama. The teams had their work cut out for them. UDT 19 from the *Knudson* reconnoitered Kuba, Aka, Geruma, and Hokaji, while UDT 12 from the *Bates* surveyed Yakabi, Zamami, and Amuro. UDT 13 from the *Barr* went to Tokashiki. Following the procedure that Kauffman and his staff had labored over on Maui and in earlier operations, each landing craft went in to about five hundred yards from its assigned beach and discharged a swimmer every fifty yards. Each swimmer took soundings every twenty-five yards, as measured by the knot in his fishing line, using either his small lead line or, if the water was shallow, his body with its black rings painted at twelve-inch intervals. "After an hour or more of reconnaissance," wrote Samuel Eliot Morison in *Victory in the Pacific,*

> depending on the width of the reef, each swimmer was picked up by his LCVP [landing craft, vehicle, personnel], which in the meantime had been planting little colored buoys on dangerous coral heads. Their method of recovering swimmers was simple and effective. A sailor held out a stiff rope to the swimmer, who grasped the "monkey's fist" at the rope's end, while the boat was making three or four knots, and was hauled on board. Landing craft then returned to their APDs where

the swimmers' data were correlated and entered on a chart. All this went on under gunfire support from destroyers and gunboats, and "really beautiful air support," as Comdr. Draper L. Kauffman USNR described it, from escort carrier planes.

One could follow these "frogmen" . . . from the ships, and as they calmly waded about the beach, they looked (as Admiral Deyo observed) like Kodiak bears fishing for salmon. (14:121)

"Half fish and half nuts," the frogmen were affectionately called by the men watching their mission from the landing craft.

The teams that looked at Kuba and Yakabi Shima ascertained that the beaches in those two outer islands were impracticable for landing craft and could only be approached by amtracs.

The UDTs made a curious discovery in the Ryukyu Islands: 260 small boats hidden away in some water caves, and not a crewman in sight. The men had never seen them used in combat before and could only guess at what they were. Japanese suicide boats? When word of the craft was sent on to Admiral Kinkaid's flagship, the intelligence analysts agreed with that conclusion. After the war it was learned that two days before the UDTs arrived, all those missing boat crews had been sent to Okinawa for an exercise and training period. The UDTs destroyed some of the boats the day they were found and made note of the remainder.

Their primary mission, of course, was reconnaissance. Once that was completed, the UDTs reconvened on the flagship *Gilmer*, compiled their report, and sent representatives from the teams over to the amphibious flagship, the *Mount McKinley*. They had done a very thorough job and the Ryukyus were easily taken by Maj. Gen. Andrew Bruce and his 77th Army Division.

On Love-minus-5 and minus-4 the UDTs had a small job of reconnoitering an island called Keise Jima, about four miles west of Okinawa. The Japanese had small units there and the army wanted to use it for artillery.

On Love-day-minus-4 the UDTs reconnoitered the beaches on Okinawa, reporting that the reef was suitable for amtracs, but that in only a few places would there be water deep enough at high tide to float landing craft. The main landings at Okinawa would take place on the island's southwestern coast on a long, straight beach stretching out to either side of the village of Hagushi. On 29 March, Love-minus-3, the UDTs went in for a day mission.

On that day every skill that the swimming scouts had been honing over the many grueling months of war in the Pacific was put to the test. The landing craft moved to within five hundred yards of the shore and released a large number of men, masked and covered in silver camouflage paint. Each one carried with him his reel of fishing line knotted at twenty-five-yard intervals, his sounding line, his stylus, and a sheet of plexiglass for making notes. The warm water off Okinawa had encouraged the growth of jagged, irregular bulwarks of coral that threatened to shred boats in the attack force. The coral's configuration had to be accurately plotted, and any other possible obstacles recorded, if the Marines were to reach the shore in one piece. The scouts went about their business, unwinding their reels, taking soundings, and recording the results while American ships shelled the island to soften up its defenses. Experience had taught the UDT men the risk they ran. They knew that at any moment stray shells from their own ships could cut them down, or they might be targeted by keen-eyed Japanese defenders who saw through their silver camouflage. But that day luck was on their side. The Japanese were preoccupied with strikes from carrier planes, and the U.S. ships, benefiting from hard-earned experience, were targeting their shells accurately.

What the UDTs discovered that day was classic proof of the value they brought to the war effort in the Pacific. For lurking under six feet of water were three thousand pointed wooden stakes laced with barbed wire and driven into the coral floor. Some had mines attached.

That lethal wall had to be removed. On Love-day-minus-2, Good Friday, the demolitioneers returned and attached two-and-a-half-pound charges to each and every stake. For three hours they glided through the water, fixing their charges and connecting them with waterproof primacord. Because the fuses were not impervious to water, the swimmers, known for their ingenuity, protected them with a device that was ubiquitous in the Pacific: the condom. Once that was completed, they set the fuses and raced seaward. On each beach about five hundred stakes were tied together. At a prearranged signal from the flagship, the fuses were pulled and the entire line of stakes blew up simultaneously. In one single, ear-splitting explosion, the path was opened that would allow U.S. Marines to storm ashore.

"To our intense surprise," remembered Kauffman, "the enemy did not reply with so much as a single rifle shot. . . . It's a very ticklish business to tie some 3,000 packs of tetrytol to some 3,000 obstacles, get them connected with primacord exactly right, and do it all under enemy fire." Fortunately for the demolitioneers, during the three hours that it took to rig all the stakes they took very little fire, although one man, sadly, was killed by a sniper.

Love-day dawned on a peaceful Easter morning. GIs and Marines waded in to a deserted beachhead. But Love-day was also April Fool's Day, and Gen. Missuru Ushijima, who was commanding the Japanese forces on Okinawa, had a surprise in store for the invaders. In those peaceful early hours, the advancing troops had no way of knowing that Okinawa would be the bloodiest battle of the Pacific war, and that there was an enemy general holed up on the island who expected to win it. One hundred thousand Japanese soldiers lurked in pillboxes in the southern region of the island, where numerous caves hid heavy artillery that could be rolled in and out on railroad tracks. Once the Marines and GIs were ashore, Ushijima planned to knock out the U.S. fleet with kamikaze bombers and then slaughter the helpless and unsuspecting invaders.

On 2 April, Love-day-plus-1, UDT 11 was responding to an army request for a deep-water channel, some fifty feet wide and three hundred feet long, that would allow wheeled vehicles to reach the beachhead at low tide. Sixteen tons of powder and primacord were laid, and by 1615 everyone but the triggermen had returned to the *Kline*. They waited until the rising tide had covered the powder, and then at just after 1800 fired the shot, resulting in an explosion so massive that some ships nearby went to general quarters. Once the channel was cleared, Japanese troops that were dug in behind the landing beach starting firing. Two men of UDT 11 reported to the first amtrac wave of Marines and guided it into the beach. Swimming scouts led in the second, third, fourth, and fifth waves of amtracs, still under heavy fire.

In another sector of the beachhead, a small unit of swimming scouts was set to guide in the first tank wave. The tank commander could not decide whether to send his tanks across the watery reef, and while he was questioning one of the scouts about depths between the reef and the beach, another scout, less patient (or more positive), jumped out of his landing craft and waded to the beach in front of the line of tanks. As Edward Higgins described it in *Webfooted Warriors,* "The others followed, ending the tank commander's dilemma. Until 1115 [3 April] these grotesque mermen, clad only in trunks and swim fins, directed tank traffic across the reef and into the beach, sniper bullets whistling around their ears and plunking into the water within arm's reach."

On Love-plus-12 the UDTs were assigned to the Ie Shima operation. Surrounded by lava rather than coral, Ie Shima was a main Japanese stronghold about ten miles east-northeast of Okinawa. It was to be assaulted on Love-plus-15 by General Bruce's 77th Division. On 13 April came word of President Roosevelt's death. That night the demolition teams went in for reconnaissance and the following night for demolition. They had a tough job—building a ramp for landing craft out of lava. Ramps were difficult enough to create out of coral (simply removing the coral by blasting was much easier), but virtually impossible to make out of lava. At 0300 on the fourteenth, greatly frustrated, Draper Kauffman went to Bruce's flagship, woke the general up, and explained the problem. As he later recalled, he pointed out that the UDTs

> were not skilled artists in the use of explosives. A proper professional demolition man would have been horrified at the way we went about demolition. We always used far more explosive than we really needed, I'm sure. But we were never certain and we certainly weren't going to cut it fine, because we had to get the job done. It takes a very refined, very professional use of explosives to produce anything like a smooth ramp with a gradient on coral, and [is] much more difficult to do the same on lava. But General Bruce was perfectly fine about shifting to the alternate beaches [which could be properly ramped] and didn't seem to mind that I had wakened him out of his good sleep!

Many UDT men remembered Ie Shima most for the loss of Ernie Pyle, the war correspondent who had won the hearts of GIs in Europe by slogging it out in the mud alongside them, and who had only recently arrived in the Pacific. "The extraordinary hold that Ernie had on my enlisted men and officers!" Kauffman marveled. "He spent almost all his time with the enlisted men, sitting and shooting the breeze with them." Kauffman always had the feeling that Pyle was interviewing him when they were together, and Pyle vehemently disagreed with him on the subject of secrecy. Kauffman had had trouble with the press after the first Saipan operation. "Well now, look," journalists would argue, "the Japanese know all about the UDTs. Why shouldn't the Americans? You've just done it in broad daylight in front of everybody, and you can't tell us they don't send intelligence back home." But the underwater demolition teams leader argued that if the Japanese learned enough about demolition work, they could easily figure out a way to wipe out whole teams by planting explosive charges in the water. "Let me put it this way," he explained to Pyle, "I'm probably like a baseball manager who has won ten games wearing the same dirty shirt, and he's not going to take that shirt off, no matter how much it smells, until he loses!"

"That's as poor a reason for the suppression of the press in the United States as I've ever heard!" Pyle retorted.

Kauffman understood Pyle's reasons for wanting to write about the UDTs. "Not just because he didn't like to miss out on a good story," he later explained, "but because he felt my men were not getting the credit with the American people that they deserved. Pyle was so intimately involved in his mind and his heart with the soldiers and sailors that that ruled everything. He was lost there at Ie Shima just a few days after President Roosevelt died and I can assure you that, at least with my enlisted men, the loss of Pyle was an even greater blow than the loss of the president." Ernie Pyle was killed by a sniper's bullet.

On 6 April, Japan began launching massed kamikaze attacks known as *kikusui* (floating chrysanthemums) against the U.S. fleet. These operations had been planned since January. As Japanese strategists had foreseen, luring the Marines on to Okinawa and then embroiling them in protracted fighting would pin down the U.S. armada offshore, forcing it to protect and supply the fighting men on the beaches and leaving it vulnerable to aerial attack. The Japanese hoped to take out large numbers of warships and supply vessels before the expected Allied invasion of Japan. But years of war had deprived the Japanese of experienced pilots. They now were forced to depend on young, poorly trained volunteers who had but one thing to offer—a willingness to lay down their lives for the emperor. The pilots were treated to a lavish feast and entertained by geishas on the Japanese island of Kyushu, then released to perform their suicidal feats.

On 12 and 13 April an especially terrible attack took place. Kauffman was standing on the bridge of the *Gilmer* talking to her skipper when a kamikaze came zooming straight at them. It was an awe-inspiring sight, he recalled,

> because the plane caught fire about 100 yards out but still continued heading right for the ship—a flaming torch coming in, and the guns of course firing everything they could. It hit the ship, the bombs skipped in the water and exploded about 50 yards away. The plane hit a forward turret; one man was killed and three seriously injured. The idea of someone literally throwing himself at you along with his bomb made for an exceedingly uncomfortable feeling.
>
> And of course at night, no matter what we were doing—unless we were actually conducting a reconnaissance or demolition—the UDTs had to go out on the picket line since the APDs they were on had guns. Besides which each of the UDTs had fifty tons of explosives on board, and that was always enough to make you a little more uneasy.

Draper Kauffman was a master of understatement. Following the 12 and 13 April attacks, the pickets enjoyed a hiatus until the sixteenth, when a *kikusui* of 165 planes was launched. In *Webfooted Warriors* Edward Higgins describes the terror of being in an APD on the picket line that night. So as not to endanger friendly carrier aircraft trying to fend off oncoming kamikazes, the gunners had to hold their fire until the last minute. Once U.S. carrier aircraft were safely back on deck, however,

> the guns on the ships let loose. Nervous trigger fingers tightened on fire-control switches and triggers. All hell broke loose in the darkening sky as [almost] every gun in the fleet . . . poured fire and steel at the skimming, darting, weaving flying bombs. It was like all the Fourth of Julys rolled into one, orange tracer patterns fingering the shell trajectories toward their targets, starting high and leveling out over the water as they closed with the suicide runs. White flashes burst with sudden brilliance in the air as shells exploded, sending

> plumes of smoke arcing . . . gracefully out from the center of the burst. Slowly growing fires, rising to white heat and burning bright red and orange, trailed black and white streamers of smoke as the kamikazes took hits and writhed in the agony of death, still trying to take a ship along as they flamed into oblivion.
>
> The gods of war must have been pleased at the celebration in their honor, but to small men on small ships the effect inspired only . . . desperation controlled by the discipline of training, controlled by the instinct of self-preservation, controlled by a savage desire to destroy those who would destroy us.

One of the many ships sunk that day was the *Twiggs,* which had rescued Kauffman at Iwo Jima. A total of 126 of her men, along with her skipper, Lieutenant Commander Philip, went down with her. "I was never so happy to leave a place as I was to leave Okinawa," Kauffman said "—and those [terrible] kamikazes."

The UDTs that had participated at Okinawa could be proud of their contribution to the largest amphibious operation of the Pacific War. But pride in a job well done could never erase the memory of how dearly that victory was bought. On 22 June 1945 the island was secured, after almost three months of fierce fighting in which American casualties totaled 48,000. The U.S. Navy alone, in its worst losses of the war, saw 5,000 men killed, almost as many wounded, 29 ships sunk, and 368 others damaged. After all this devastation, the United States finally had its giant air and naval base close to Japan's heartland. The next step was the invasion of Japan.

9

End of the War

U.S. PLANNERS IN THE PACIFIC HAD NO REASON TO EXPECT THAT THE atomic bomb, which was being secretly developed at a remote site in New Mexico, would soon bring the war with Japan to an end. And so with Okinawa secured, they set about planning for Operation Olympic, the invasion of Japan. Draper Kauffman was sent to the Philippines, first to Manila, where he could visit with his father, and then to work with the staff of Gen. Robert Eichelberger, who commanded the Eighth Army.

Three landing areas were planned for the Japanese Islands, two of them to be commanded by UDT officers, Comdrs. Donald Young and Draper Kauffman. Kauffman had recently been promoted and, like Young, would be given a spot promotion to captain. He was scheduled to lead an invasion in the southeast corner of Japan, at Kyushu, the region where Japan's war industry was concentrated. For the first time ever, he felt pessimistic for himself and his men. And he was hardly the only one.

V-E Day—victory in Europe—came on the eighth of May 1945, in the midst of the battle for Okinawa. As soon as peace was announced, delirious dancing broke out in the streets of New York, London, Paris, Moscow. But in the Pacific there was little elation, only the weary hope that reinforcements would soon come from Europe. As far as the veterans in the Pacific knew, they would be lucky to get home in 1948—if at all—after landing in Japan. The closer the Allies got to Japan, the fiercer and more fanatical the Japanese defenders became. Clearly these people, who had tried to cast their net over eastern Asia and the vast Pacific region, were willing, now that that net was ripped wide open, to lay down their lives for emperor and homeland. The Americans could not ignore the fierce level of resistance at Iwo Jima and Okinawa. If those two small islands in Japan's outer ring of defense could result in the loss of many thousands of American lives, then how many men would become casualties of fighting in the 140,000 square miles of the five home islands? Surely those would be much more fiercely defended.

Gen. Douglas MacArthur, Supreme Commander for the Allied Powers in the Pacific, predicted that the assault on Japan would be the greatest bloodletting in history. MacArthur expected fifty thousand casualties just in establishing the initial beachhead on Kyushu, an operation planned for 1 November. He warned Washington that the Japanese might take to the hills and fight as guerrillas—in which case, he cautioned, the Allies might be embroiled in a ten-year war with no ceiling on losses. Presented with that dire prediction, President Truman approved the dropping of an atomic bomb, America's secret new weapon, with the hope of limiting casualties and bringing a rapid end to the war. On 6 August 1945 a B-29, the *Enola Gay,* dropped its deadly cargo over the Japanese city of Hiroshima; three days later another B-29, the *Bockscar,* dropped an atomic bomb on Nagasaki. If the Japanese did not surrender, they were warned, another bomb of similar destructive force would be used.

Just before Hiroshima, and while he was still expecting to participate in the invasion of Japan, Draper Kauffman was sent to Washington for one week of duty and two weeks' leave. "I had dropped from my normal 175 pounds to 126," he recalled,

> and was pretty tired, and he [Admiral Turner] was very sharp in observing things like this. Now, you would never know he was being compassionate. His idea of doing you a favor always included swear-

ing at you while he was doing it, for fear you'd think he was compassionate. He never told me that my trip to Washington included leave. The trip required that I deliver, amongst other messages, a sealed envelope to the head of the Bureau of Personnel, and the sealed envelope told Admiral Jacobs to give me two weeks' leave.

While I was home the bomb was dropped, and, listening to the early descriptions of the weapon and its damage, I was convinced that that was it, that we would not have to land in Japan. The first reaction Peggy and I had was to hightail it down to the Cathedral and say just a few words of thanks.

I am convinced to this day that the losses on the part of the Japanese in defending their own homeland against an invader would have been many times more than losses they suffered from the bombs, and, of course, our losses would have been comparable. I listen to discussions of the morality of dropping the bomb and I am never able to concentrate on the theory. My mind immediately goes to the more practical aspects, particularly as I was one of the people who were going to be involved.

On 29 August 1945 the USS *Missouri* sailed into Tokyo Bay in preparation for the Japanese surrender on 2 September. The UDTs were sent in to ensure that all would be calm for the ceremony, hence Kauffman was ordered back to the Pacific. The atmosphere in Tokyo Bay was tense. Along with the *Missouri* came an armada of U.S. battleships, cruisers, and destroyers, as well as a variety of other vessels from Allied fleets. Every heavy gun in the fleet was trained on the shore. Japanese government officials had urged that the American landing be delayed, for the homeland was a hotbed of potential rebellion by military elements not yet reconciled to surrender. Some kamikaze pilots had been boasting that they would dive-bomb the *Missouri* when she entered Tokyo Bay. The Americans also worried about the presence in the bay of motor torpedo boats, the suicide weapon first encountered at Okinawa. It was a fifteen-foot boat that carried its torpedo in the bow; the boat's pilot was to speed headlong into a ship, wreaking destruction and taking his own life in the process. Some two thousand such boats were said to be lurking in Japanese bays at the end of the war.

Several days before the surrender ceremony, Kauffman led a demolition team to investigate this latest menace. They swam toward the beach in standard UDT form, spread out, while two cruisers and four destroyers stood off with their guns trained directly at the Japanese on shore. What the swimmers discovered came as no surprise: a cache of suicide boats and torpedoes. Kauffman recalled the mission:

> I didn't do U.S. prestige any good that day. I was absolutely certain that this was going to end up as a combat operation. I couldn't visualize that these people would give in. . . . Just about in the center of the beach there was a pier. So I said, "All right, I will head for the pier." There was a ladder and I climbed up to the top and walked along the pier.
>
> If you can walk gracefully with swim fins on, you're a better man than I am. I looked pretty odd because I had swim fins on, swim trunks, and my face mask down over my neck. . . . And there were about 420 Japanese, all in immaculate uniform, drawn up in formation. A Japanese captain in his formal whites came down the pier. He said, "I wish to see your commanding officer." I didn't look much like a commanding officer. I said, "I am the commanding officer." . . . We went through this again—he repeated himself, and then I repeated myself, three times.
>
> He finally accepted the fact that I was the commanding officer, and stuck out his hand. If somebody sticks out their hand, you almost automatically raise your own to shake hands. I started to do that and then I thought, "Well, wait a minute now, that's a hell of a way to accept a surrender." So I put my hand back and his hand was still out. . . .
>
> We looked at each other for what seemed like hours but probably was a minute or two, and I told him what I wanted him to do, which was to assist me and my men in blowing up the boats and torpedoes and he agreed and we got on with it.
>
> But it was really about the most undignified surrender that was ever accepted. You know, I should have asked for his sword and so forth and so on.

Kauffman's demolition experts finished off the boats that evening. The next morning he came back with four men and dealt with the torpedoes, which were concealed in well-recessed caves at the end of a seven-mile-long railroad track. The men arrived in a landing craft and entered the caves in a jeep. "We went in very early, and about 0530 we had all the torpedoes blown up," he recalled. "I must say, they made a hell of a racket!"

When the torpedoes had been disposed of, Kauffman suggested that they "go down the road and see what it looks like." That was absolutely against orders. But with irrepressible curiosity, he and the other four set off in their jeep, and soon they came to Yokohama. A road led to Tokyo, and on either side of it were signs of utter destruction from U.S. fire bombings. "We didn't intend to do this; it was one of those things," he remembered. "We went a little way, and then thought, Well, we'll go a little farther." They made it to the outskirts of Tokyo, at which time a large group of Japanese began gathering around them. At that point Kauffman grew a little leery, and he said, "We've got to turn around and go back before we get into any trouble." But first they stopped in a small store. The store had five dolls for sale—one for each UDT man in the jeep. Of course, the Americans did not speak Japanese, and the Japanese certainly spoke no English, but both were good enough at sign language. The UDT men offered the proprietors five dollars and took the dolls. They then went back to their ship, and they thought everything was fine.

Two weeks later Adm. Jesse Oldendorf, now in command of the U.S. naval base set up on shore after the surrender, sent for Kauffman. When the UDT leader walked in to the admiral's office, Oldendorf threw a long dispatch across the table with the command, "Read this!" It was from General MacArthur, and it said, "I understand that a group of Navy men dressed in Marine fatigues went into Tokyo . . . and this was absolutely against all orders." MacArthur wanted Oldendorf to find the perpetrators, punish them severely, and inform the general that he had done so. As Kauffman repeated the story:

> I read only about the first sentence or two, and it was obvious from my expression . . . that I was guilty.
>
> He said, "Dammit to hell! I knew it was these damned UDTs. I knew nobody but you guys would do such a damned thing as that. Now you listen to me, Draper Kauffman, don't you ever go into Tokyo ahead of General MacArthur again! Do you understand me!"

I've heard him [Oldendorf] tell this story many times. Boy, he practically had me in the emperor's garden the way he told the story afterwards.

The war had ended and Draper Kauffman was sent back to Coronado, California, with orders to resume his old job as UDT training officer. He arrived in October and immediately Peggy and Cary joined him. For the first time since his wedding Kauffman was not under pressure, and the three of them finally settled down to enjoy family life together. Kauffman was bone tired and underweight—at 126 pounds, 3 pounds lighter than Peggy—and her immediate objective became to fatten him up. Without a pressing need to contemplate the future, Kauffman mused about his wartime career. He commented to Peggy that every one of his jobs had been with volunteers. He did not hold to the old bluejacket saw, "Don't never volunteer for nothing." Volunteers, he truly believed, were the best people—and in wartime, especially, the best people made all the difference.

On 13 October 1945, with the veil of secrecy lifted, an article entitled "They Hit the Beach in Swim Trunks" appeared in the *Saturday Evening Post*. It was the first publicity the UDTs had received since they had been born at Fort Pierce in Florida in 1943. They had earned it many times over. The author, Comdr. Harold Bradley Say, likened the underwater warriors with their black painted circles and bizarre swimwear and gear to "heathen idols." There was a moving photo of a swimmer slipping from his rubber boat into the water "like a Norseman," shots of enemy-constructed obstacles rearing out of the water while bobbing swimmers affixed explosives to them, and a picture of Adm. Reggie Kauffman pinning the Navy Cross on his son, Draper Kauffman. The article described UDT operations in the Pacific—Commander Say had consulted Draper Kauffman on the details—and concluded that "thousands of Americans home alive today would never have returned, save for these men in swim trunks."

By that time Draper's sister, Betty Lou, and her husband, Pres Bush, had moved to Rio de Janeiro, where they were living at one end of Copacabana Beach in the shadow of Pão de Asucar (Sugar Loaf) and expecting their first child. Her mother visited in November shortly before the baby was due. Admiral Kauffman was still in the Philippines, trying to track down his son who with typical forgetfulness had neglected to keep him informed of his whereabouts. At the end of October Draper received a forwarded letter from the Philippines.

Dear Draper:

I have just received a copy of the article in the *Saturday Evening Post* for 13 October. My congratulations, I think it is an excellent article and I must say that you were inordinately modest in regard to your contribution to UDT. I hope that you were properly reimbursed for your arduous efforts, not for UDT, but for helping to write the article.

I have endeavored to find some trace of you since I returned here two months ago. You might drop me a line . . . now and then, to let me know where you are and what you are doing.

As you probably know, your mother has gone to Rio and should have arrived there about a week ago. I am most anxious to learn something about your sister. However, I am glad your mother went down there for it is simpler for Betty Lou to have the baby in Rio than in Washington.

On my arrival here on 17 August, I walked into lots of employment. I look back nostalgically on those days when there was an active war on, as I then knew what was to be done and I had a pretty good idea as to how to do it. The sudden stoppage of the war certainly caught us unprepared in many ways. First, we were jammed with ships getting ready for Olympic, and then had thousands of men dumped on us, all wanting to go home immediately. Receiving stations built for five thousand had twelve thousand men thrown upon them. Staging centers were thrown together with anything we could make available. Ships going to Japan and China dumped their personnel ashore without the necessary records or processing which, of course, slowed everything down.

In addition to the above troops, large numbers of our own prisoners of war came in and not only had to be taken care of, but, as I ordered, . . . given the very best possible treatment and further, given top priority on going home. . . .

I haven't the slightest idea as to what is going to happen to me. I wrote Washington, but have yet to hear.

I suppose you have been formulating some plans of your own and I trust you have not asked to be released immediately. From the limited information I have, I think you could stay on for at least another year and that you could have duty in Washington [where Peggy's family lived] for a greater part of this time.

I thanked the Good Lord when V-J Day came. The more I thought about your job at Olympic and the beaches you were to cover—the less I liked it. You had had wonderful luck for five years and I was afraid it might run out.

Lots of love and lots of luck, Dad

P.S. I have just received a cable from Rio from Pres, announcing the birth of Prescott Bush III!

Draper Kauffman's job—training UDTs that had just completed intensive wartime demolition operations—was not a serious assignment. The demolitioneers were amused when, after receiving complete physicals, 40 percent of them were judged unfit for duty. Kauffman found one of his most difficult problems was "bringing those distinguished young gentlemen back down to earth again and making them realize that they had to live as part of the Navy." And he was not always successful. One case in point was Gordon Leslie, the fine Marine who had been loaned to the UDTs for the Saipan operation. Leslie really liked underwater demolition work—so much so, in fact, that he deliberately became lost in the bureaucratic shuffle. He had received the Navy Cross at Tarawa, and after he helped UDT 5 at Saipan, he persuaded Kauffman to keep him on at Tinian. Kauffman left the Marianas and turned over command of UDT 5. He was amazed, later in the Philippines, to discover that Leslie was still with UDT 5 as the official marine observer. By the end of the war Leslie was still a marine observer and had also become executive officer of the team. He had not been with the Marine Corps since the time of the Tarawa operation, nor had he drawn a dollar of pay from it. To prevent the Marines from discovering his whereabouts, he depended on an allowance from his father to tide him over. So the leathernecks just lost Gordon Leslie. They never asked where this guy was who had been lent to the UDTs before Saipan. In fact, the marine bureaucracy was so confused that during Leslie's absence it had promoted him twice. Now he was a captain, albeit an unpaid one.

When the underwater demolition people got back to Coronado, they decided they had to return Leslie to the Marine Corps. Kauffman tried to persuade the senior Marine there, a colonel, to take back this prodigal son. Balking at the paperwork involved in untangling the situation, the colonel would have no part of it.

But Leslie then made the problem worse: he put in a request to transfer from the Marine Corps reserve to the regular navy. No Marine, he was informed tartly, ever requested transfer to the regular navy. No Marine would even *think* of doing such a thing. Kauffman went to marine headquarters at Camp Pendleton, California, and asked to see Gen. Holland Smith. He explained the problem to the general, who wasn't at all sympathetic. Smith sent for several colonels, ordered them to handle the situation, and told them in no uncertain terms that they were to cure the young man of the brainwashing he had "obviously" received from the navy.

But Leslie bucked the system. He did get transferred to the regular navy, and he finally got his back pay for all those months of combat service. With a check for four thousand dollars in his hand, he went to the manager of the Hotel del Coronado and said, "I want to give a party, and it's up to you to end the party before the $4,000 is spent because that's all I'm going to give you."

The hotel had peninsulas of rooms that opened out onto an interior garden. Leslie took three suites. As Kauffman recalled

> [Leslie] would order about four gallons of milk and four quarts of brandy and mix them. I think they added sugar. As far as I could make out they lived only on milk punches. The party went on for thirteen days and twelve nights.
>
> Well, to say that I was worried was putting it mildly, because we had five admirals staying at the Hotel Del, including my immediate boss. So I went around to each of the admirals and told them what was about to happen, and I told them that the only rule that I had laid down was that there had to be one sober UDT officer sitting outside of the only unlocked door in the corridor, in full uniform, at all times.

Luckily for the partygoers, the laudatory *Saturday Evening Post* article had just come out, and the manager of the hotel made a smart move: he distributed copies to the occupants of all the nearby rooms and personally explained what was taking place. The hotel did not burn down, and the reputation of the UDTs was not destroyed.

When Christmastime came, Peggy and Draper asked every member of the UDTs who was in Coronado to come to their home for Christmas dinner, as well as Peggy's brother-in-law, Bob Williams, a Marine. They lived in a Quonset hut. It was one long room. In the front was the kitchen with a small sink and a small stove and oven. In the very back was a double bed and Cary's crib. In between was the living and dining area. The sink was used for every purpose—brushing teeth, bathing the baby, and washing everything from diapers to vegetables, dishes, and pots and pans.

Peggy got a large turkey and managed to squeeze one half of it into the little oven; she roasted that and then turned it around and roasted the other half. For the dinner table they borrowed some sawhorses from the navy, put wooden planks over them, and requisitioned benches to sit on. After setting out the plates buffet style, they arranged tall sawhorses on either side of the bed and suspended planks over the mattress to put dirty dishes on. Cary was in her playpen to greet the guests as they came in. The day raced by, full of stories, jokes, and songs; it was such a success that the last person didn't leave until after 5 A.M. Peggy and Draper were so tired they crawled into bed under the planks and the dishes and went to sleep.

Something that pleased Draper Kauffman greatly during those halcyon days was his ability to convince roughly a quarter of his UDT men and officers to transfer to the regular navy. One of his favorite demolitioneers, Bob Marshall—who later became CEO of Turner Construction Company—told Betty Lou Bush that one night over drinks her brother had tried to convince him that the navy was *the* career for him. "One more martini," Marshall related, "and I would have signed up!"

After two months of his low-key job, Kauffman began thinking about a career in the regular navy for himself. As always in such matters, he went to his father for advice and said that he did not want to transfer unless he had a reasonable shot at making captain. Furthermore, he did not want to make the move in any way that would completely rule out making admiral.

Admiral Kauffman, who by that time was commandant of the Fourth Naval District in Philadelphia, wrote his son a long letter. One of his points took Draper by surprise: "Now when it comes to higher rank, your Navy Crosses will do you practically no good at all. Keep in mind that the Navy has no desperate need for a captain or an admiral who can take a bomb apart, and its need for a captain or an admiral who can swim into somebody's beach is also remarkably limited. At the other end of the scale, your three commendation medals will do you a great deal of good because they were for organizing Bomb Disposal, organizing UDTs, and organizing JANET [the Joint Army-Navy Experimental Testing Board]."

The only hope his father could offer was for Draper to become involved in strategic planning. Furthermore, he should not even consider transferring to the regular navy unless he could persuade somebody to give him command of a destroyer in the very near future. In fact, Draper Kauffman would need as much time as he could wangle in command of a ship, and his dad did not think he would be able to get it.

While Kauffman contemplated his possibilities, U.S. Lines, the steamship company he had worked for before the war, offered him a job as its number two man in Europe, with headquarters in London. The salary was highly appealing, especially when compared to what he would make if he continued in the navy, and it greatly tempted Peggy.

On a trip to Washington in early September 1946 to visit his in-laws, Kauffman had dinner with Capt. John Webster, who was in charge of detail for commanders at the Bureau of Personnel. Webster promised that if Draper transferred to the regular navy, he would ensure him one year on a large ship such as a cruiser, followed by command of a destroyer. Kauffman was dumbfounded. "You know, Johnny," he said, "if I run that destroyer aground, I'm not going to be the only person at the end of the long green table. You're going to be there with me."

The captain responded, "Don't worry about that. I'm not as big a fool as you think I am. I'll make sure you go to a destroyer that has a superb executive officer, and I'll make you promise that you'll listen to your exec." Kauffman did not know whether Webster ever checked this out with his superior officer—and he never wanted to ask.

Then came one of those strange coincidences that can change a person's life. Following his talk with Captain Webster, Kauffman went to take his physical exam. A corpsman gave him the eye exam, and he failed it. So he phoned Peggy at her parents' house, and then he phoned the U.S. Lines and told them he would be with them in six weeks. But when he returned to the Tuckermans' house, there was a note to call the doctor who headed the dispensary at the Navy Department. Draper called him and then went over. The doctor sat him down and said, "Are you the Kauffman who was with the underwater demolition teams at the Marianas?"

"Yes, sir."

"Did you go in on reconnaissance with the teams?"

"Yes, sir."

"I was at Saipan. I thought I remembered that name," the doctor said. "I see you did not do well on your eye exam for transfer this morning."

"I think that's an understatement. I think I failed it."

"I tell you, son," the doctor went on, "I can't help but think that if your eyes were good enough for reconnaissance in wartime, they ought to be good enough for paperwork in peacetime. Now, let's take that exam over again."

So the good Samaritan took Draper Kauffman into the examination room and there on the wall was the old chart that he knew by heart: D E F B O T E C, A E L T Y P H E A L T.

"And lo and behold, I passed it," Kauffman recalled. "Now that's a series of coincidences. The doctor happened to be at Saipan. He happened to remember my name. He happened to notice it in the paperwork that he was signing, which failed me on my physical, and then, bless his heart, he did something about it."

At long last Draper Kauffman had reached his goal—to become a line officer in the regular United States Navy!

When Betty Lou and Pres Bush returned from Rio with Pres III in tow, they moved to Greenwich, Connecticut, where the Bush family lived. One day they decided to give a "Suppressed Desires" party and started drawing up the guest list. Pres's parents, who were away, lent their nice big house. Each guest was to come dressed as the person he or she had always wanted to be. Betty Lou wore a ballet tutu, and Pres appeared as golfer Bobby Jones. Many of the costumes were ingenious. Peggy, who had come a day early to help prepare for the event, dressed as Madame

Curie. Abraham Lincoln was there, as well as Madame de Pompadour, Caesar and Cleopatra, and at least two Babe Ruths.

The war's end had not put an end to Draper Kauffman's general absent-mindedness about family affairs, and that night was a case in point. True to form, the UDT commander showed up at the very last minute without any special outfit—just in service dress blue. Everybody crowded around him. "Where's your costume, Draper?" they teased. His immediate response was, "There's only one desire I ever had, and now it's fulfilled—to wear the uniform of the regular U.S. Navy!"

Epilogue

DRAPER KAUFFMAN HAD AN EVENTFUL AND DISTINGUISHED CAREER IN the navy after the war. In 1946 he volunteered for the joint scientific-naval task force preparing to conduct atomic tests at Bikini Atoll in the Pacific. Following those momentous explosions Kauffman was ordered to start a school for radiological safety monitors. Trips to Los Alamos followed and an extended acquaintance with two scientific giants of the time, Enrico Fermi and Ernest Lawrence, Nobel Prize winners and key pioneers of the nuclear age.

It was unusual, if not remarkable, that as a junior reserve officer Draper Kauffman started four naval organizations, three of which are still in existence today. Bomb disposal, UDT/SEALs, and the Radiological Safety School are currently active. Only JANET (Joint Army-Navy Experimental Testing Board) is no longer operational.

Kauffman finally got his destroyer in 1948 when he took command of the USS *Gearing*. He agreed with his father that it was the ideal ship.

He had many things yet to learn about the navy that he had missed while heroically serving as a frogman during the war, perhaps first among them the key role of navy chiefs in maintaining the morale of a ship's crew. Draper Kauffman never did become a particularly gifted ship handler like his father, but his natural talent for leadership soon imparted to all the men under his command a sense of purpose and a desire to do the best possible job for the navy.

Following time at the Naval War College, tours in Washington, and additional ship commands, Kauffman was selected early for rear admiral while he was skipper of the heavy cruiser USS *Helena*. One of his junior officers aboard the *Helena,* Bruce Beam, later remembered that "Captain Kauffman demanded and always got the best from every man aboard, but he did so in a way that made you happy to work for him and ashamed not to." Not long after, Kauffman was given the flag command of Destroyer/Cruiser Flotilla 3, headquartered on the West Coast.

In the early 1960s Admiral Kauffman was ordered to Washington as chief of the Strategic Plans and Policy Division of the Joint Chiefs of Staff. Formulating a five-year plan for all military forces, he found himself in a true joint interservice operation where he worked with many civilians, including Secretary of Defense Robert McNamara and his numerous brilliant young interns, often referred to as the whiz kids. Kauffman was impressed by the group's grasp of facts and figures but often dismayed by their lack of interest in experience, personnel, and morale. He did not relish the uncomfortably sensitive job he was then given (the worst in the navy, he believed) as head of the newly created Office of Program Appraisal, where he was required to review navy programs and report the deficiencies of bureau chiefs who were many ranks and years his senior. But working with outstanding people, including Secretary of the Navy Paul Nitze; his assistant, Capt. (later admiral) Elmo Zumwalt; and Alain Enthoven, McNamara's Assistant Secretary of Defense, who had become a friend, made the task less onerous.

Later in the decade Draper Kauffman served as superintendent of the U.S. Naval Academy. It was not an easy time. American society was marked by drug problems, race issues, and strong antiwar and often antimilitary sentiment. But Kauffman applied his leadership abilities to move the academy away from its trade-school tradition and strongly in the direction of academic excellence by supporting the move toward a largely civilian, academically trained faculty who were teaching a broad range of practical and academic courses. He aggressively recruited minority midshipmen, and he and Peggy placed the highest importance on mentoring these young men, some of whom went on to become among the navy's first black admirals and Marine Corps generals. One of them, Tony Watson, who donned his stars as a rear admiral in 1993, recalled that "I knew his hands were on my shoulders, that his spirit was with me. Rear Adm. Draper Kauffman had mentored me well, and I shall never forget his stature, his strength, and his kindness. He was the admiral of all time."

When Kauffman's tenure at the Naval Academy was completed in 1968, he was posted to the Pacific as Commander, U.S. Naval Forces, Philippines, and as Representative Commander, U.S. Forces, Pacific. It pleased him to feel he was following in his father's footsteps in the Philippines. He not only excelled as a naval diplomat but also worked closely with Admiral Zumwalt to increase the UDT/SEAL presence in Vietnam. Those forces operated with the all-important River Patrol Forces (riverine) and were also attached to MACV-SOG (U.S. Military Assistance Command Vietnam—Studies and Observation Group) for highly sensitive operations. In the mid-1980s UDT units were absorbed into the SEAL program.

Kauffman's last job in the naval service was as commandant of the Ninth Naval District, the Great Lakes Naval Training Center north of Chicago. The base was at the epicenter of racial unrest in the navy during the early 1970s. In a difficult social and political time, Kauffman tackled the problem head-on. Demanding equality for all navy personnel regardless of race, Kauffman insisted that local housing be open to all or none. His actions were credited with substantially reducing the tension at Great Lakes and were highly praised by Adm. Elmo Zumwalt (at that time, chief of naval operations) in his autobiography *On Watch*.

Draper Kauffman retired from the U.S. Navy in 1973. For two years, he had a very successful term as president of Marion Institute, the military school in Marion, Alabama. Four years later, on a cruise of the Danube River, sponsored by the Naval Academy, he suffered a heart attack and died in Budapest. Following the funeral service in the Naval

Academy chapel, conducted by an old family friend, Frank Sayre, dean of the National Cathedral and Reggie Kauffman's chaplain in the Philippines during World War II, Kauffman was buried next to his mother and father in the Naval Academy cemetery. Top midshipmen today receive the Rear Adm. Draper L. Kauffman Leadership Excellence Award.

Draper Kauffman has also been honored since his death by the naming of the Draper L. Kauffman Naval Special Warfare Operations Facility at Norfolk, Virginia, and the Kauffman Explosive Ordnance Disposal Training Complex at Eglin Air Force Base, Florida. No doubt the commemoration that would have pleased him most was the launching in 1986 of the guided missile frigate USS *Kauffman*, named for both him and his father.

Draper Kauffman's men remember him as an exceptional leader who led by example. He trained and fought alongside them, seemingly impervious to danger. It was he who was assigned the task of establishing the first training program for underwater demolition units, which would fight their way ashore at Normandy and clear the island beaches in the Pacific for marine and army landing forces. During some of the fiercest island battles Kauffman would serve as a UDT commander and was awarded his second Navy Cross for his heroic actions during the Saipan campaign. Because of the high standards he set for those who became frogmen, thousands of American lives were saved in World War II, Korea, Vietnam, and other military conflicts. Today, the early established UDT traditions of perseverance, spirited teamwork, and a lasting brotherhood of men of extraordinary courage is carried on by Navy SEALs. This is Draper Kauffman's legacy to the U.S. Navy and his country.

Appendix A

Summary of Duty Assignments for Rear Admiral Draper Laurence Kauffman, U.S. Navy, Retired

ACADEMIC

January 1942: Organized and became first commanding officer of the U.S. Navy Bomb Disposal School in Washington, D.C. As additional duty assisted in organizing the U.S. Army Bomb Disposal School at Aberdeen Proving Grounds in Maryland.

June 1944: Organized and became first commanding officer of the U.S. Naval Combat Demolition Unit training UDTs in Fort Pierce, Florida.

August 1946: Organized and became first commanding officer (temporary additional duty) of the U.S. Navy Radiological Safety School on Treasure Island, San Francisco. In October 1946 assisted army in establishing similar school at Edgewood Arsenal in Maryland.

July 1950: Student at the Naval War College.

July 1951: Staff, Naval War College, instructing in strategy and tactics.

June 1965: Superintendent, U.S. Naval Academy.

COMMAND

April 1944: Commanding Officer, Underwater Demolition Team No. 5, and Commander, UDT Group, Marianas Operation (Saipan, Tinian, and Guam).

November 1944–June 1945: While serving as chief staff officer to Commander, UDTs, Pacific, acted as Commander, UDTs, for Iwo Jima and Okinawa Operations.

December 1948–July 1950: Commanding Officer, USS *Gearing* (DD-710).

June 1953–June 1954: Commander, Destroyer Division 122.

August 1957–August 1958: Commanding Officer, USS *Bexar* (APA 237).

February 1960–February 1961: Commanding Officer, USS *Helena* (CA 75).

February 1961–February 1962: Commander, Cruiser-Destroyer Flotilla Three.

July 1969–May 1970: Commander, U.S. Naval Forces, Philippines, additional duty as Commander in Chief, Pacific Representative, Philippines.

June 1970–May 1973: Commandant, Ninth Naval District, with additional duty as Commander, Naval Base, Great Lakes.

June 1973: Transferred to the retired list of the U.S. Navy.

DUTY INVOLVING PLANNING

July 1954–July 1955: Strategic Plans Division, Office of the Chief of Naval Operations.

August 1958–February 1960: Fleet Plans Officer for Commander in Chief, U.S. Pacific Fleet.

April 1962–July 1963: Joint Staff of the Joint Chiefs of Staff.

July 1963–June 1965: Organized and became first director of Office of Program Appraisal on the Staff of the Secretary of the Navy.

ADDITIONAL DUTIES

August 1943: Organized and became first chairman of JANET (Joint Army-Navy Experimental and Testing Board).

February 1946–September 1946: Radiological Safety Operations Officer, Joint Task Force One (Bikini tests).

September 1946–October 1947: Chief, Defense and Protection Section, Atomic Warfare Division, Office of the Chief of Naval Operations.

December 1947–October 1948: Gunnery Officer, USS *Valley Forge* (CVA-45).

July 1955–July 1957: Aide to Under Secretary (and then Secretary) of the Navy Thomas S. Gates.

Appendix B

Selected Documents

UNITED STATES LINES

UNITED STATES LINES COMPANY

PANAMA PACIFIC LINE
AMERICAN PIONEER LINE

PIER 60 NORTH RIVER, NEW YORK

OFFICE OF THE GENERAL MANAGER

March 18, 1940

read P.S. first

Dear Dad:

I am enclosing a letter to mother in this letter because I think it would be better for you to tell her. I am going to do something which may worry her quite a bit if she lets her imagination run away with her. Also it will be very difficult for her to understand why I am doing it and I know you will. Enough preliminary I will get down to facts.

I am enlisted in the American Volunteer Ambulance Corps. My present orders are to leave on the ~~sixteenth~~ twentieth of April for France. My duties will be driving an ambulance, assisting in field hospitalx though not medical work. There will probably be very little da nger or you probably wouldn't find me there. That is the important point I am hoping you can get over to mother. The safest place in all Europe is just behind the Maginot line. I understand the loss of life at the front is less than the automile accidents at home by about 80%. They have promised me that I can get into the first section to go into the Balkans (if the war breaks there) because I have had some military discipline and education. Too bad they dont have hospital ships. I dont want to tell mother the Balkan stuff because the word Balkan would probably worry her more. Just tell her that I have the softest and safest job there is with red crosses plastered all ove me and the car.

Now as to why I am doing it. I know perfectly myself but I find it very difficult to put it into words. First I believe there is a right and a wrong side to this war. Second I think there are times when a thing

Draper Kauffman wrote his father about his plan to drive an ambulance with the French Army. By the time his father received the letter it was too late for Draper to change his mind (had he wanted to). While he was in a German prison camp, he realized he had never written either parent (his mother in California or his father at

UNITED STATES LINES

UNITED STATES LINES COMPANY

PANAMA PACIFIC LINE
AMERICAN PIONEER LINE

PIER 60 NORTH RIVER, NEW YORK

OFFICE OF THE
GENERAL MANAGER

is worth fighting for even if it is not in your best self-interest of the moment. Third, I think it is very much in our self-interest that Russia and Germany do not win the war. Fourth, as I believe number three to be true I do not believe we shoud let England and France fight our war for us. Fifth, The thing I always liked best about the Navy was that along with the Army and Marines ttxix they are called the services. I realize that my e contribution is going to be small and unimportant, but I know that it will be a heck of a lot easier to live with myself if I go. In other words I know I have to go.

Needless to say, I have given this a tremendous amount of thought over the last three months. I wanted to join the volunteers in Finland last January but put it off because I thought I ought to finish the job I was doing with the company. That war is over and I heard that they needed volunteers desperately up there particularily in the ambulance corps. The more I thought about it on the way back from Italy, we heard about the peace two days out, the more I realized I was the type that would use every possible excuse to keep from giving up what amounts to a darn good job, with a reasonably good salary and work that I like. As soon as I arrived I went right up to the office of the corps and enlisted. They wanted me to go Sat this Saturday but I pled for more time to let mother know. I think you will agree that it is best to tell mother afterward as it will prevent recriminations etc. and she will not exhaust herself fighting it.

I am only in it for six months, you sign a contract for six at first and then for three months each time thereafter. I will be able to go into the naval reserve, this doesn't affect that at all. All my papers for

sea) about his impressions of Hitler and wartime Germany. While in Germany he became convinced that Hitler planned to conquer all Europe and would easily defeat France and England unless America pledged its help. Draper was upset about the deteriorating situation in Europe and made numerous speeches around New York City in an effort to persuade people to tell Congress that the United States must go to war, but he neglected to pass his feelings along to his family.

UNITED STATES LINES

UNITED STATES LINES COMPANY

PANAMA PACIFIC LINE
AMERICAN PIONEER LINE

PIER 60 NORTH RIVER, NEW YORK

OFFICE OF THE
GENERAL MANAGER

the reserve went in three weeks ago, so Ishould have definite word on that before leaving the country.It is going to be funny to be an officer in the American Navy and a private in the French army at the same time. I will get no pay at all and must get myself to Paris which I can arrange somehow but it sure would help if that money of Fred Greenwood's came thru. I also hope I can wangle a year's leave of absence from the company instead of resigning.The war may be over in six monthe or even before I sail.

I know that everyone is going to think I am crazy with the heat so please you back me up on this even if you agree with them as I am going to need some moral assistance desperately particularily from you. If you cant make mother understand at least make her realize that there is no danger and cut down her worrying as much as possible.

Lots of love,

Draper

P.S. I dont know where you are & as I got no reply from telegram & letter addressed Destroyer squadron 36, San Diego feel you may be on your way East. Will get your address from Navy Dept tomorrow & am sending other letter to mother c/o Betty Lou. It contains nothing not here.

Schedule
Arr Panama – 1 April
Lv. " – 5 "
Arr. Galveston, Tex. – 9 April
Mail Address. U.S.S. Shubrick, Galveston, Tex.

U.S.S. Shubrick
Enroute Panama
30 March

Ask Captain Stevens Capt. of Yd. New York To send me a radio when you get this

My dear Son:

A few days ago I received a radio (Copy enclosed) from your mother saying you were going to France on 3 April to drive an ambulance. I was absolutely stunned and still am. Nothing as far as you are concerned has upset me as much since you were nearly fired at the Academy.

I sent Lem Stevens a radio asking him to please tell you to wait until you heard from me and the reply stated you were "under orders to sail on the Washington 6 April impossible change".

The whole thing is incomprehensible to me. You have worked long and hard and successfully in the shipping business - even if you are fired you can live with us until you get another job. They do not need men in France; I know several Frenchmen in San Francisco who were told they were not needed. --- Why should you volunteer? What if you were disabled? --- No kindly government to take care of you the rest of your life. --- You are not violently Pro-French or Pro-Allies either. --- Why? Why?

I have thought about it for three days (and about precious little else). I have come to the conclusion my information must be incorrect; or, you have been fired (or layed off) and have too much pride to come to me; or, you are in some kind of trouble and going away is the easiest way out; here again you should come to me as I have never let you down in the pinches.

You have often admired our system at the War College of making an "Estimate of the Situation". I sat down and made one. It is not very comprehensive and is incomplete due to my lack of accurate information. --- Here it is.

Statement of Problem.

You are a young man well beyond the age of adolescence; have seen considerable of the world and by the "Bill of Rights" you are entitled to Life, Liberty and Pursuit of Happiness.

Mission: To live your life according to your own ideas having due regard for the rights of others.

Apr. Your Mother's birthday is May 3rd

Reggie Kauffman, completely in the dark about his son's motives for joining the American Volunteer Ambulance Corps, wrote back to Draper almost frantically, completely unable to understand why he was choosing this course of action.

(A) Own Forces

(a) Good health (I hope)
(b) Good moral background and religious training.
(c) Devoted family
(d) Excellent education
(e) Pleasing personality
(f) Good business training
(g) Seven years of training in one line of business
(h) Important social and business contacts
(i) In shipping business which has brightest prospects in 80 years.

(B) Enemy Forces

(a) No responsibility except to yourself
(b) No real incentive to succeed in a business way
(c) No family life in recent years
(d) Natural youthful desire for excitement
(e) Boredom with present life
(f) Unduly influenced by people in high position
(g) 29 years old without attaining financial stability.

Possible Enemy Forces

(h) Loss of job
(i) Financial difficulties
(j) Woman trouble

- -

According to rules I should discuss each of the above; however I will let them stand simply as my opinion.

"Courses of Action Open To You". In this case you have restricted them to two; namely

(C) To go abroad as a volunteer in the Ambulance Corps.

Advantages: (a) Excitement. (b) Glamour. (c) Change of scene. (d) No responsibilities. (e) Easiest way out in case of: (1) Loss of job. (2) Financial difficulty. (3) Women.

Disadvantages: (a) Failure to utilize to fullest extent your "Own Forces". (b) Throwing away 7 years hard work and effort. (c) Growing older every day without regard for the future. (d) No necessity of doing work for Allies as they do not need man-power at this time. (e) When war is over you will have no job and will have lost what you have done so far. (f) No kind government to take care of you in case of injury. (g) Chance of being killed or permanently maimed without any sound reason therefore. (h) Eyes too poor to make a successful driver under stress. (i) Severe nervous strain on your mother.
Note: Not the same as in 1914 when Allies needed man-power: Volunteers were mostly young men out of college; most with money and no regular job.

(D) "To remain in United States and carry on".

Advantages: (a) See "Disadvantages" under (C) (Going abroad). (b) To make something worth while out of yourself as an American Citizen. (c) Prepare yourself to assume greater responsibilities in your chosen profession. (d) Remaining close to where the "Powers that be" are developing our shipping. (e) Remaining where your family have some chance of seeing you, and keeping alive that "love of family" without which you will miss a lot in this life.

Note: Our plans were based on being with you a great deal after this spring.

Disadvantages: (a) See "Advantages" under (C). (b) Seeing "Life" in foreign lands. (The grass is always greener in someone's else backyard). (c) Getting into a "rut". (We make our own ruts).

I should discuss the advantages and disadvantages but do not see the necessity. Therefore, as to my mind the "Disadvantages" under (C) and "Advantages" under (D) are so self evident to an educated person like yourself that you could only arrive at the

Decision: To Remain in the United States.

1. Minor Decisions:

(1) To carry on in the shipping business.
(2) To inform me if: -- (a) You are out of a job. (b) Need money badly. (c) In Trouble of any kind.

Note: I promise to straighten matters out without loss of prestige to you. If you must go on now I hope you will return within two months. I will arrange for you to go west, drive the family east where you all can establish yourself near the place that best suits you.

(3) Analyze yourself so as to take full advantage of all "Your own forces" and become a credit to yourself and those that love you.
(4) Marry a nice girl; get busy and provide a home and all that goes with it.

On reading over the above I can't really believe ~~my~~ my information is correct and that you are seriously considering driving an ambulance in France. From what I read and hear confidentially and otherwise they have relatively little need for ambulance drivers except around the North Sea: When anything does happen they need undertakers and hearses.

However if this letter is to reach you before sailing I must send it airmail immediately on my arrival in Panama and before I have a chance to get mail from you or your mother.

If ~~any~~ my information is incorrect or garbled, just take the part that fits. If you have signed up in the Ambulance Corps get out of it just as soon as you possibly can and come back here and "be yourself".

We have had a pretty good trip. Nine breakdowns but nothing serious so far. Had Lou Snider to dinner tonight and enjoyed him. He is working hard and doing well. We decided that if any information is correct you have gone slightly crazy.

I am very fond of you and I always have
admired you and had the greatest confidence
in you. Regardless of what you intend to do,
or what I may think of your decision or
action I want you to know I will do anything
I can for you. All I ask is that you play
ball and let me know the true state of
things. — To touch on an old subject:—
One of the last things your grandfather told
me, was that he appreciated my thoughtfulness
in writing him and never forgetting them no matter
where I was or what I was doing — I shall like to
remember that, I never knew my mother — you
have and do. Everything you got until you were
on your own she arranged — Kent, N.C. — many
other advantages. She is getting on in years, she has
a slightly enlarged heart and her blood pressure was
up pretty high when I left, she is a big woman:—
Sudden shocks and excess worry will not help her.
If you cannot find time to write her every week
you will ultimately regret it. When you were young
your thoughtlessness could be overlooked — you are
no longer young. — Anyway Son — lots of love
and a great deal of good luck — Please send me a
letter giving me your forwarding address before you leave — — Dad

Index

Page numbers in italics indicate photographs

About the Author

Elizabeth Kauffman Bush, a typical navy daughter, attended fourteen schools in thirteen years and enjoyed the ever-changing navy life.

She cares most about faith, family, and friends. She also enjoys reading, travel, politics, and dance; she is deeply committed to Family ReEntry, a prison ministry.

She and her husband, Prescott, live in Greenwich, Connecticut, and Vero Beach, Florida (near the SEAL museum). They have three children and six grandchildren. Prescott is the brother of former President George H. W. Bush and the uncle of President George W. Bush.

The Naval Institute Press is the book-publishing arm of the U.S. Naval Institute, a private, nonprofit, membership society for sea service professionals and others who share an interest in naval and maritime affairs. Established in 1873 at the U.S. Naval Academy in Annapolis, Maryland, where its offices remain today, the Naval Institute has members worldwide.

Members of the Naval Institute support the education programs of the society and receive the influential monthly magazine *Proceedings* and discounts on fine nautical prints and on ship and aircraft photos. They also have access to the transcripts of the Institute's Oral History Program and get discounted admission to any of the Institute-sponsored seminars offered around the country. Discounts are also available to the colorful bimonthly magazine *Naval History*.

The Naval Institute's book-publishing program, begun in 1898 with basic guides to naval practices, has broadened its scope to include books of more general interest. Now the Naval Institute Press publishes about one hundred titles each year, ranging from how-to books on boating and navigation to battle histories, biographies, ship and aircraft guides, and novels. Institute members receive significant discounts on the Press's more than eight hundred books in print.

Full-time students are eligible for special half-price membership rates. Life memberships are also available.

For a free catalog describing Naval Institute Press books currently available, and for further information about joining the U.S. Naval Institute, please write to:

Membership Department
U.S. Naval Institute
291 Wood Road
Annapolis, MD 21402-5034
Telephone: (800) 233-8764
Fax: (410) 269-7940
Web address: www.navalinstitute.org